Petroleum Taxation

Petroleum taxation is the universal instrument through which governments seek to determine the crucial balance between the financial interests of the oil companies and the owners of the resource. This book addresses how governments have and continue to approach this problem, the impacts of different policy choices and how these are being adapted to changing business conditions. Carole Nakhle presents the reader with an illuminating and robust analysis of the entire taxation story, from the basic theoretical considerations through to advanced computations applied to various tax regimes.

Nakhle's main argument is that petroleum taxation is a subject of complexity, variety and exposed to continued evolution, being surrounded and shaped by multi-faceted geological, technical and market factors together with unpredictable political influences. The author challenges the assumption that perfect models of petroleum taxation can be designed and applied to countries and circumstances around the world, arguing that an ideal structure exists only in theory but can be nonetheless a useful benchmark against which to test proposed fiscal systems.

This book will be of world-wide interest to practitioners and policy makers directly engaged with petroleum taxation, as well as students and researchers interested in energy economics, policy and public finance.

Carole Nakhle is Energy Research Fellow at the Surrey Energy Economics Centre, University of Surrey and also acts as Special Parliamentary Adviser on Energy and Middle Eastern Issues in the House of Lords.

Routledge Studies in International Business and the World Economy

1 States and Firms
Multinational enterprises in institutional competition
Razeen Sally

2 Multinational Restructuring, Internationalization and Small Economies
The Swedish case
Thomas Andersson, Torbjörn Fredriksson and Roger Svensson

3 Foreign Direct Investment and Governments
Catalysts for economic restructuring
Edited by John H. Dunning and Rajneesh Narula

4 Multinational Investment and Economic Structure
Globalization and competitiveness
Rajneesh Narula

5 Entrepreneurship in a Global Context
Edited by Sue Birley and Ian Macmillan

6 The Global Structure of Financial Markets
An overview
Edited by Dilip K. Ghosh and Edgar Ortiz

7 Alliance Capitalism and Global Business
John H. Dunning

8 Multinational Enterprises from the Netherlands
Edited by Roger van Hoesel and Rajneesh Narula

9 Competition, Growth Strategies and the Globalization of Services
Real estate advisory services in Japan, Europe and the United States
Terrence LaPier

10 European Integration and Foreign Direct Investment in the EU
The case of the Korean consumer electronics industry
Sang Hyup Shin

11 New Multinational Enterprises from Korea and Taiwan
Beyond export-led growth
Roger van Hoesel

12 Competitive Industrial Development in the Age of Information
The role of cooperation in the technology sector
Edited by Richard J. Braudo and Jeffrey G. MacIntosh

13 The Global Restructuring of the Steel Industry
Innovations, institutions and industrial change
Anthony P. D'Costa

14 Privatisation and Liberalisation in European Telecommunications
Comparing Britain, the Netherlands and France
Willem Hulsink

15 Multinational Corporations
Emergence and evolution
Paz Estrella Tolentino

16 Foreign Direct Investment in Emerging Economies
Corporate strategy and investment behaviour in the Caribbean
Lou Anne A. Barclay

17 European Integration and Global Corporate Strategies
Edited by François Chesnais, Grazia Ietto-Gillies and Roberto Simonetti

18 The Globalisation of Corporate R & D
Implications for innovation systems in host countries
Prasada Reddy

19 Globalization of Services
Some implications for theory and practice
Edited by Yair Aharoni and Lilach Nachum

20 A Century of Foreign Investment in the Third World
Michael J. Twomey

21 Global Capitalism at Bay
John H. Dunning

22 Foreign Direct Investment
Research Issues
Edited by Bijit Bora

23 Ford and the Global Strategies of Multinationals
The North American auto industry
Isabel Studer Noguez

24 The World Trade Organization Millennium Round
Freer trade in the next century
Klaus Deutsch / Bernhard Speyer

25 Consultancy and Innovation
The business service revolution in Europe
Edited by Peter Wood

26 Knowledge Economies
Clusters, learning and co-operative advantage
Philip Cooke

27 The Role of Resources in Global Competition
John Fahy

28 Globalization, Employment and the Workplace
Diverse impacts
Edited by Yaw A. Debrah and Ian G. Smith

29 Transnational Corporations
Fragmentation amidst integration
Grazia Ietto-Gillies

30 Growth Theory and Growth Policy
Edited by Harald Hagemann and Stephan Seiter

31 International Business and the Eclectic Paradigm
Developing the OLI framework
Edited by John Cantwell and Rajneesh Narula

32 Regulating Global Trade and the Environment
Paul Street

33 Cultural Industries and the Production of Culture
Edited by Dominic Power and Allen J. Scott

34 Governing Interests
Business associations facing internationalization
Edited by Wolfgang Streeck, Jürgen Grote, Volker Schneider and Jelle Visser

35 Infrastructure Development in the Pacific Region
Edited by Akira Kohsaka

36 Big Business and Economic Development
Conglomerates and economic groups in developing countries and transition economies under globalisation
Edited by Alex E. Fernández Jilberto and Barbara Hogenboom

37 International Business Geography
Case studies of corporate firms
Edited by Piet Pellenbarg and Egbert Wever

38 The World Bank and Global Managerialism
Jonathan Murphy

39 Contemporary Corporate Strategy
Global perspectives
Edited by John Saee

40 Trade, Globalization and Poverty
Edited by Elias Dinopoulos, Pravin Krishna, Arvind Panagariya and Kar-yiu Wong

41 International Management and Language
Susanne Tietze

42 Space, Oil and Capital
Mazen Labban

43 Petroleum Taxation
Sharing the oil wealth: a study of petroleum taxation yesterday, today and tomorrow
Carole Nakhle

Petroleum Taxation

Sharing the oil wealth: a study of petroleum taxation yesterday, today and tomorrow

Carole Nakhle

Routledge
Taylor & Francis Group
LONDON AND NEW YORK

First published 2008
by Routledge
2 Park Square, Milton Park, Abingdon, Oxon OX14 4RN

Simultaneously published in the USA and Canada
by Routledge
270 Madison Avenue, New York, NY 10016

Routledge is an imprint of the Taylor and Francis Group, an informa business

Typeset in Times New Roman by
RefineCatch Limited, Bungay, Suffolk

British Library Cataloguing in Publication Data
A catalogue record for this book is available from the British Library

Library of Congress Cataloging-in-Publication Data
Nakhle, Carole.
Petroleum taxation : sharing the oil wealth : a study of petroleum taxation yesterday, today and tomorrow / Carole Nakhle.
p. cm—(Routledge studies in international business and the world economy ; 43)
Includes bibliographical references and index.
1. Petroleum—Taxation. I. Title.
HD9560.8.A1N35 2008
336.2′78338272—dc22 2007044275

ISBN10: 0–415–43379–7 (hbk)
ISBN10: 0–203–92789–3 (ebk)

ISBN13: 978–0–415–43379–2 (hbk)
ISBN13: 978–0–203–92789–2 (ebk)

Contents

List of variables

CE_t	Capital Expenditures (CAPEX) in period t
C_{et}	Certainty Equivalent of the expected total costs cashflow at time t
CIT_t	Corporate Income Tax in period t
C_t	Total Cost in period t
CT_t	Corporation tax in period t
D_{ac}	Depreciation
DF	Discount Factor
D_{ns}	Depreciation
EMV	Expected monetary value
$e^{-\varphi ot}$	First discount factor
e^{-it}	Second factor
$E_0\,(P_t)$	Current expectation of the oil price evaluated at time zero
FYA_t	First Year Allowance in period t
i	Nominal risk-free rate
K	Payback Period
$Lossc_{t-1}$	Loss Carried forward from period t–1, for CT purpose
$Loss_{t-1}$	Loss carried forward from Period t–1, for PRT purpose
λ	Speed of reversion or mean reversion factor of oil prices, associated with a half life, HL
N	Number of years over which profitability is calculated
NCF_t	Net Cash Flow in period t
NPV	Net present value
OA_t	Oil Allowance in period t
OE_t	Operating Costs (OPEX) in period t
P'	Long-run mean price to which the price will tend to revert
P_t	Oil price in period t
PRT_r	Mainstream Petroleum Revenue Tax in period t
$PRRT_t$	Petroleum Resource Rent Tax in period t
π_a	Adjusted profit
π_{ct}	CT assessable profit
π_{pt}	PRT assessable profit
Q_t	Oil production in period t

R	Discount rate
RDF	Risk Discount Factor
ROY_r	Royalty in period t
R_t	Oil Revenue in period t
S	Safeguard period
SPT_t	Special Petroleum Tax in period t
ST_t	Supplementary Charge in period t
σ	Volatility of oil price expectations
t_{ac}	CIT rate
t_{ap}	PRRT rate
t_c	Corporation tax rate
TDF	Time discount factor
T_e	Present value of the total tax cash flow at time t
t_{ns}	SPT rate
t_{nci}	CIT rate
t_p	PRT rate
t_r	Royalty rate
t_s	Supplementary Charge rate in period t
T_t	Total Tax Take in period t
φ	Price of risk
up_{at}	Uplift rate
up_{nt}	5 per cent uplift for 6 years
up_t	Uplift rate on capital expenditure in period t
$V_0(P_t)$	Value of the claim to be received at time t
WDA_t	Writing Down Allowance in period t

List of Figures

List of Tables

Foreword

Foreword by The Right Honourable Lord Howell of Guildford, UK Secretary of State for Energy 1979–81 and President of the British Institute of Energy Economists

When oil was first discovered in commercially recoverable quantities in the North Sea in the late 1960s and early 1970s an intense debate began in British political circles. This debate concerned the way in which the British nation might best benefit from the proceeds of these discoveries. In particular the extent of Government involvement in North Sea development became the object of heated discussion. How was this new and unknown industry which was springing up at the heart of the British economy to be managed and regulated and, above all, how were the British people to obtain their 'fair share' of the wealth which was due to flow from North Sea oil (and gas) production?

Unfortunately, the discussion was impeded by a number of serious obstacles. Not the least of these was a distinct lack of experience and expertise about petroleum fiscal issues and the most suitable kind of tax regime to be applied to the new North Sea activity. There were no obvious models to follow and history offered no clear guide in what were unique and novel conditions. Nor were there any truly comprehensive surveys or overviews of the whole field of petroleum taxation round the world to which to refer. Just across the North Sea the Norwegian oil and gas policy, also still emerging, was thought at first to have some possible lessons to offer, but even there conditions, both political and geological, were soon seen to be substantially different. In short, there was no track record to follow and no guide-book to the future.

Since then, while the British eventually reached some initial decisions about the best fiscal arrangements (frequently altered thereafter), similar debates have continued in many other oil producing provinces, new and established around the world.

The oil industry has undergone significant change since the first North Sea developments – a process which continues apace, reinforced by big shifts on the geo-political stage. Some oil producers have moved towards much more state involvement and control, ejecting the international oil companies and building up their national companies. Some, such as the de-Sovietised Russians, have moved in the opposite direction, with giant new private sector oil corporations bursting onto the world scene. Some, such as Iraq, have sought to design completely new relationships with their oil sectors. In all cases the issue of the fair or appropriate 'take' by the state has been a central preoccupation and in most cases it is the question of the right level and structure of taxation which has been in turn at the heart of that discussion.

Now the whole range of highly complex issues surrounding petroleum taxation world-wide, has been vigilantly drawn together in this major and comprehensive study by Dr. Carole Nakhle. This is a work which not only describes and analyses in great detail what has already happened in the world of petroleum taxation but also, fascinatingly, what could have happened had different paths been followed, and, most important of all, what could or should happen in the future. It does so by taking the reader step by step through the entire taxation story, from the basic theoretical considerations through to advanced computations applied to various tax regimes and finally adding the all-important political and social dimensions lying behind tax policy in many countries. It therefore constitutes a valuable and illuminating guide not only for those who wish to study the oil industry and its progress from outside, but also, and perhaps even more so, for the practitioners involved – namely, oil industry investors and decision-makers, government policy-makers and tax experts, revenue officials and the general public who are the oil industry's customers and consumers.

I am therefore very proud to be able to write a foreword to a work of such marked relevance and value. Not all parts are for the lay person. Some sections are inevitably highly technical, given the nature of the subject. But together they combine between one set of covers a highly authoritative survey of the entire issue in all its aspects – the history, the underlying politics, the mechanics and computation, the errors, the successes and the opportunities. It is a volume of clear and indisputable value to all concerned with petroleum taxation in the modern world.

David Howell
House of Lords
2007

Preface

The purpose of this book is to illuminate the subject of petroleum taxation and to cast fresh light on the complex pattern of the taxation of oil and gas production which continues to evolve and adapt in response to a variety of critical factors such as volatile commodity prices, basin maturity, and resource nationalism.

The global oil and gas business is undergoing significant change, under the triple impact of geopolitics, competitive pressures and technology. Access by international oil companies (IOCs) to resources in the traditional, 'big reserve' areas of the Middle East are becoming more difficult and expensive, the costs of new investment in oil exploration, development and production are rising fast, especially in more remote regions and deeper deposits, where increasingly the IOCs are focussing their efforts. At the same time technological innovation is opening up vast new possibilities particularly in unconventional hydrocarbons such as oil sands in Canada. Meanwhile, the thirst for oil has continued climbing at a formidable rate as the developing world speeds up its growth and multiplies its energy needs.

Against this fast-changing backdrop, the responses of governments, both in the producing and in the consuming countries (sometimes the same), have been to re-assess their relationships with the oil industry and to adopt new policies which encourage diversification of sources and of fuels. Higher oil and gas prices have also encouraged host governments to scrutinise closely and reform their tax regimes to increase government take with a view of creaming off a greater proportion of the price upside. The IOCs in their turn have had to re-think and re-balance their interface both with governments and national companies, particularly from India, China and the former Soviet Union.

The pattern of change can be broadly summarised under the following headings:

- Whilst the IOCs objectives continue to be securing oil supplies from regions with relative political stability, reliable commercial environments, and equitable and predictable regimes, the reality is proving more elusive. The IOCs are having to face a combination of threats ranging from adverse legislative change, an auction of ever higher access costs and a variety of fiscal terms for new licences, and from general policies influenced by growing resource nationalism.

- Main consumer countries are building increased storage capacity for oil, oil derivatives and gas to maintain secure supply and reduce producer bargaining power in the short term.
- Systematic policy encouragement is being given to oil savings and general energy saving and measures to favour alternative fuels such as renewables and nuclear power.
- Substantial expansion of natural gas consumption is taking place, using a wider geographical spread of resources both for pipeline deliveries and frozen (LNG) imports.
- Much closer co-operation between consuming and producing countries is being sought, in efforts to maintain both demand and supply security.

The common thread running through all these upheavals is the matter of sharing the wealth between the investors and enterprises seeking a return on their money on the one hand, and the owners of the resource – the world's oil-producing nations and their governments – on the other. Petroleum taxation is the most common instrument through which governments seek to determine the crucial balance between the two interests, and to do so over a prolonged period.

How governments have approached this problem in recent decades, how they have sought to make their calculations, what effects and outcomes different policies might have had and how they are now adapting their policies to new conditions – these are the matters addressed, and hopefully illuminated and explained, in the following pages.

Acknowledgments

In writing this book, I have been indebted to the many talented and caring people who have helped my work in one way or another. I want to use this opportunity to convey my genuine gratitude for their assistance.

First, I want to thank Lord Howell, the former Secretary of State for Energy in the Thatcher Government in 1981, for his valuable wisdom. His authoritative observations on British politics, mainly those related to petroleum taxation and the North Sea, have been invaluable. But Lord Howell's inputs have not been limited to the dry world of politics and taxes; being the co-author of my first book *Out of the Energy Labyrinth*, he is very familiar with my style and my authorial strengths and weaknesses, enabling him to give me reliable advice on how to bring the whole subject of the book into focus.

I also owe a great deal of gratitude to Raymond Hall, who helped me to evolve and expand the ideas of this book. With his remarkable experience within the oil industry, he helped me put some flesh on the bones and frame of this work.

I cannot fail to mention the help and encouragement given to me freely by my colleagues at Surrey Energy Economics Centre, especially Professor Lester Hunt, who was also my second supervisor during my PhD in Energy Economics at the University of Surrey. In fact, many of the ideas in this book first saw the light of day in my PhD thesis. As such, I want to thank all those who helped me complete my degree, back in 2004. In particular, I want to acknowledge the support of David Hawdon, Brendan Shevlin and Marc Wastell for their timely advice; they all went above and beyond the call of duty to help me, WoodMackenzie for providing me with GEM, and Marco Dias for giving me access to his model on real options.

I also want to thank my great friend Sania Mirza, not only for her commitment to our friendship and her endless support and encouragement, but also for helping me bring this book to life, working for long hours on perplexing graphs and tables, adding colours to the overall format of the book. She did many wonderful things for this book. What started almost light-heartedly – Sania's attempt to relief the pressure on me – soon became a skilful and necessary element in finalising the manuscript and bringing the whole project to completion.

I also have to thank my parents for teaching me how to work hard. My endless indebtedness goes to my mother for all the stress she endured trying to protect me and my brothers during the war in Lebanon, and still succeed in providing us with the best education, even when it involved helping us with our homework in a tiny refuge studying by candlelight. My lasting gratitude goes to my father too; he didn't have the chance to see his kids growing, as he was forced to live far away from his family during the years of war, to earn his living and fund his children's education.

I want to dedicate this book to the memory of my precious grandmother, Teta Renee, who moulded my personality, taught me how to attain fulfilment and pride in working hard and made me always want to be a better person. I will never forget the last time I saw her back in August 2003, how she begged me to spend one more day with her, on my last summer break day in Lebanon, but I had to leave her to go back to London to work on my PhD thesis. I will always regret my decision and if I had the chance, I would give away everything I have achieved so far to spend that one more day with her.

I also want to thank my friends Paul Hawa and Shafic Hitti, who have been very enthusiastic about my book and have given me lots of confidence.

Last but not least, my gratitude goes to my late friend Campbell Watkins, who reviewed every single line of my work, even commenting on the punctuations. Campbell's consummate professionalism and friendly words of encouragement inspired me to keep working for my book's improvement. His loss was a big grief for the community of energy economists.

To the list of those who have been ready with advice and assistance during the production of this volume many more names could be added. Inevitably, this acknowledgment falls short of a full roll-call of everyone to whom I am indebted. I hope to overcome that shortfall by thanking everyone who contributed, directly and indirectly, to the accomplishment of this work.

Finally, I would like to say that while the ideas, wisdom and insights in the pages draw on the help and minds of many others, the opinions and factual material are entirely my own, and for these, and any errors (of which there are bound to be some) I take full and personal responsibility.

Carole Nakhle
2007

1 Petroleum taxation

Art and science

1.1 INTRODUCTION AND APPROACH

This work seeks to offer to the reader a comprehensive and up-to-date analysis of petroleum taxation and its impact. Round the world petroleum taxation is the principal mechanism for sharing hydrocarbon wealth between host governments and investors and has, in particular, been a central feature of both UK fiscal policy and UK energy policy since the early nineteen-sixties and pre-dates this for many long established provinces.

However, the analysis and commentary go beyond the UK scene and examine both the theoretical background to petroleum taxation and the many varieties of taxation that can be, are, or indeed might have been, applied in any country or oil province.

Petroleum fiscal regimes consist of a variety or mixture of tax instruments. Essentially the most popular choice is between Tax and Royalty regimes (T&R), predominant in OECD countries and Production Sharing Contracts (PSCs) typically favoured by developing countries. Thus the UK, for example, operates a concessionary regime, companies being entitled to the ownership of the oil extracted. By contrast a country like Azerbaijan applies a contractual regime where the government retains the ownership of the resource. The book reviews the two most common types of fiscal regime which operate all round the world and looks at their main strengths and weaknesses.

In addition, the book explains how many of the world's fiscal regimes can be evaluated quantitatively and develops a general cash flow model that can be applied to each country's circumstances. This procedure is then applied (as an example) to six countries – the UK, Norway and Australia, where concessionary regimes apply, and India, China and Iraq, which have contractual regimes.

Specific focus is given to the UK North Sea and its fiscal history because the lessons from this regime, which has been one of the world's most unstable and frequently altered regimes, are generally relevant to oil production and applicable world-wide. The UK North Sea and indeed the whole North Sea province play a highly important part in Western Europe's energy supply. The North Sea provides an interesting example of how fiscal terms can and do change through the lifetime of a province (from high production to maturity and decline), and in tune with changes of policy approach and in particular changing oil prices (from very high in the nineteen seventies and early eighties to low levels in the nineties and back to high points in the new century).

The uniqueness of oil taxation when compared to the taxation of other commodities lies in the oil industry's special characteristics, e.g. the significant contribution oil makes to numerous national economies, the high operating and development costs, high uncertainty in exploration activities, volatility of oil prices, and the maturity of certain oil provinces such as the North Sea.

These all add challenges to both the government and the industry. Consequently, the field of oil taxation requires specific knowledge by any regulator. A study such as this can therefore hopefully yield new insights into the investment decision process and the way it is influenced by the different oil industry fiscal packages and regimes to be found today around the globe. Others are still in the making. It is hoped that the messages from this work can also aid decisions for changing or creating new fiscal regimes, such as that struggling to emerge in Iraq, where future change is clearly and urgently needed, but can only come about in practice at a pace dictated by the rate of improvements in the security situation.

National tax policies can greatly influence the petroleum industry long-term global sustainability. The research in this book has been carried out against the background of a helpfully timely feature, namely the current maturity of the UK North Sea province. The larger fields (such as Forties, Brent and Ninian) were discovered in the early phases of exploration and brought into production between 1975 and 1979. Fields found during subsequent periods have become progressively smaller. This fact vividly illustrates further the significance of taxation in its effect on the trade-off between the opposing viewpoints of the government and companies. As the great French finance minister, Jean-Baptiste Colbert, observed 'the art of taxation consists in so plucking the goose as to obtain the largest amount of feathers with the least possible amount of hissing',[1] to which a modern commentator has added 'it is also important not to frighten away the geese so that they lay no eggs, golden or otherwise, let alone present themselves for plucking.'

As world oil demand continues to climb inexorably, driving oil prices to levels well beyond predictions of only a few years back, the importance of heeding these adages increases. It is the tax authorities above all who can determine how much hissing there will be, how many golden eggs will be laid now and how many more will be laid in the future. They need to get it right.

1.2 PURPOSE OF THIS BOOK

The message of this book is that petroleum taxation is a decisive factor in oil and gas investment decision making and ultimately will have a material impact on basin production. At a time when oil prices are high and countries and companies want to maximise revenues from the oil and gas sectors, the design of fiscal regimes is a critical factor in shaping perceptions of basin competitiveness. All round the world many countries are seeing their production aspirations undermined, and in some cases production declining, because their fiscal terms are poorly designed for the character and features of the province in question.

Since there is no objective yardstick for sharing economic wealth between the various interests involved in petroleum activity, controversy and tensions will always prevail between investors and the host government. A trade-off is bound to exist, since both government and oil companies want to maximise their own rewards. Tax rates that are set too low leave the government, the owner of the resource, a small and inequitable portion and are unlikely to be sustainable. Yet, if tax rates are too high, investment will be discouraged, not only in new projects, but in sustaining the capital investment required to maximise future value added from existing operations.

The exploration and exploitation of oil require significant financial resources that can exceed the capability of most of oil producing countries. This becomes more than ever the case as deeper and more remote wells are drilled. The ever higher risks involved, as a result of geology and oil price volatility, make a purely national approach to the exploitation of petroleum increasingly outdated. It follows that exploration and exploitation activities present delicate legal, technical, financial and political problems and any solution requires a balancing act between the respective interests of the producing countries and the oil companies.

But despite the competing objectives of both government and oil companies, a balance can still be reached. The right choice of fiscal regime can improve the trade-off between each party's interests. A small sacrifice from one side may be a big gain for the other.

There is no final, fixed or universal solution to the ever-changing and evolving set of problems and challenges which oil industry taxation presents. But the aim in the following pages is to suggest how a balance can be most effectively sought and how the inevitable adjustments which are constantly needed to secure that balance can best be devised and applied.

1.3 CONTENTS OF THE BOOK

Our subject – the pattern and impact of petroleum taxation round the globe – is approached by first, in Chapter 2, examining the theoretical background to petroleum taxation then, in Chapter 3, making an in-depth analysis of some of the principal fiscal packages that have been applied around the world. Chapter 3 compares six internationally representative petroleum fiscal regimes; UK, Australia, Norway, Indonesia, China and Iraq. Chapter 4 looks at the UK experience and case in detail, together with the many controversies and policy attitudes surrounding this subject.

In Chapters 5, 6 and 7, we then move on to predominantly technical issues. Chapter 5 develops a cash flow model for each of the six selected countries, further highlighting the complexities behind petroleum taxation. Chapter 6 covers the impact of different fiscal packages on selected oil fields' profitability and government revenues under different price scenarios. It also evaluates the possible outcomes of previous fiscal rates and structures, had they still applied today, and researches the way in particular in which the designers of the UK's petroleum fiscal regime and its subsequent amendments have affected the trade-off between the UK government and the oil companies. Particular attention is paid to the question of how differing tax regimes might have worked out through time, had they been left unchanged, how they affect different field sizes and what impact different crude oil price levels have had, and might have had, on the overall results.

Chapter 7 examines alternative possible methods for evaluating oil projects' profitability and revenue outcomes. By applying hypothetically different accounting conventions to the various examples selected it enables the reader to judge how significant these different techniques have proved, and would have proved useful to both oil companies' and government's appraisals, estimates and decisions. The choice of financial evaluation technique is of particular significance to both oil companies and government. An inappropriate technique can generate a misleading figure for profitability and taxable capacity leading, in turn, to incorrect decision making and an inappropriate assessment of a particular fiscal structure or instrument. In addition, major controversy still surrounds the choice of an appropriate evaluation technique.

Chapter 8 sets these detailed considerations of petroleum taxation in the broader political and attitudinal background from which they originate and by which their shape is heavily influenced. A final Chapter 9 summarises the main findings and conclusions of the whole book.

2 The taxation of oil

Theoretical background

A good tax – principle and characteristics of an effective tax system

2.1 GENERAL APPROACH

This chapter addresses the basic principles underlining petroleum taxation. It looks at the elements and qualities required for an ideal oil tax system, and examines the extent to which the various instruments discussed in previous studies match up to these basic criteria for an ideal system.

The basic proposition underlying petroleum taxation is easily stated. It is to acquire for the state in whose legal territory the resources in question lie, a fair share of the wealth accruing from their extraction, whilst encouraging investors to ensure optimal economic recovery of those hydrocarbon resources. However this general statement leaves all the key questions to be answered. What is fair? What is a share and of what total stream of output and income? At what point in the extraction and production process is the state's take to be levied?

These issues, and many others, arise in almost all taxation policy activities. But in the case of petroleum they assume a special character and complexity. Of central relevance are the uncertainties associated with petroleum geology, the specific characteristics of individual oil fields and the possibility of re-investment. The costs of petroleum projects tend by their nature to be incurred up front. The time lags can be considerable, often of many years and even decades, from the initial discovery of oil or gas reserves to the time of first production. Such characteristics impose numerous difficulties in the design and implementation of an appropriate tax system aimed at achieving a balance between both government and industry objectives.

In the case of minerals in the ground, and petroleum in particular, governments and state authorities see themselves as the legal owners of these resources and therefore fully entitled to collect a revenue stream from what they own. This ownership status can be translated into policy in a variety of ways. One traditional method has been to charge royalties on all units extracted, regardless of associated costs or actual net revenues – a method understandably unpopular with the industries incurring the costs and likely to act as a strong deterrent to investment and production. In the high noon of socialism the leading authoritarian countries, notably the former Soviet Union, bypassed the ownership and taxation issues by maintaining total state ownership of oil producing activities, by ignoring normal profit criteria and the true cost of capital, and by siphoning off surpluses, often on an arbitrary basis – with of course a damaging impact on the flow of investment.

Most common, and the main focus of this work, (but by no means free of arbitrary political influences), are patterns which recognize oil enterprises as separate entities with proper accounts and are taxed at arm's length, without the state's underlying assumption of ownership rights (and therefore rights to participate in the benefits) being in any way surrendered.

Governments of oil producing countries face important challenges when designing a tax system that meets two fundamental objectives; namely to ensure a fair share of revenues for themselves whilst simultaneously providing sufficient incentives to encourage investment. These two objectives are often competing rather than complementary. The need for balance between taxpayer and tax-levying authority is unavoidable but hard to achieve in practice particularly at times of volatile prices. A fair share at $20/barrel may be seen as unfair at $40/barrel. In the petroleum case, as in others, tax rates that are set too high will eliminate field value and create investment disincentives; hence both the producer and the government are left with nothing.

The general proposition is well illustrated by the concept of the Laffer Curve, which illustrates the trade-off between tax rates and tax revenues. As Professor Arthur Laffer famously maintained, governments can maximize tax revenue by setting tax rates at an optimum point. Lowering tax too much will produce less revenue but setting the tax rate too high – beyond the optimum level – can decrease revenue as well. When the Laffer doctrine was applied during the first Reagan Administration in the US it was found that lower taxation increased the tax flow from higher tax bracket earners. The same outcome occurred in the UK when top tax rates were dramatically lowered in Margaret Thatcher's first administration (1979–83). But pressed beyond its limits the Laffer curve can be counterproductive. When the same medicine was applied to the much larger standard rate brackets, both in the US and the UK, the outcome was a marked decline in total revenues, leading, in the American case, to a dramatic widening of the annual budget deficit.

Nevertheless, confirmation of the validity of the Laffer lesson in a reverse sense – that higher taxes do not always increase revenues – can be detected in UK government North Sea tax policy. In 2002, the UK government introduced a 10 per cent supplementary charge on top of the standard 30 per cent corporation tax and in 2005, doubled the charge to 20 per cent. The latter changes to the North Sea tax regime were introduced in order, it was hoped, to maintain a balance between oil producers and consumers, by promoting investment and ensuring fairness to taxpayers in view of the significant increases in oil prices and the upwards shift in expectations of the medium term outlook for future oil prices.[1] The UK government expected to generate an additional £2bn. from oil activity in 2006–7 as a result of the increase in tax. However, six months after the increase in tax, estimates were revised and the government wrote off three-quarters of the £2bn. originally expected revenues, in the light of decreasing North Sea production. Then, in the space of a further six months following the March 2006 budget the government further reduced the yield expectations from the North Sea by £2.8bn. in the tax years 2007–8.

The clear lesson of both these past and more recent experiences is that pitching tax rates and designing tax regimes carefully and in a balanced way can yield a positive rather than a zero-sum outcome. With rates set at a competitive level both the government and investors benefit respectively from a fair share of revenues and appropriate profitability. Set too low, government returns are weakened; set too high the incentives to oil companies to invest in exploration drilling, in development and in production can be severely damaged with the result that investment flows to countries offering a more attractive fiscal regime.

2.2 STRUCTURE OF THE CHAPTER

This chapter is organized in six sections. Following this introduction, Section 2 addresses the main functions of taxation with reference to petroleum industry activity. Section 3 studies the key features of an appropriate tax system, particularly as applied to an exhaustible resource such as oil. Section 4 includes a discussion of the concept of economic rent and examines the different types of rents recognizing that each has different tax policy implications. Section 5 analyses the main tax instruments considered for the upstream petroleum sector and qualitatively assesses the tax instruments proposed in the literature of petroleum taxation. Closing remarks on the main lessons of petroleum taxation are made in Section 6.

2.3 THE FUNCTIONS OF TAX

Taxation is the means by which a government obtains the resources with which it operates. But, taxation regimes in general, and taxation of petroleum in particular, reach well beyond the simple process of providing revenue to government. Since natural resources are frequently owned or controlled by governments, petroleum taxation, the surplus annexed by government, can be considered as the owner's claim to net resource value, defined as the net value of revenues received from the sale of the recovered product less all claimed production costs. It is, at least in theory, the means that divides rewards between the investor and the government.

The main functions of oil taxation can be listed as follows:

Financing government expenditures

Taxes are the principal source of revenue that governments use to finance public expenditures. Energy taxation, in particular, provides substantial revenue to virtually every advanced economy. Petroleum taxation has traditionally generated large revenues for government. In the UK, more than £215bn. or approximately $430bn. (2005 money terms) has flowed to the Treasury between 1968 and 2006 thereby contributing to health-care, education and various other services funded by government. Much bigger sums have flowed into the coffers of major Middle East oil producer governments, as well as into Russian state revenues, despite the apparent diversion of colossal sums away from the state and into the pockets of Russia's legendary oligarchs who have succeeded in becoming, in the space of a few years, some of the richest individuals on the planet.

Rent extraction

Taxation is used to capture a large share of the economic rent accruing from the production of a scarce resource, such as oil.[2] The concept of economic rent is discussed in section four.

Distribution of benefits

'The art of government consists in taking as much money as possible from one party of the citizens to give to the other' (Voltaire, 1764). The distribution of benefits from natural resources is at the heart of many resource taxation policies. Many tax instruments have been adopted almost entirely on distributional grounds. A key distribution of benefit is between government and the producer, especially as the natural resource is deemed to be owned by the state which is entitled to a fair share of the value of the depletable resource.

Taxation also has other important objectives such as:

Impact on the economic environment

Taxation is a key instrument by which governments affect and control economic decision and outcomes. By increasing or decreasing the amount of income it collects, a government can encourage, or discourage, different economic activities. Taxation affects a company's profits, the country the company chooses to invest in and the type of projects a company undertakes. Taxation can also be used to mitigate certain economic problems such as the 'Dutch Disease', where the petroleum industry can adversely impact upon the international competitiveness of the non-oil sector.[3] It can also be used to moderate the pace of exploration and exploitation of petroleum and at the same time reduce the depletion rate. In other cases where, for instance, there is chronic balance of payments problem, the government can use taxation to accelerate the development of export oriented natural resources, as occurred in the UK in the late 1970s. However, petroleum taxation is not a tool for macroeconomic policy, since it forms only one part of public sector funding.

Demand management

For energy-producing countries, if the cost of domestic production of an energy source is very low compared to that in the international market then prices in the local market will be low. In this case, indirect taxation (at the point of purchase) can be applied to reduce the differential, hence discouraging wasteful energy use as well as counteracting distortions in investment choices.

In contrast, domestic political pressures can lead the other way, namely to severe under-pricing of the oil resource and related products, usually for reasons of political and popular pressure. Thus in certain Gulf countries the price of gasoline is set so low that wasteful consumption is inevitable (and of course export revenues which would otherwise have accrued from the sale of oil at world market prices foregone). Governments which persistently under-price, or fail to tax, gasoline can find themselves in considerable difficulties. Thus it is reported that Iran, a major oil producer, is nevertheless being forced to import petrol and petrol products – a fact which becomes less surprising when it is learnt that petrol in Teheran costs 12 US cents a litre!

By contrast in some of the industrialized economies, especially in Europe, taxes represent a large fraction of oil prices. In the UK, there are three main components to the price of petrol at the pump: Price of the product, excise duty and value added tax (VAT). Excise duty is a fixed charge of 47.1 pence, VAT is set at 17.5 per cent and the price of the product covers, inter alia, the crude oil itself, the refining, the additives, the transportation, the marketing. Assuming the price of the product of 34.7 pence, the final price of petrol will be 96.1p. In this case, the price of the product represents 36.1 per cent of the final price. If the oil price increases by 20 per cent from 34.7p to 41.6p, the petrol price will increase to 104.32 p, which is the equivalent of an increase of only 8.5 per cent. It can be seen that the main feature of the high fixed tax, the excise duty, is this damping effect of product price variations. In countries with little or no element of fixed duty variations in the product price would have a much greater affect at the pump.

Control of pollution emissions from energy

Environmental concerns related to energy have been addressed through the use of tax instruments and many proposals have been made for the use of taxes to control pollution from energy. 'Green' taxes such as on CO_2 emissions are designed to mitigate or prevent pollution and other adverse effects on the environment.

The policy issue here is whether such taxes should be a substitute for existing taxes, with a zero net impact on overall government revenues, or whether they should be regarded as part of an enlarged tax base. Thus, if additional taxes are to be applied to those such as manufacturing businesses, who are deemed to be imposing external costs on the environment, the question is whether they are to be offset by reductions in other business taxation, or whether they constitute a net increase in the overall tax burden. Individuals faced with higher taxes for motoring or air trips are inclined to ask the same question.

An important presentational issue is also whether 'green' taxes are to be regarded as general incentives to increased energy efficiency and low-energy usage, or whether they are in some way part of the 'punishment' for carbon dioxide emissions and for inflicting climate damage on generations to come. A government which simultaneously urges high fuel prices to help future climate control, while applauding lower prices to ease fuel poverty and heavy household utility burdens, can find itself exposed to the accusation of inconsistency and may find it challenging to explain to a bewildered public where its priorities lie.

Government accountability

It is often argued that the lack of a viable tax regime can impede broad economic growth and the development of democracy. Two contentions arise – both of some validity. One concerns the situation of a government in a normal oil-consuming country which simply seeks to impose too demanding and too complex a tax regime generally on its citizens, bringing about widespread protest or evasion and the collapse of the broad compact between taxpayer and the state which balanced growth and social stability require. Such discontent may bring more draconian tax-collecting methods and worsen the overall fiscal climate further, creating a downward spiral in public finances which spills rapidly over in political unrest.

The other familiar pattern arises, especially in oil-rich producer states, where a government draws so much revenue from its petroleum resources, that it has no need to visit ordinary citizens for tax purposes. No taxation can, and does, lead to no representation and in the long run is unsustainable. With no requirement to explain to citizens what it is doing or how it spends money a government becomes literally unaccountable. Dangerous political conditions can then develop, usually slowly, leaving a yawning divorce between the well-funded authorities and the general populace – a classic recipe in the end for political upheaval.

In either circumstance it is the consequent political instability which weakens investment and undermines growth. It can, and does, happen.

2.4 A GOOD TAX? THE CRITERIA FOR ASSESSMENT

The performance and robustness of any tax system or regime needs to be measured against certain basic attributes or qualities. In effect these constitute the benchmarks, or basic criteria, against which the soundness of any particular tax can be initially measured and which can provide a framework for evaluation.

Below are listed and discussed the most important of these attributes. Obviously the list is not comprehensive and could be almost indefinitely extended to cover such a vast subject. The levying of taxation has, after all, been a central activity in human affairs since organized social groupings first appeared in history. But here are six of the most fundamental criteria against which any tax, if it is to succeed in its basic purposes, requires to be appraised.

Efficiency

This criterion refers to the impact of any tax on the allocation of resources in the economy, as determined by the tastes and preferences of individuals. It is often referred to as the social optimal position. The allocative efficiency concept has been the main point of departure for the economic theory of optimal taxation.[4] Reduced efficiency implies reduced output and a lower standard of living, when as a consequence of a tax being imposed investments are not placed where the productivity of capital is highest. An efficient tax neither impedes nor reduces the productive capacity of an economy, nor does it create distortions in the allocation of resources by favoring one industry or type of investment at the expense of others. The concept of efficiency is often combined with the neutrality criterion, explained below.

Neutrality

The neutrality criterion determines whether the tax system interferes with investment and operational decisions in such a way as to cause them to deviate from what is the social optimum. A neutral tax will reduce disposable income but does not otherwise affect decisions on consumption, trade or production.[5] It will also generate revenues when a company earns profits and nothing when it makes losses. A neutral tax does not distort investment decisions while a distortionary tax affects the decision making process, so that individuals make inferior choices to those that would have been made in the absence of the tax; consequently, resources are not allocated efficiently. In the petroleum sector, for instance, a non-neutral tax can adversely affect decisions relating to the development of marginal fields. A neutral tax neither deters exploitation of a full range of field sizes, nor alters project rankings nor interferes with price and production decisions. Thus, if project A is more attractive than project B before tax, it should remain so after tax. In such a case, a rational investor will implement exactly the same investment policies as in the absence of taxation.

Equity

Equity issues can be considered from a number of different perspectives. Firstly, equity can be assessed in both a 'horizontal' and a 'vertical' sense. The concept of horizontal equity implies that tax payers with equal abilities to pay should pay the same amount of tax. Also, firms in the same economic circumstances or oil fields with the same characteristics, including similar cost structures, should be taxed in the same way if a degree of 'horizontal' equity is to be achieved. By contrast 'vertical' equity requires that taxpayers with a greater ability to pay should pay more tax. It also refers to the equivalent treatment of companies or resources with different characteristics. A progressive tax is more likely to satisfy this criterion. Firms that exploit more valuable resources have a greater ability to pay and so their tax liabilities can be greater. Similarly, fields with high profitability can be taxed more heavily than those with low profitability. Some authors like Stauffer and Gault (1985) emphasize the equity issue and argue that one way of improving a tax system is to reduce taxes on marginal fields and equalise each participant's after-tax return across all fields.

Secondly, extracting and consuming natural resources now will reduce the stock available for future generations. Some argue that a tax system, which satisfies the intergenerational equity criterion, is one that discourages rapid depletion of resources when prices are low at the expense of future generations. In this sense, an equitable tax will ensure that future generations get a fair share of the resources or compensation for those that are depleted. 'Fair' however is a difficult word, and especially so when it involves attempted predictions about the circumstances which future generations may face.

Finally, equity considerations arise from the assumption that since the state (or in the UK case, the Crown) is the basic owner of all a nation's natural resources it should receive a fair and equitable payment for all concessions, licences to exploit or any other 'rights' transferred to operating entities, whether these entities are themselves state-owned bodies, or part state-owned companies, or companies entirely within the private sector.

Risk sharing

Risk can be defined as the variation in the investor's expected returns. When the investor evaluates the profitability of a project, the required rate of return combines both a risk free rate and a risk premium.[6] The lower the premium the lower the required rate of return and vice-versa. There are several sources of risk in oil activity. Exploration activity is dominated by risks related to the geological and geophysical attributes of a project, namely the probability associated with finding substantial and economic deposits when drilling. However, risk is not only limited to the exploration phase; 'only when the deposit is exhausted do you know precisely what the reserve was'.[7] The volatility of oil prices is also an important source of risk, affecting all projects in the same direction.

The attitude of the investor depends not only on the level of tax, but also on the extent to which the government shares the project's risks. There is no doubt that companies have the means to diversify certain levels of risks through, for instance, a large, worldwide portfolio, but they obviously try to avoid those situations where the potential rewards are outweighed by the perceived risks.

There is also the matter of fiscal risk. In this sense, taxation can increase the risk of a project if it increases the political risk by means of additional fiscal risk. The latter issue is considered in the context of the criterion of stability, explained further below.

Stability

This is an intangible yet crucial attribute of a fiscal regime. It directly affects the confidence of investors in government policy, particularly in the case of petroleum extraction activity, where long-term projects are the norm. If a tax system changes frequently and *prima facie* in an unpredictable manner, it may seriously affect future development projects. A tax system subject to continuous tinkering tends to increase political risk and reduce the value placed by investors on future income streams. If the variation of taxes over project life can be minimized – that is if the tax regime is stable – there is one less variable to worry the investor. One risk factor is either reduced or eliminated. That is why authors like Boskin and Robinson (1985) argue that temporary taxes are likely to be inferior to permanent ones.

Stability can be also considered in the context of government revenue. A tax system should have some level of predictability and reliability to enable governments to know how much revenue will be collected and when. Tax revenues should not rely on volatile exogenous factors such as the crude oil price, otherwise this can undermine Budget arithmetic, creating the need for tax rises elsewhere in the economy if revenue forecasts prove over-optimistic. Stable government revenue clearly assists with reliable expenditure forecasting and budgeting.

Clarity and simplicity

These criteria are relevant to the administration and monitoring of the tax system, also referred to as administrative efficiency. An ideal tax is simple to understand and inexpensive to administer. It is levied on a well-defined tax base that is simple and easy to collect. The simpler a tax base is, the lower the administrative costs are, for both administrations and the taxpaying businesses. A simple tax system makes it easier for taxpayers to judge the tax consequences of their actions. Transparency is equally important; it allows taxpayers to know the true cost of transactions. Also, the more transparent the means by which the government obtains revenues, the better informed the investors and the less the scope for manipulation and administrative discretion – behavior which is bound to increase industry's perception of risk.[8]

2.5 MEETING THE CRITERIA – CONFLICTS AND COMPROMISES

As in most areas of taxation there are inevitable compromises in satisfying the evaluation criteria. The most prominent of these potential clashes are analyzed below.

Neutrality and simplicity

Several studies have questioned the suitability of neutrality as a major characteristic of tax systems.[9] A major disadvantage with neutral taxes is their complicated administration, especially in the case of petroleum extraction where the individual characteristics of oil fields (size, location, quality, etc) have to be recognized. To maintain neutrality, the government is required to calculate different levels of rent and expected yields in order to value each individual field properly, subsequently imposing what would be called a fully differentiated tax. Such a task is impractical since it can be significantly complicated to administer.

Neutrality versus revenue generation

There can be a conflict between revenue collection and neutrality. A neutral tax system provides incentives for companies to exploit marginal fields. However, because marginal fields do not generate resource rent, they do not generate revenues for the government. As Mommer (1996) debates, under a neutral tax regime the company can exploit the resource without paying any tax.

Equity versus simplicity and efficiency

Governments often try to incorporate tax allowances and reliefs to reduce the tax burden on marginal fields as a means of ensuring equity. Such allocations, however, can impose additional administrative costs, thereby making the tax system complicated. Also, these allowances can generate misallocation of resources, thereby creating inefficiencies. Furthermore, the concept of fairness, like beauty, is subjective. It has different meanings to people. For instance, some would view an income tax system as fair if there were deductions for basic items such as medical expenditures and child care. Applied to the oil industry and indeed to extractive businesses generally, this 'grey area' can and does lead to endless disputes as to what constitute legitimate and therefore deductible costs. One firm's situation can be quite different from another's. A 'simple' tax system applied to all invariably seems unfair to some. Others would view the system as fair if there were almost no deductions. Some view an income tax as fair if it represents a higher percentage of a high income taxpayer's income relative to lower income taxpayer (that is the system is progressive). On the other hand, some view an income tax as fair if everyone pays the same rate (the tax is the same percentage of every taxpayer's income yet high income taxpayers pay more because they have more income).

Stability versus fiscal risk

Although stability of the tax regime is often advocated, in reality it cannot be fully achieved. Circumstances are constantly changing. Governments seeking stable revenue flows will adjust tax regimes to suit their needs. From their viewpoint, what is considered stability – i.e. a steady incoming tax flow – may feel to the taxpayer like change and uncertainty. Much as taxpaying enterprises would like it, governments cannot be expected to cast their tax systems in stone. Flexibility there has to be in any tax system if it is to respond to differing conditions and to evolve as a result of major changes in the external environment. All this inevitably increase the sense of risk associated with any particular project or investment. What looks a profitable investment at the outset, with attractive rates of return, can be turned sour by unanticipated changes in tax arrangements which, to the government, may look entirely reasonable.

Risk-sharing

The criteria of risk sharing can be argued in terms of the extent to which the risk can be shared between the government and investors. However, it is noteworthy that companies have a portfolio of activities and are able to diversify certain forms of risk.

It can be concluded that there is always, of necessity, a degree of compromise between the various criteria which an optimal tax would require when trying to design and implement a practical tax system. Compromise is also inevitable because of the competing objectives and interests of government and the private investor. The government usually seeks to achieve high revenues and receive a portion of the fiscal take relatively early in the life of a petroleum project, while at the same time accepting an appropriate amount of project risk. The private investor has to accept the need for a reasonable overall level of tax take, especially in fiscal systems that adopt a risk sharing attitude, whilst nevertheless seeking to recover project costs at an early stage.

Given all the compromises between criteria and trade-offs between objectives, it is not surprising to find that the principal tax instruments suggested in previous studies fail to satisfy all the main criteria of optimal taxation. Different authors have accorded varying weights to the main criteria discussed. For example, according to Heady (1993), the equity concept has to be the main consideration, and it is certainly true that amongst economists it has been widely discussed and forms a major part of the evaluation of any tax policy. By contrast, Kemp and Rose (1983) emphasize the importance of efficiency and risk sharing attributes, whereas Dickson (1999) ignores the concept of risk sharing and focuses on efficiency/neutrality and equity. Raja (1999) concentrates on the concept of neutrality and Watkins (2001), whilst respecting the majority of the key criteria, chooses to give most emphasis to the concept of risk sharing.

Despite such divergence in interests, the majority (if not all) of the work undertaken in the area of optimal taxation in the petroleum and wider energy sector follows a common theme, that of economic rent. In general, the studies contend that a tax based on economic rent is likely to be an ideal tax. To assist in understanding the validity of such views the concept of economic rent is defined and discussed in the next section.

2.6 ECONOMIC RENT

The concept of economic rent is central to the petroleum taxation debate. This section starts with the definition of economic rent in order to understand the reasons why previous studies have considered it the most suitable base for an ideal tax. The section further emphasizes the different types of economic rent and discusses their implications on taxation policy.

Economic rent can be defined as the true value of the natural resource, the difference between the revenues generated from resource extraction and the costs of extraction. These costs include the costs of employing factors of production and their opportunity costs.[10] In other words, economic rent represents the surplus return above the value of the capital, labour and other factors of production employed to exploit the resource. It is the surplus revenue of the resource after accounting for the costs of all capital and labour inputs.[11] In addition to the capital and labour inputs referred to, further inputs in respect of entrepreneurial reward and risk taking are also usually incorporated.

2.6.1 Types of rent

Several types of rent can be identified. These need to be highlighted before further explaining the suitability of economic rent as a tax base, since such differences can be of particular significance in taxation policy. The three main types of economic rent are as follows:

Scarcity rent

This type of rent results from the natural scarcity of the resource, which limits the output available. It represents the foregone future profits as a result of extraction today. Harold Hotelling, an American economist, argued, in an important article published in the early 1930s, that a mining firm or enterprise with a given stock of reserves will behave differently from other and different kinds of business. Normally, competitive firms continue to expand their output until the cost of producing the next unit – the marginal cost – equals the market price it receives. But a mining operation, in addition to its production costs, must also consider the opportunity cost associated with producing one more unit of output during the current period, because reserves exploited today are not available in the future. This cost, which is also referred to as scarcity rent or user cost, equals the net present value of the loss in future profits associated with producing one more unit of output today. It can also be expressed as the difference between marginal revenue and marginal production cost that can only come about as a result of the natural or policy induced scarcity of the resource.[12] Non-renewable resource projects that cannot recover their production costs plus user costs have an incentive to alter their behaviour by ceasing production. If the market price is not high enough to cover both the production and user costs a firm is better off keeping the reserves in the ground for use in the future. In general, user cost is often considered as a cost rather than a rent.

Differential or Ricardian rent

David Ricardo, a British economist writing in the nineteenth century, was one of the first to apply the concept of rent. He argued that arable land could be separated into different classes according to its fertility. Increasingly greater levels of rent accrue to land of increasing productivity, with land at the margin receiving no rent. This is illustrated in Figure 2.1.

AC and MC respectively represent the average costs and marginal cost of food production. Land A enjoys the largest rent as it can produce food at the

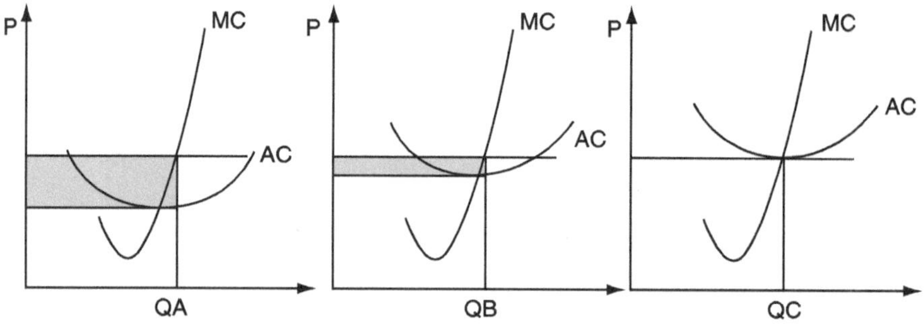

Figure 2.1 Ricardian rent.

lowest cost. The next best land, B, has somewhat higher costs, but still earns rent as its unit production cost is lower than the market price. The marginal land, C, does not, since its AC is too great and is equal to the unit price. The rents accruing to A and B are determined in comparison to C, as they benefit from greater productivity or better soil quality as compared with C. That is why such rent is referred to as differential rent or quality rent; it normally arises because extraction costs depend on differences in the quality of the resource and location.

This is analogous to the returns accruing to oilfields. Mineral deposits such as oilfields can be grouped by ascending cost of production. Fields with unit costs below market prices – because of efficiencies or favourable physical properties – enjoy Ricardian rent, reflecting greater profitability. The marginal field is the field with a unit cost equal to the market price; it has no rent.

In Figure 2.2, wellhead prices and unit costs are measured on the vertical axis; field production is measured on the horizontal axis in terms of ascending cost. Field A has a unit cost ***cA*** and a unit rent of (p-cA), where (p) is the market price. Field B, with a unit cost equal to price (p) has no rent.

Quasi rent

The third type of rent represents the returns that accrue to firms from past investment and innovative practice or as a result of changes in the market. Such rents only occur in the short-run before they are competed away. They are earnings over and above that required to maintain a firm in business in the short run. The existence of sunk costs, representing past expenditure, is a necessary but not sufficient condition to generate quasi rents. Short-run rent, then, is the difference between the market price and the supply prices of variable inputs (labour, power and the like). Normally, short-run rents can be expected to exceed long-run rents. In the case of petroleum, short-run rents for an already discovered and developed field – the difference between the wellhead revenues and extraction costs – would typically be large, since extraction costs tend to be relatively small. Rents on discovered but

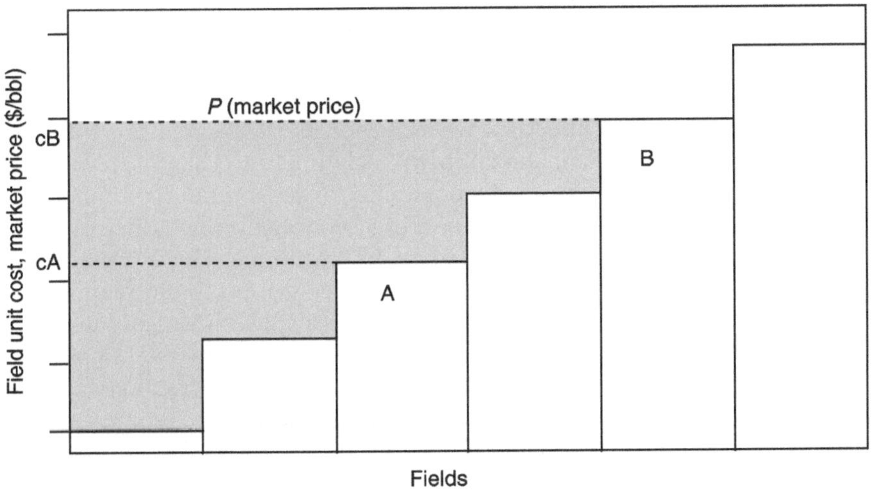

Figure 2.2 Oil field Ricardian rent.

undeveloped resources entail deduction of development costs in addition to extraction costs. Rents on unexplored land involve deduction of finding costs, as well as development and extraction costs. In short, economic rent can vary between costs and returns necessary to sustain ongoing production from existing fields, development of discovered fields, and new exploration costs. Calculations or estimates of economic rent are bound to depend on the stage of development reached by any particular petroleum property.

2.6.2 Issues raised by economic rent: simple theory but complex reality

Determining taxable income from oil and natural gas production has long been a source of controversy. But because economic rent is best considered as a bonus – a financial return not required to motivate desired economic behavior[13] – there is a general presumption that a tax based on economic rent is optimal since it satisfies the tax criteria. Since the magnitude of such 'rent' profits is seen as unrelated to management skills or the wisdom of economic decisions, it is judged to be a fully justifiable base for taxation. In theory, therefore, economic rent tends to be viewed as an important and legitimate source of government revenue since its appropriation, again in theory, can take place without destroying economic incentives.

Here, for example, are some of the arguments and contentions which tend to be most commonly advanced in favor of taxing economic rents – often very heavily – as the ideal means of taxation; of plucking the goose without losing the golden eggs.

First and foremost, it is very often claimed that if taxes are only levied on economic rent, there will be no effect on the incentive of firms to undertake any activity since rent is not required by the firm to continue or initiate operations. Additionally, because the true value of the resource will be collected, the consumption of future generations will not be sacrificed cheaply. Further, if the tax seeks to capture economic rent, then the tax take falls when economic rent decreases and rises when it increases. As such, the tax base responds in the appropriate direction to variations in costs and crude oil prices. A stable system increases the possibility of substantial economic rent. A fair progressive tax, aimed at absorbing economic rent, is neutral and stable. A tax system, which collects as much economic rent as possible, is fair to the community. A neutral tax should fall on economic rent which, at the same time, will allow for risk sharing between government and investor. The exploitation of exhaustible natural resources can generate significant economic rent. Oil, in particular, is not only an exhaustible resource but also a commodity which for most of the oil industry's recorded lifetime has had no perfect substitute (although this could now be changing). This implies that the extraction of oil can earn substantial amounts of economic rent, and that has inevitably become the widely held assumption in the minds of petroleum tax policy makers.

Yet, many complications arise when estimating the quantum of economic rent. The complications include distinguishing between various types of rent. Scarcity rent and differential rent generate the total resource rent.

However, the classification between scarcity and differential rent is somewhat artificial, since any rent could be understood to be generated by either scarcity or differential effects alone and in reality governments find it difficult to distinguish between the two types. The resource rent (i.e. scarcity rent and differential rent) is an appropriate tax base since taxation of this rent does not affect the behaviour of the firm. This is not the case with quasi rent. Although quasi rent is part of economic rent, it only occurs in the short run. The capture of quasi rent can alter the long run efficiency behaviour of firms, often causing them to reduce investment and therefore the social optimum level of output. Naturally, any firm strives to retain the quasi rent generated by its more efficient behaviour in comparison to other firms. But it will be competed away in the long run since competitors will learn from the firm generating quasi rent. As such, quasi rent is not to be included in the tax base but the question is how to identify or quantify that rent and distinguish it from other types?

A second complication is the difficulty governments have in determining acceptable rates of return for all companies, especially oil companies, as they do not normally reveal directly their required rate of return on investment. The question therefore arises as to how the rent element is to be sensibly judged as between different enterprises which may well have varying views about what constitutes an acceptable rate of return.

Thirdly, measuring economic rent requires knowledge of the differing costs of the individual factors of production as well as their opportunity costs. The difficulty in measuring each of these components is what makes the determination of economic rent and its capture complex and controversial. Further, because the size of a given discovery and its related exploitation costs can vary substantially, economic rent will vary from field to field. Although this problem can be partly overcome by a progressive tax system, it is difficult to make conventional fiscal systems sufficiently flexible and focused on resource rent across a wide range of variables, such as price and different cost structures.

Two further troubling issues arise in relation to economic rent calculation. First, rents are found in many sectors. Ricardo focused on agriculture land. Forestry, fishing and other important sectors using natural resources also generate sizable rents. If mining rents are to be taxed, should not the same apply for all rents? Yet rarely do those advocating the taxation of mining rents extend their proposals to other rents. Second, and more importantly, it is the discovery of rich deposits or technological developments that permit the profitable exploitation of known but previously uneconomic resources that create rents. Of course, favourable geology is necessary. But prior to their discovery and the development of the necessary production technologies, mineral resources have no value.

As a result, in the very long run there are no true rents in the mining sector. We have already seen that the quasi rent, if taken by the state, will reduce or eliminate the incentives that companies have to invest. In the case of pure rent it is the hope of discovering a bonanza, a deposit so rich it can generate huge amounts of pure rent, that drives exploration. Similarly, the quest for pure rent motivates the research that creates new technologies, allowing the mining and processing of known, but previously uneconomic, mineral resources. So governments that tax pure rent (even though they carefully leave the quasi rent) are doomed to watch their mineral sector slowly decline over time as their known deposits are depleted. The presence of substantial Ricardian rent in the short-run, coupled with the absence of such rents in the very long run creates a danger of short-sighted public policy. Higher taxes on mining will almost always appear to work successfully for a time. Their adverse effects on mining production and government revenues may take years to become apparent.

In summary, and taking the problems outlined above into account, it emerges that economic rent capture is not, in practice as opposed to theory, quite so simple and straightforward after all. Given the issues of complexity, variations through both time and circumstances and the difficulties of design and definition, it suggests that other forms of oil taxation, to which we now turn, could provide a better route in many instances – although, as we shall see, these, too, have their distinct disadvantages.

2.7 TAX INSTRUMENTS[14]

Oil taxation can take many forms. As has been shown, a variety of tax instruments have been proposed in the literature on energy taxation in order to capture the economic rent from oil activity. This section defines these instruments and analyses their main characteristics. Four tax instruments are selected namely Gross Royalty, Brown Tax, Resource Rent Tax (RRT) and Income Tax. Royalty is an output-based tax because it is levied on the unit or the value of production, whereas the other three instruments are profit-based taxes or cash-flow taxes, because they are imposed on net profit or operating income after capital investment. A description of each of these instruments follows.

Gross royalty

A Royalty is a payment made for the right to use another's property for purposes of gain. It is a payment for the use of a wasting asset,[15] though to most investors it is simply a tax like any other. Authors like Mommer (2001) argue that a country is entitled to earn a Royalty on the extraction of its natural resources. This entitlement arises from the reward of ownership; this is similar to a piece of land being taken away, hence compensation is necessary. The Royalty can be a per-unit tax, which is a uniform fixed charge levied on a specified level of output or an ad-valorem tax, which is a fixed charge levied on the value of the output. In other words, GR is determined with reference to the volume of production or to gross revenues.

Brown tax[16]

This tax is levied as a fixed proportion of a project's net cash flow in each period. When net cash flow is positive firms have to pay the tax but when negative firms receive a rebate. In other words, BT involves the payment of a proportional subsidy or tax credits on annual cash losses and an equivalent tax on annual cash profits. If the BT rate is set at 50 per cent, the government would supply half of the project cash outflows and obtain half of all cash inflows. In this case, the government has become an equal project partner or an equity participant. Consequently, the BT is a tax on net cash flow – with full contribution by the government where the net cash flows are negative.

Resource rent tax (RRT)

RRT was introduced by Garnaut and Clunies Ross (1975) and was developed primarily for application in less developed countries, particularly those that rely on external sources of capital investment. It is a modified version of BT but instead of paying tax credits in years with negative cash flows, the government allows such negative amounts to be carried forward and deducted from positive cash flows in later periods. However, the negative net cash flows are uplifted by a minimum rate of return requirement (the 'floor level' also called the 'threshold rate') and added to the next year's net cash flow. The accumulation process is continued until a positive net cash flow is generated.

No tax is payable until the firm has recovered its costs inclusive of a 'threshold rate' of return which is compounded from year to year. As such, RRT involves carrying forward losses, whereas the Brown Tax provides a rebate for losses. With RRT, the government makes no direct contribution to a project's capital's cost; tax kicks in only when positive cash flows emerge, the project investment is recovered and a threshold return on the investment is made.

Income tax

Unlike the previous two types of cash flow taxes, income tax applies to a company's profits. The tax is levied at a corporate rather than oil field level, as such it is generally known as corporation tax (CT) or tax on corporate net income. IT in most countries allows current expenses, interest expense and historic cost depreciation to be deducted. In fact, all forms of income tax allow relief for capital expenditure, but extra reliefs are sometimes given to provide incentives to develop high cost 'marginal' projects and are called 'uplift allowances on capital expenditure'.

In general, a country's oil taxation system can draw on any of these tax instruments, possibly with some adjustments and often using a combination of two or more of them. The UK petroleum fiscal regime is a typical example as it has included (over time) a Royalty, PRT (similar to RRT) and CT (IT); these are described in detail in Chapter 4.

2.8 QUALITATIVE ASSESSMENT OF MAIN TAX INSTRUMENTS

Royalties

Royalty is a simple tax. Its computation is straightforward since it is imposed on the amount or the value of the output. It also ensures a share of revenue for the government as soon as production commences. This is in contrast to profit-based taxes where the government obtains its first tranche of revenues only when the net cash flow begins to turn positive. In the case of GR, however, the government is less at risk, because the costs of exploration and production do not affect the Royalty base. In this sense, Royalty ensures that some of value of the resource, concurrent with extraction, flows to the state.

But since Royalty is imposed on gross revenues (or the amount of output) it ignores costs and profits associated with the project. As such, Royalty is not targeted on economic rent – indeed at low prices Royalty can take all the value of the project leaving the investor in a loss making position. Royalty is often referred to as classic example of a non-neutral tax, which can affect investors' behaviour and create distortions for several reasons.

Royalty has an up-front effect because it is imposed concurrent with the commencement of production. It is imposed irrespective of the size of the field and it is equivalent to an increase in the resource extraction cost, affecting the depletion decision of the investor. This may cause operating income to become negative even when gross revenues exceed extraction costs and consequently can lead to a premature abandonment of the field. Just as with any tax which is based on production not on profit, Royalty pushes more of the commercial risk on to the investor with little protection arising from cost increases or reduced oil prices. In fact, a high tax rate on production is more likely to cause distortions and disincentives to continuous production than a profits-tax at the same rate.

That is why there is a general agreement in the literature that Royalty is a regressive tax, which can render profitable projects unattractive on a post-tax basis. Royalties will eventually deter marginal investment as they are not profit based; this explains why in many mature basins such as the UK and Norway Royalty has been abolished.

However, distortions caused by the imposition of Royalty can be reduced by the application of a sliding scale Royalty. This Royalty is based on charging different rates of tax depending on the level of production or on oil prices. In this case, the Royalty rate will be low when production or the oil price is low and vice versa, thereby decreasing the possibility of negative cash flows when production or oil prices are low. Such a tax incorporates the benefit of normal Royalty, which is the generation of early revenues, and also combines a progressive aspect in contrast to the impact of a fixed rate. As such, the sliding scale Royalty can extend economic field life with both government and the investor sharing the overall gains. But there is one additional burden which cannot be avoided by any such schemes, which is the sheer administrative complexity of the sliding scale tax.[17] In some regimes allowances are made for costs in the computation of Royalty, and Royalty rates may vary with production, water depth and other proxies for profitability.

The Brown tax (BT)

BT is a cash-flow tax and consequently incorporates the different costs an investor incurs in each period. It is based on economic rent and satisfies principally the criteria of neutrality and risk sharing. It is usually described as the oldest type of neutral tax imposed on extraction industries. It is financially equivalent to the government having contributed equity in an oil field.

Despite such advantages in theory BT is an unpopular option in practice, not least because it imposes an unacceptable level of risk on the government. In fact, its biggest problem is the requirement for the government as owner to contribute capital up front. Furthermore, since companies are aware that in the case of unsuccessful exploration the government will subsidize their investment, they have less incentive to reduce costs and increase efficiency.

Resource rent tax (RRT)

RRT is a modified form of the BT, designed to capture economic rent and therefore considered a neutral tax. Furthermore, it is a progressive tax that responds automatically to a variety of outcomes. It is based on deemed profitability after allowance for a threshold rate of return representing normal profits. As with any tax based on profits, RRT tends to share risk with the government; if costs rise or oil prices fall taxable profits change in sympathy, as does the tax burden. Further still, as a company only pays tax when a profit is made the payback period of the investment will be shorter than if a Royalty is applied. It is often argued in the literature that RRT is an appropriate tax instrument to collect economic rent without distorting investment decisions. Consequently, it may be appropriate to apply RRT at significantly higher rates to capture a bigger share of rent given that it has less distorting effects at the margin than alternative forms of taxation. It is also relevant that RRT is levied on a project basis rather than on aggregate company income. Again in theory the appropriate threshold rate ought to vary across projects. But in practice, a uniform threshold rate often applies.

Despite these positive aspects RRT has some weaknesses. It is thought to give rise on occasion to over-investment, hence affecting the rate of resource depletion. Since it is targeted on economic rent it is difficult to raise large amounts of revenue and preserve neutrality, especially in view of the difficulties inherent in determining economic rent, as previously discussed.

In fact, problems result from the determination of the threshold at which RRT should be levied. The threshold represents the rate of return that investors require to undertake a project. In other words it represents the level of normal profit. However, this raises the issue of whether companies are motivated by the prospect of normal profit, since businesses usually seek to maximise profits. Furthermore, since the threshold reflects the investor's required rate of return, this can vary from one project to another.

As regards the generation of early revenues, if the government applies RRT it is unlikely to receive revenues until several years after first production. This is principally because the threshold rate has to be achieved before RRT becomes payable. Consequently, some authors argue that RRT is politically unacceptable since it may delay tax payments and can only be imposed in conjunction with corporation tax. A further complexity arises from the controversy over the pricing of the services from long-lived capital assets, and the implications for the definition of profit.

Income tax (IT) – some varying views

Since IT is a profit-based tax, it is also assumed to be neutral. Some authors describe IT as a typical example of a neutral tax because when profits are zero IT revenues are zero. This is unlike Royalty where if profits are zero the tax revenue will still be positive. A proportional IT can leave undistorted the choice among projects of different economic lives and time-line profiles. With full and immediate loss offsets, IT is therefore neutral in its impact on different projects.

Although, Dasgputa and Stiglitz (1971) argue that no differential taxes should be used, (otherwise they will affect the allocative efficiency of resources), the authors advise the use of differential taxes (e.g. special petroleum taxes) if economic rent exists. If differential taxes are not feasible, high rates of corporate taxes can be applied to the energy sector to tax rent indirectly. Garnaut and Clunies Ross (1975) recommended an adjusted version of IT, known as the higher rates of proportional income tax (HRIT), which is targeted more on economic rent than on profits and requires payment of normal corporate IT but at a higher rate than would be applicable to non-resource income.

IT also has some limitations in the case of resource taxation – a major one being that it does not allow any threshold return on equity capital. In fact, it is a tax on the total return to equity. Consequently, several authors conclude that IT is neither directly targeted at economic rent, nor is it progressive, hence it can distort investment decisions. Further, if tax reliefs are very large, a gold-plating effect may be induced whereby the investment in capital equipment may result in tax relief exceeding the original investment. The main debate surrounding IT is more likely to be focused on the immediate deductibility of costs. In practice, IT does allow for the deduction of capital costs but over a period of time using depreciation, which can apply over the life of the project. In contrast to BT and RRT, with IT, investors usually do not recover their costs immediately; this can result in early payments of revenues to the government. Thus for the investor the pattern of cost recovery relates to the economic life of the asset.

The conclusion of this section is that each tax has some benefits and some limitations, as summarized in Table 2.1. As such, it is not surprising that several oil producing countries have in practice adopted a combination of two or more tax instruments in an attempt to capture the economic rent and minimize distortions in the investment decision.

2.9 INTERACTION OF TAX INSTRUMENTS

Although a tax instrument can create distortions, it cannot be ruled out solely for this reason. The most appropriate tax instrument is one which creates the least distortion, and the more a tax is targeted towards economic rent, the less the distortion created. Often, the combination of several taxes is advisable – in fact this is the pattern which prevails in oil producing countries, such as the UK and Australia. Sometimes two taxes with opposite effects can be used to counterbalance each other. Often, the government has to choose a combination of fiscal arrangements, but it should be careful in determining the relative weights given to different elements in the structure of the system.

Table 2.1 Tax instruments summary

Tax Instruments	*Advantages*	*Limitations*
Royalty	– Simple – Early source of revenue	– Regressive – Non neutral – Not targeted on economic rent – Less risk sharing
Brown Tax	– Neutral – Risk sharing – Targeted on economic rent – Progressive	– High risk on government – Late source of revenue – Over-investment – Complicated
Resource Rent Tax	– Neutral – Progressive – Risk sharing – Targeted on economic rent	– Complicated – Requires knowledge of threshold rate – Late source of revenue – Over investment
Income Tax	– Simple – Neutral – Progressive – Risk sharing at the corporate level – Homogeneous treatment among industries	– Earlier revenue generation – Gold plating – Not project related – Often no immediate 100 per cent relief for Capital Expenditures

Authors like Garnaut and Clunies Ross (1979) argue in favor of a combination of RRT and IT where the company pays in each period the higher of either RRT or IT. In this situation, the company will pay IT even in early years, since with RRT the payments are delayed. At the same time, when RRT applies, both government and companies will benefit from the advantages of this tax. Other authors like Lund (2002) maintain that it is optimal to combine a tax on gross revenue, such as Royalty, with a tax on economic rent.

Stauffer and Gault (1985) maintain that an ideal tax substantially reduces perceived risk without any loss of revenue to the company. The authors compare the ideal tax to the following four fiscal packages: a Corporate income tax (CIT) with a deductible Royalty, a production-sharing contract[18] (PSC), a carried interest system superimposed on a CIT and Royalty, and a rent skimming surtax superimposed on CIT. The authors argue that while the Royalty and IT package is the highest risk scheme, the rent skimming scheme is the lowest (i.e. it allows high risk sharing). Carried interest systems are second while the PSC is third. However, despite its superiority to other tax systems, the rent skimming system is far from ideal, as it allows larger returns to the larger or more profitable discoveries.

2.10 SUMMARY AND CONCLUSION

In this chapter we have been able to survey and highlight the main functions and effects of petroleum taxation. The principal criteria of an ideal tax, against which all tax instruments relating to petroleum extraction activity are normally assessed, have been duly set out and examined. Six criteria in particular have been identified – efficiency, neutrality, equity, risk sharing, stability and simplicity – all of which are desirable when designing a tax system. A tax targeted on economic rent plainly has its attractions, as it is believed to meet the optimum criteria – although some downside problems of economic rent taxes have also been pointed out. Both the concept and type of economic rent have been explored since these have important implications for taxation policy. Additionally, the main tax instruments proposed in previous studies have been examined and analysed.

Several complications have been identified. In practice, designing an optimal tax system that meets different considerations, some of which are contradictory and which vary between countries and evolve over time is a challenging task. This is particularly true in the case of petroleum taxation, which is a complex issue in its own right, both in terms of economic theory and political economy. Natural resources, such as petroleum, have special characteristics that complicate the design of an optimal tax system. Oil is an exhaustible resource, with an uncertain level of reserves before any investment takes place. It is both a raw material input as well as a final product with no obvious close substitutes so far – especially in the transportation sector.

More importantly, as this chapter has demonstrated, the main source of complication lies in the difficulty of determining economic rent and the distinction between the various types of rents, namely resource rent and quasi rent. Another source of complication is the inevitable compromise between the various criteria of an optimal tax. Such difficulties make it complex to design and impose a tax that captures the resource rent exactly.

None of the tax instruments put forward in previous studies offers an optimal tax. The main tax instruments often suggested are Royalty, BT, RRT and IT. Each tax has both advantages and limitations.

The concept of an ideal tax is useful primarily as a paradigm against which to test actual or proposed fiscal systems. In practice, the perfect fiscal regime has yet to be invented. It is impossible to conceive of a fiscal regime that meets all the required characteristics at all prices, at all times for all sizes of fields and cost structures likely to be encountered in a given basin. Fiscal regimes have to be designed to match the nature of the investment opportunities and competitive interest from investors. Nevertheless, although compromise seems to be inevitable and an ideal tax is not practical, the trade-off can be improved and a balance can be reached in terms of generating a fair share of revenue for the government while keeping the country in question attractive for investment.

Designing the optimum tax regime requires that a delicate balance be struck between the needs of the oil industry and other stakeholders, including government and the community. If the proper balance is not achieved, the result can be a tax regime that serves neither the consumer, the investor nor the nation. Just as a competitive oil tax regime will attract investment, it follows that an unattractive regime can drive away investment. An adverse change to a country's petroleum tax rules can result in reduced exploration activity, well and field closures and deferment of expansion plans.

Great care must therefore be exercised in designing and maintaining a country's oil taxation regime. This is a dynamic process and the fiscal regime will need to evolve with the development and maturity of the basin and reflect competitive pressure in alternative hydrocarbon provinces. It should never be forgotten that oil investment can always move elsewhere. Even those countries with the most accessible and plentiful reserves must necessarily recognise, in designing their tax regimes, that the oil industry has completely special attributes.

There is no such thing as the perfect oil tax regime. A country's tax regime is the product of balancing the need to have an internationally competitive regime with government policies that reflect the nation's unique priorities – priorities which will certainly include the primary one of security of domestic supply. Failure to ensure secure and reliable flows of affordable energy and to avoid supply interruptions, has toppled too many governments for any authorities to feel secure unless they can deliver on this front. As a result, oil producing nations have implemented oil tax regimes that include a wide range of varying features round the world to suit their individual conditions and political and social environments. It is to a comparison of these regimes, and of their variety, efficiency and durability, that the next chapter now turns.

3 Comparing fiscal regimes

An examination of six petroleum tax packages and policies, either developed and now operating, or being developed, round the world.

3.1 ORIGINS AND ROOTS

Tax systems have their roots in the culture, history and socio-political conditions of the countries or jurisdictions in which they are imposed. This applies as much to petroleum taxation in oil and gas producing countries as to any other forms of tax. No two countries' conditions are the same. Attempts to export and replicate the fiscal patterns of one state in another invariably fail.

The story is told of the world-famous British tax expert, Nicholas Kaldor, a star disciple of Lord Keynes and key adviser to the British Government back in the 1950s. Kaldor had elaborate and ingenious views on tax reform which were applied with limited success within the UK. However when other governments called on his advice and tried to introduce his ideas the results were catastrophic, leading in several cases to governmental overthrow, revolution and violence. For example there were riots in India when his tax advice was applied. In Sri Lanka there were also violent protests. In Mexico the government fell, also in British Guiana. In Ghana there was a coup, in Turkey, riots, in Venezuela a change of government – quite a record. The lesson is that while the study of other regimes can provide lessons and standards, adopting or copying fiscal systems wholesale can end in tears.[1]

In the case of petroleum, while it is true that the oil industry has a strongly international character, local influences, both external and internal to the industry itself, such as province maturity, field size, self sufficiency, security of supply considerations and specific characteristics can still be decisive in shaping the tax regime and in turn influencing the overall attractiveness of the province.

Also, fashions change and evolve about the preferred relationship which governments may wish to have with their oil and gas extraction sectors. The case history of oil production in the UK North Sea shows how at one stage partial state ownership of the resource was favoured, with all oil being produced either by a giant state corporation – the British National Oil Corporation (BNOC) – or under tight contractual terms (under a Socialist-inclined government), while at another stage the approach favoured greater delegation and a concessionary regime. Round the oil-producing world a variety of relationships exist – and change – along this spectrum, from complete state ownership at one extreme, to total private enterprise operations at the other.

Other key variables determining the differing pattern of tax regimes are the age and maturity of the province and the general trend and expected pattern of world crude oil prices. In countries with oil provinces where production has peaked and is declining, fiscal regimes can be shaped (although policy-makers may be slow to adjust) to compensate for the decline by encouraging existing and new companies to sustain output, develop less profitable fields and revisit fields previously deemed to have been exhausted. The tax impact can be decisive in these areas. For instance in Norway, in an attempt to ease the fiscal regime in line with production profiles, royalty was tapered off in 1986 for fields that were still liable to it.

Price obviously plays its part as well. Where governments reach the view that prices have moved on to a higher plane, and will stay there, attitudes to tax also change. Of course the inclination of tax-gathering authorities is to assume that higher prices will stay and therefore regimes can be tightened up to divert more of the benefits to the state, and of course governments can be wrong. To take a UK example again, in 2002 the UK tightened its fiscal regime by imposing a supplementary tax (ST) on North Sea operators. This was doubled in 2005, driven, no doubt by soaring world crude prices and in defiance of the fact that the UK North Sea had become a fully mature province.

All these influences help explain the extraordinary variety of fiscal regimes and packages which exist around the world, despite a large pool of common experience and some powerful underlying principles. Johnston (1998, p.5) has rightly observed that 'there are more petroleum fiscal regimes in the word than there are countries' – a point well illustrated by the fact that even within one nation, such as Canada, provincial variations in the management and taxation of resources occur and differing patterns co-exist.

In the previous chapter, the difficulties were discussed both of achieving the best balance between the competing objectives of a 'fair' government share of oil revenues and the imperative of oil company profitability and of the practical barriers to an optimal petroleum tax system. In this chapter, six different national petroleum tax regimes, both established and evolving, are analysed and compared. The countries chosen are the UK, Norway, Australia, Indonesia, China and Iraq. The aim is to evaluate the ways in which these countries are addressing their specific petroleum taxation problems. All of them are facing widely differing circumstances, with three of those selected following concessionary and three following contractual regimes. As we shall see, variety is the keynote.

3.2 CONCESSIONARY AND CONTRACTUAL SYSTEMS: A PRELIMINARY NOTE

In the pattern of relationships between governments and the exploitation of petroleum resources two basic categories of agreement have developed over the years – the concessionary system and contractual agreement. The concessionary system originated with the very beginning of the petroleum industry (c. 1850), while the contractual system emerged a century later (c. 1950).

Mommer (2001) describes the two categories of fiscal regime as the liberal and the proprietorial regime respectively. The author argues that in liberal regimes, oil companies are in a much stronger position compared with the proprietorial systems, where the government exercises a stronger control over the exploitation and production of the natural resource. But the reality which has emerged behind these different approaches is one of ideology and political fashion.

In the high noon of twentieth-century socialism, the doctrine of state ownership applied with special vigour in the petroleum sector. In the twenty-first century age of decentralisation this has become diluted by and mixed with the desire to delegate and to mobilise the energies of private enterprise in the service of public and governmental aims. However, the instinct within governing circles, especially in the weaker democracies, is to retain closely both ownership and control of oil resources, and therefore to adhere to contractual type schemes, tightly circumscribed.

But this instinct may be misleading. As the pioneers of privatisation in the UK discovered in the 1980s and 90s, moving from the old pattern of nationalized state ownership to privatised industries by no means led to weaker control. Conversely, full public ownership could mean loss of political control, poor accountability and the progressive transfer of direction and influence to unelected boards with their own powerful constituencies. The clear lesson of that era, both for petroleum extraction in the North Sea and for other previously nationalized concerns, was that privatisation, and concessions granted to private enterprise firms, could be combined with the appropriate fiscal and regulatory systems to provide *more* and not *less* control and accountability than state ownership had ever afforded.

3.3 CONCESSIONARY SYSTEMS: THE DETAIL

A concession is an agreement between a government and a company that grants the company the exclusive right to explore for, develop, produce, transport and market the petroleum resource at its own risk and expense within a fixed area for a specific amount of time. The degree of 'concession' can certainly vary. Under one type of concessionary arrangement, while resources in the ground (or seabed) remain the property of the state or crown, oil companies take title to produce oil at the wellhead and then pay the appropriate royalties and taxes. The company is entitled to ownership of the production and can freely dispose of it, subject to the obligation to supply local markets.

A broader type of concession, such as found in the United States, goes further and assigns rights of ownership to the actual reserves in the ground to the discoverer of those reserves. This is still the case in some other countries. However, in Europe especially, the reserves are considered as constituting inalienable natural resources and the concessionaire acquires the ownership of the production at the wellhead. The minerals remain the property of the state until produced.

A striking example of this earlier pattern was the concession granted to W.K. D'Arcy by the Persian monarchy in 1901. This covered very large areas, indeed the entire national territory, and with a very long duration, up to 60 and 75 years. Similar 'long-lease' concessions were granted in earlier years (sometimes up to 99 years in Kuwait), providing exclusive ownership to the IOC of the reserves found in the area covered by the concession. The financial benefits accruing to the host government were limited and consisted primarily of payments based on volume of production and labelled royalties at a flat rate rather than a percentage of the value of the oil produced. The concessionaire retained control virtually over all aspects of the operations, including the rate of exploration, the decision to bring new fields into exploitation, the determination of production levels, among others. This type of early concession agreements did not provide for any possibility of renegotiation of the terms and conditions of the agreement, should a change of circumstances warrant it. It did not enable the government to participate in the ownership of the petroleum produced and left it with basically a passive role.

Such one-sided arrangements were bound to be called in question as the balance of power changed in favour of ruling authorities and governments. After World War II, a second generation of concession agreements was developed, providing for more active role for the host government and a corresponding decrease in the rights of the IOCs. The concession areas began to be limited to blocks, and the awarding of concessions restricted to a limited number of blocks. Modern concession agreements also include provisions for the surrender of most of the original area and the duration of the concession tend to be far more tightly limited. They also comprise bonuses payable on signature of the agreement, on discovery of a petroleum field or on reaching certain levels of production.

Since the 1970s, as a consequence of the oil crisis, the trend has intensified to devise more and more complex tax regimes, for example through the introduction of special taxes, in order to increase the host government's take in relation to the profitability of petroleum operations. Host governments, where there has not been outright reversion to state ownership, have nevertheless assigned to themselves the authority to exercise increasingly intrusive monitoring and control over a private sector concern's decisions, for example, by requiring minimum exploration work programmes, participation in the decision-making process and approval of the exploration costs and expenses. Russia is one example of 'moving the goal posts' in this way. Also, in early days in the North Sea, the Norwegian government selected a model in which foreign companies carried out all petroleum activities on the Norwegian continental shelf. Over time, the Norwegian involvement was strengthened through the creation of a wholly owned state oil company, Statoil.

There are now 55 countries applying a concessionary system to petroleum activity.[2] The usual way of taxing oil companies in a concessionary regime involves a combination of IT, special petroleum tax (SPT) and royalty. That is why concessionary regimes are commonly known as 'Royalty/Tax Systems'.

Royalties, which originated in the United States, are typically either specific levies (based on the volume of oil and gas extracted) or ad valorem (based on the value of oil and gas extracted). Royalty rates are generally set at a level close to 12.5 per cent (1/8th) of production. Some countries have introduced a profit element in royalties by having them depend on the level of production. This is known as a sliding scale royalty.

Income tax is generally the most frequently deployed instrument used in oil producing countries of the world. IT systems usually consist of a basic rate structure i.e. a single rate, plus provisions for deduction of certain items from the tax base, supplementary levies and tax incentives. The overall corporate IT rate in several countries lies in the range 30 to 35 per cent. Various countries provide an incentive for exploration and development by allowing exploration costs to be recovered immediately and allowing accelerated recovery of development costs (tax depreciation), for example, over five years. Accelerated cost recovery brings forward payback for the investor. In addition to tax deductions, losses carried forward and/or back are commonly allowed tax incentives. Invariably the income tax regime for oil and gas companies is the same regime that applies to all corporate activities for all industries in the country in question.

In addition to income tax, most oil-producing countries impose a special petroleum tax, such as RRT, in order to capture a larger share of economic rent from oil production. This special tax is normally based on cash flow but is imposed only when cumulative cash flow is positive. In countries where the special petroleum tax exists, the tax is usually imposed as a supplement to the general corporate IT. An issue arises as to whether the special tax should be imposed before or after the IT. If imposed before, then it can be treated as a deductible cost (as in the UK), but if imposed after, the payment of IT can be treated as a cash outflow in calculating the special tax's income base.

Other payments can also be made to the government. These include bonuses, which are lump sum payments made to the government. They can be signature bonus, payable upon signing the agreement with the government, discovery bonus, payable when a commercial discovery is made, or production bonus, payable at an agreed amount upon the achievement of a stated level of daily production. Production bonuses are normally on a sliding scale of production, therefore if daily production reaches a certain level the government takes a fixed sum, which increases if daily production reaches higher levels. Depending on the tax regime, bonuses may be deductible for income tax purposes. In most cases, discovery and production bonuses have little effect on the profitability of a field. Signature bonuses would appear to have a negative effect; whilst they are not taxes in the strict sense, they recover the economic rent up front. The sums today are very large (circa $1 billion per block); they comprise a material proportion of overall government take and are paid before discoveries are made.

Some countries ring-fence their oil and gas activities whilst others ring-fence individual projects. Ring fencing imposes a limitation on deductions for tax purposes across different activities or projects undertaken by the same taxpayer. These rules matter for two main reasons. Firstly, the absence of ring fencing can postpone government tax receipts because a company that undertakes a series of projects is able to deduct exploration and development costs from each new project against the income of projects that are already generating taxable income. Secondly, as an oil and gas area matures, the absence of ring fencing may discriminate against new entrants that have no income against which to deduct exploration or development expenditures.

This brief catalogue of the instruments of control which governments can and do apply to concession-receiving companies amply confirms that control can come in many forms. State ownership is by no means the necessary condition for such control. Nevertheless, a number of governments cling to ownership patterns, contracting out only the operational tasks of surveying, developing and extracting petroleum. To these we now turn.

3.4 CONTRACTUAL SYSTEMS

Under the typical contractual based systems, the oil company is appointed by the government as a contractor on a certain area. An essential characteristic of this system is that the government retains ownership of production hence all production belongs to the government, while the IOC operates at its own risk and expense under the control of the government.

The two parties agree that the contractor will meet the exploration and development costs in return for a share of production or a fee for this service, if production is successful. If the company receives a share of production (after the deduction of government share), the system is known as a PSC or production sharing agreement (PSA), and in this case the oil company takes title to its share of petroleum extracted. If it is paid a fee (often subject to taxes) for conducting successful exploration and production operations, the system is known as a service contract, also called risk-service agreement (RSA). The latter is so-called because in a service contract, the host government (or its national oil company) hires the services of an international oil company and in the case of commercial production out of the contractual area, the oil company is paid in cash for its services without taking title to any petroleum extracted.

In contractual regimes, the oil company bears all the costs and risks of exploration and development. It has no right to be paid in the event that discovery and development does not occur. However, if there is a discovery the company is allowed to recover the costs it has incurred, and this is known as cost recovery or cost oil.

Cost recovery is similar in outcome to cost deductions under the concessionary systems. It includes mainly unrecovered costs carried over from previous years, operating expenditures, capital expenditures, abandonment costs and some investment incentives. Financing cost or interest expense is generally not a recoverable cost. Normally, a pre-determined percentage of production is allocated on a yearly basis for cost recovery. However, in general there is a limit for cost recovery that on average ranges from 30–60 per cent of gross revenue; in other words, for any given period the maximum level of costs recovered is 60 per cent of revenue.

Contractual systems normally offer certain investment incentives. For instance, unrecovered costs in any year can be carried forward to subsequent years. Also, some contracts allow these costs to be uplifted by an interest factor to compensate for the delay in cost recovery. Investment credits can also be provided to allow the contractor to recover an additional percentage of capital costs through cost recovery. There is usually a ring fence on petroleum activities, hence all costs associated with a particular block or licence must be recovered from revenues generated within that block.

The principle of cost recovery applies in the case of both PSCs and RSAs. However, the basis of the contractor's remuneration after it has recovered its cost differs in type.

In a PSC, the remaining oil after cost recovery is termed 'profit-oil' or 'production split' and is divided between the government and the company according to a pre-determined split set out in the contract. The split can be a sole profit-oil split or a progressive split. Hence, in this case, the remuneration of the oil company is a share of the production.

In a service agreement, the government allows the contractor to recover its costs. Additionally, the government pays the contractor a fee based on a percentage of the remaining revenue. Because the remuneration of the contractor is in cash in a service contract, the system has met some resistance on the part of some oil companies who would prefer a PSC as it provides them with a ready access to all or part of the production process. Since the contractor does not receive a share of production, terms such as production sharing and profit-oil are not appropriate even though the arithmetic will often carve out a share of revenue in the same fashion that a PSC shares production.

Additionally, in a PSC, the company's share of profit-oil can be subject to IT, while in a service contract the fixed fee remuneration of the contractor can be subject to tax. RSAs are similar in their principles to PSAs and present similar features. The main difference lies in the mechanism for the recovery of costs and the remuneration of the contractor.

Royalty is not a common instrument in contractual regimes. However countries like China still apply it. In this case, royalty is paid to the government before the remaining production is split. Nevertheless, an alternative to royalty is to have a limit on 'cost oil', to ensure that there is 'profit-oil' as soon as production commences. Such a limit on cost recovery has a similar economic impact to a royalty, with the government receiving revenue – its share of profit-oil – as soon as production commences.

In some countries, the government has the option to purchase a certain portion of the contractor's share of production at a price lower than the market price. This is called domestic market obligation (DMO). There can also be an additional government take in form of bonus payments, whether signature bonus or production bonus.

Many authors see the contractual regime as an alternative to concessionary regime – the main difference being of legal nature and lying in the key issue of the title to production ownership. But the expanded concept of government ownership of the production is one of the most striking characteristics of the contractual regimes. Government ownership of production is considered as an essential corollary of its claim to sovereignty over its petroleum resources.[3] In concessionary regimes, the government can maintain some of its entitlement to production through the national oil company but that entitlement is relatively limited. In theory contractual regimes enable governments to exercise more control over both petroleum operations and the ownership of production. In practice, as indicated earlier, this is not always so.

Contractual regimes are relatively new systems for defining the relationships between the government and the oil company. They were first applied in Indonesia in the 1960s. There are 64 countries adopting a PSC system in their petroleum activities and only 12 countries following a service contract.[4]

3.5 CONCESSIONARY SYSTEMS IN PRACTICE

3.5.1 The UK petroleum fiscal regime[5]

The UK ranks high in the global league of oil and gas producers. It is a major non-OPEC oil producer. In 2006, it had 4.0 bnbbl of proven crude oil reserves, the most of any EU member country and between 16 and 27 bnbbl of oil equivalent of overall oil and gas resource potential. In 2004, the UK produced more oil and gas than Venezuela, Nigeria, Indonesia or Kuwait;

producing 1.3bnbbl of oil and gas from the UKCS, sufficient to provide over 80 per cent of the nation's total energy needs.

Oil production in the UK peaked in 1999, and production is expected to decline to 1.38mmbbl/d by 2009. The two main reasons for this decline are first, the overall maturity of UKCS oil fields, and second, the declining field sizes for new discoveries and developments. Additionally, increasing unit extraction costs, in what is acknowledged to be one of the highest cost basins in the world, are damaging project economics and basin competitiveness. A shift of basin production to more remote and inhospitable areas of the UKCS is also a factor. Crude oil exports have followed a similar path to production, albeit that they initially levelled off between 1999 and 2000 before slowly declining. Crude oil imports have risen steadily to substantially narrow the gap with exports although the UK remains a net exporter of crude, as of 2007.

Petroleum taxation has received considerable attention since the discovery of oil in the 1960s in the UK sector of the North Sea. The structure of the current fiscal regime was first set out in a 1974 White Paper and was formally legislated through the Oil Taxation Act of 1975. The regime consisted of three main instruments, royalty, PRT and corporation tax (CT). At the outset the UK Government had two key objectives. These were to secure a fairer share of profits for the nation and ensure a suitable return for oil companies on their capital investment.

The royalty rate was fixed at 12.5 per cent on the gross revenues of each field with a deduction for conveying and treating costs, which represent the cost of bringing the petroleum ashore and its initial treatment. Royalty was abolished in 1983 on fields that had received development consent after 1983, and then abolished on all fields in 2002.

PRT is a special petroleum profits tax assessed on a field-by-field basis with all fields treated equally irrespective of ownership. PRT was charged initially at a rate of 45 per cent on the value of oil and gas produced. The tax base broadly equates to revenue receipts less the expenditure incurred in developing and operating the field. PRT was introduced to capture economic rent from the more profitable fields. PRT also offered different allowances and reliefs, namely uplift, oil allowance and safeguard. Uplift is an additional allowance equal to 35 per cent of capital expenditures. The oil allowance grants 250,000 tonnes for each six month to be exempt from PRT up to a cumulative maximum of 5 million tonnes (Mt). The safeguard provision limits the PRT liability in any chargeable period to 80 per cent of the amount by which gross profits exceed 15 per cent of cumulative expenditure. In 1993, PRT was reduced to 50 per cent on existing fields and abolished on all fields receiving development consent after April 1993. Incentives for exploration and appraisal drilling were also removed.

CT was initially set at 52 per cent then reduced gradually over many years to 30 per cent on company profits. Exploration costs were deemed fully deductible, while development costs were made subject to various tax depreciation allowances. CT is the standard company tax on profits that applies to all companies operating in the UK. However, in the case of petroleum activity, there is a ring fence that prohibits the use of losses from other activities outside the ring fence to reduce the profits originating from within the UKCS ring fence. Nonetheless, losses and capital allowances inside the ring fence may be set against income arising outside the ring fence.

In 2002, the UK government introduced a 10 per cent supplementary charge on profits subject to CT. This charge was calculated on the same basis as normal CT, but there was no deduction for financing costs. Additionally, a 100 per cent capital investment allowance was introduced against both CT and the supplementary charge, replacing the previous 25 per cent per annum writing down allowance. In 2005, in view of the significant increases in oil prices, the upwards shift in expectations of the medium term outlook for future oil prices and the dramatic increase in public spending, the UK government decided to increase the level of the supplementary charge by 10 per cent, with effect from 1 January 2006.

3.5.2 The Australian concessionary system

The Australian tax regime that applies to offshore activities has the following features:

Royalty used to apply at a rate of 10 per cent but was abolished in 1990. CIT is currently charged at 30 per cent, and is the same general income tax that applies to all companies operating in Australia. Capital expenditures are depreciated on a straight-line basis over field life. Petroleum projects are also subject to a special taxation, the Petroleum Resource Rent Tax (PRRT), which is deductible for CIT purposes.

PRRT applies at 40 per cent on net cash flow, but only when net cumulative receipts turn positive. Hence it is levied after the company has recouped all exploration and development costs. Undeducted capital expenditures are compounded forward at an uplift rate, which is a specified return on capital that supposedly will yield a fair return on investment. The uplift rate can be considered as the threshold rate that was referred to in Chapter 2 in the case of RRT. For exploration costs the uplift rate is approximately 23 per cent, while for development costs, it is equivalent to 15 per cent. As such, compounded capital expenditures are carried forward and deducted from positive cash flows in later periods. The accumulation process is continued until a positive net cash flow is generated. No PRRT is payable until the firm has recovered its costs inclusive of the uplift rate, although CIT may still be incurred.

For IT, deductible expenses are offset against income from any source. For PRRT, however, there is a ring fence around all offshore activities for exploration expenses and around the field for development expenses. Furthermore, the Australian regime does not provide abandonment costs reliefs. Capital expenditures are depreciated on a straight-line basis over field life.

3.5.3 The Norwegian concessionary system

The Norwegian regime has often been compared with the UK oil tax regime.[6] But although Norway and the UK share the same sea, a divergence in government policies has often occurred. In the UK, the 1980s were characterised by a reduction of government participation, unlike Norway where the period up to 1986 was one of continuous tightening and increased government intervention. However, in 1998, while the UK was thinking about tightening its regime, the Norwegian government was seeking to relax its system. The size of oil reserves, the low exploration cost and the high political risk make the petroleum fiscal regime in this country worthy of note.

The claim has been made that Norway is Europe's Saudi Arabia. Norway ranks as the world's fifth largest oil exporter and the tenth largest oil producer (as of 2007). The country is a significant oil exporter; because it consumes a relatively small amount of oil each year. Thus it is able to export the vast majority of its oil production. In 2005, Norway was the third largest gas exporter and the seventh largest gas producer in the world.[7] Despite more than 30 years of activity, the Norwegian side of the North Sea still has substantial oil and gas deposits to develop. Norway contains the bulk of oil reserves in the North Sea (57 per cent). It is also the largest producer of oil with 2.5 mmbbl/d or about 57 per cent. In 2005, Norway exported 2.2 mmbbl/d of oil, supplying 17 per cent of the EU total gas demand and 13 per cent of its oil demand.[8] Together with the Netherlands, Norway accounts for over three-quarters of gas reserves in the North Sea. Most Norwegian gas is sold through long term deals to Britain and other European countries.[9]

When the North Sea was opened up for petroleum activity, the most promising areas were explored first. This led to world class discoveries which were then put into production. These fields have been and still are of great significance for the development of the Norwegian continental shelf. The large fields have contributed to the establishment of infrastructure that subsequent fields have been able to tie into. Although Norwegian oil production in the North Sea started to decline in 2000, there is still a considerable potential for value creation in these areas if the recovery rate in producing fields is increased, operations streamlined and resources near existing infrastructure are explored. According to the Norwegian Ministry of Petroleum and Energy (2006), Norway has a potential for maintaining profitable oil production from the North Sea for another 50 years and its gas production for another 100 years. Since Norway exports more than 90 per cent of its oil production this makes it a continuing and significant factor on the global energy supply scene. In the words of Norway's Foreign Minister (2007) 'We seek to produce more of the fossil fuels that the world needs – and no matter how successful the breakthroughs may be in alternative energies, the world will continue to rely on fossil fuels for decades to come'.

The Norwegian petroleum fiscal regime is based mainly on CIT and SPT. Prior to 1986, GR (also called 'the Production Fee') used to apply. Before

1972 Royalty was applied at a 10 per cent flat rate. After 1972, it was applied on a sliding scale, ranging from 8 to 16 per cent, depending on production. However, in 1986 it was abolished for all fields receiving development approval from 1 January 1986.

CIT currently applies at a rate of 28 per cent. It was reduced from 50.8 per cent in 1992. This is the general IT that applies to all companies operating in Norway. SPT applies to offshore production income at 50 per cent. Unlike PRT in the UK, and PRRT in Australia, the SPT is not deductible for CIT purposes.

For both CIT and SPT purposes, depreciation for capital expenditures is allowed on a six year straight-line basis. Hence, SPT deductions and depreciation are the same as for CIT, except that for SPT an additional uplift applies. For all fields approved before 1986, the SPT uplift is an extra 100 per cent on expenditures incurred for each asset used in production and pipeline transportation. For fields whose development plan was accepted after 1 January 1986 the uplift applies at a rate of 5 per cent over six years.

For SPT purposes, there is a ring fence around the field. For CIT purposes, losses from operations on the continental shelf may be offset against profits from producing fields. Only 50 per cent of losses from other activities may be offset against profits from continental shelf activities.

SPT and CIT allow losses to be carried forward; hence no tax is paid unless all losses have been absorbed. Abandonment costs are not fully deductible, but a grant exists, which allows the deduction of abandonment costs at a rate equal to the effective tax rate.

3.5.4 Concessionary systems: qualitative comparison

Table 3.1 summarises the main characteristics of the concessionary systems as they apply in the UK, Australia and Norway. It can be seen that a certain harmonisation exists between the concessionary regimes applied in the three selected countries. First, none of the UK, Australian and Norwegian regimes currently apply royalty. Second, the IT rate is around 30 per cent. However with the additional 20 per cent supplementary charge imposed in April 2002, the UK has the highest IT rate at 50 per cent. Third, this IT is the general tax that applies to all companies operating in the three countries respectively. Hence, for income tax purposes, oil companies are treated on the same basis as any other company in the country. But fourth, given the special characteristics of the oil industry (availability of economic rent, high risks, long time lags involved in prospecting and extraction and high capital intensity), there is a special treatment of the oil sector. That is why the three countries have incorporated a special resource tax, which is between 40 and 50 per cent. Additionally, the three countries provide tax incentives and extra expenditure reliefs, such as uplift and the ability to carry losses forward. In fact, the UK, Australia and Norway regimes allow losses to be carried forward and taxes to be paid only when net cash flow turns positive.

Table 3.1 Concessionary systems: summary

Country		*Royalty*	*Income Tax*	*Special Petroleum Tax*	*Tax Reliefs*
Australia	1990–2007	—	30%	PRRT 40%	Uplift (15–23%)
	Pre 1990	10%		Deductible from CIT taxable base	Abandonment cost not deductible
Norway	1986–2007	—	28%	SPT 50%	Uplift (5%)
	Pre 1986	8–16%		Not deductible from CIT Taxable Base	Abandonment Relief (<100%)
UK	2002–2007	—	50%	PRT 50%	Uplift 35% Allowance (A) Safeguard (S)
	1993–2002	—	30%	PRT 50%	Uplift 35% A,S
	1983–93	—	33%	PRT 75%	Uplift 35% A,S
	Pre 1983	12.50%	52%	PRT 70% Deductible from CT taxable base	Uplift 35% A,S Abandonment cost deductible (100%)

However in terms of expenditure reliefs and where PRT still applies (i.e. on fields that received development consent before 1993), the UK offers the most generous reliefs compared with Australia and Norway. For instance, the UK PRT offers three significant reliefs, namely uplift (35 per cent), oil allowance and safeguard, compared with uplift of 15 and 5 per cent in Australia and Norway respectively. Furthermore, the UK offers 100 per cent relief against PRT and CT for abandonment costs, though the effective relief depends upon the PRT history of the field and access to taxable profits at the time of decommissioning. In Norway, decommissioning relief is based upon the effective fiscal take (i.e. on average 76 per cent) and is allowed for deductions, while in Australia there are no abandonment costs reliefs. Norway does not allow the SPT to be deducted for IT purposes, unlike the UK and Australian regimes.

The comparison is further expanded in the quantitative part of the analysis, covered in Chapter 6. The following section evaluates the other common type of fiscal regimes in oil producing countries, where divergence is more noticeable compared with the concessionary regimes.

3.6 CONTRACTUAL SYSTEMS IN PRACTICE

3.6.1 Indonesia's production sharing agreement

Indonesia is one of the most active countries in the South-east Asia. The country is a pioneer of the PSC, with the first contracts signed in the early

1960s. It has been famous for the 85/15 per cent split in favour of the government. Several changes have altered the Indonesian regime, among others the reduction in the split rate to 64/36 per cent. Additionally, the system (based on the 1990 PSC model) has the following characteristics.

The Indonesian system does not charge a royalty. Instead, it imposes what is known as the first tranche petroleum (FTP) contract, which requires that 20 per cent of the production be shared at 64/36 per cent in favour of the government before cost recovery. The FTP acts like a royalty since it is imposed on gross revenue and guarantees the government a minimum income just as production commences. The government FTP share is then added to the total government take, while the contractor FTP is added to his taxable income, and is subject to IT.

An interesting peculiarity of the Indonesian regime is that there is no limit for cost recovery. But in reality, the 20 per cent FTP acts as a cap since it reduces the available gross revenue for cost recovery to 80 per cent. In other words, the FTP is similar to an 80 per cent cost recovery limit.

The Indonesian PSC offers a 15.5 per cent investment credit, which is cost recoverable but not tax deductible. Depreciation on oil capital expenditures is at 25 per cent per year using the declining balance method with the undepreciated amount written off in year five.

IT applies at a rate of 44 per cent. It was reduced from 48 per cent in 1994. Furthermore, there is a ring fence for each licence.

Production bonuses apply as follows:

- If daily production reaches 50,000 barrel per day (bbl/d) the contractor pays the government £10M;
- If daily production exceeds 50,000 bbl/d but less than 100,000 bbl/d, the contractor pays the government an additional £10M;
- If daily production exceeds 250,000 bbl/d, the contractor pays the government an additional £25M.

The Indonesian DMO requires the contractor to sell 25 per cent of its share of oil to the national oil company Pertamina. After 60 months of production from a given field, the price the contractor receives for the DMO crude is 25 per cent of the market price.

3.6.2 The Chinese production sharing model

With 1.3 billion people, China is the world's most populous country and the second largest energy consumer, after the United States. Rising oil demand and imports have made China a significant factor in world oil markets. As the source of around 40 per cent of world oil demand growth over the period 2000–2004, Chinese oil demand is a key factor in world oil markets. Although during the 1970s and 1980s China was a net oil exporter, it became a net oil importer in 1993 and has greatly increased its foreign purchases.

Over the first five years of the twenty-first century, domestic crude output in China grew only very slowly while oil demand surged, fuelled by rapid industrialisation. Imports of crude oil grew alarmingly in 2003 and 2004 to meet demand, increasing nearly 75 per cent from 1.38 mmbbl/d in 2002 to 2.42 mmbbl/d in 2004. By 2006, imports accounted for 40 per cent of Chinese oil demand. By 2020, China might produce 3.65 mmbbl/d but will likely require more than twice that to meet its needs. China's oil demand is projected by the IEA (2006) to reach 14.2 mmbbl/d by 2025, with net imports of 10.9 mmbbl/d.

China adopts a PSC for its petroleum activity, but also combines with this system royalty and IT. Such a combination makes the system an interesting case to study as royalty is not common in PSCs. Furthermore, the royalty applies on a sliding scale where it varies with the level of production, unlike the fixed rate on gross revenue in the UK (prior to 2002). Table 3.2 summarises the royalty rates as they have applied since 1989. The maximum rate is 12.5 per cent, while a lower royalty can be negotiated for medium sized fields if commercially marginal.

Another important feature of the Chinese PSC (based on the 1996 model) is that profit oil is split at a negotiable rate, depending on the annual level of production and as such the rate varies from one field to another. A factor 'X' is determined for each field in accordance with the successive incremental tiers on the basis of the annual gross production of crude oil from an oil field during that calendar year, as presented in Table 3.3. To determine the single 'X' factor for each field, firstly the annual production (Q_n) is multiplied by the corresponding 'X' factor (X_n), secondly the total amount ($Q_n * X_n$) is divided by the total production of the field and multiplied by 100. The resulting figure is the rate at which the profit oil is divided between the government and the contractor for a particular field.

Cost recovery is limited to 62.5 per cent of annual gross revenue. Operating costs incurred are recovered first, then capital costs are fully recovered; any unrecovered balance is carried forward to the following period and is compounded at a 9 per cent interest rate.

VAT of 5 per cent is applied to gross revenue and CIT applies at a rate of 33 per cent. A ring fence exists around the contract area for cost recovery only but not for IT.

Table 3.2 China sliding scale royalty

Field size *Barrels of oil per day*	*Royalty rate* *%*
Up to 20,000	0.0
20,001–30,000	4.0
30,001–40,000	6.0
40,001–60,000	8.0
60,001–80,000	10.0
>80,000	12.5

Table 3.3 China 'X' factor

Production (thousands barrel per day) (Q_n)	*Factors (X) applicable to each production tier (X_n)*
Up to 9,999 b/d	X1 = 4%
10,000 b/d-19,999 b/d	X2 = 8%
20,000 b/d-39,999 b/d	X3 = 15%
40,000 b/d-59,999 b/d	X4 = 20%
60,000 b/d-99,999 b/d	X5 = 28%
100,000 b/d-149,999 b/d	X6 = 45%
150,000 b/d-199,999 b/d	X7 = 55%

3.6.3 The Iraq service contract: a special case and a system under construction

In Iraq, the fiscal arrangement that applies to petroleum activity is an RSA. This is also known as a buyback contract, and is similar to the system adopted by other countries, such as Iran. In these countries, the arrangements with foreign companies 'shall in no way entitle the companies to any claims on the crude oil'.[10]

Under the Iraq service agreement (based on the 2000 buyback model), the oil company undertakes all development work at its own cost and receives a sum that reimburses it for its costs plus interest and agreed remuneration. Cost recovery is allowed at 50 per cent of gross revenue, and a remuneration index is introduced in order to enable the contractor to make return on its cumulative investment. The remuneration index is also called the 'R factor', which is typical in service contracts.

The R factor can be determined as follows:

$$R = \frac{\text{cumulative contractor's cost recovery payments} + \text{cumulative contractor's profit payment}}{\text{cumulative contractor's cost recovery payments}}$$

where cumulative contractor's profit payment is the cumulative 10 per cent of gross revenue. On average, 1.5 is assumed as a remuneration index. As soon as the contractor recovers 1.5 times his cumulative investments, the handover date is reached and if at that date there are any unrecovered costs, the sum is paid by equal instalments over eight quarters or two years after the handover date. After that, the Iraqi State is entitled to all the future net incomes. As such, the Iraqi government take can be on average between 85–90 per cent. A government take of 95–97 per cent is considered typical under an RSA.[11]

The contractor is exempt from any IT. There are, typically, negotiable production bonus payments payable if production reaches 50,000 bbl/d, 100,000 bbl/d and 200,000 bbl/d.

3.6.4 Contractual systems: qualitative comparison

Table 3.4 summarises the characteristics of the contractual systems as they apply in Indonesia, China and Iraq. Several similarities exist in the way the systems work but the process of sharing revenue is different.

The three basic economic and fiscal elements of a PSC are cost recovery, the profit oil split between the contractor and the government and the IT. The four basic economic and fiscal elements of a service contract are cost recovery, the remuneration fee, the handover date and the IT.

In concessionary regimes, the international oil company usually owns the oil production. In contractual regimes, the government maintains ownership of the production; however, it maximises its control under an RSA. Blinn et al (1986) argue that the service system emphasises the principles of government sovereignty and for that reason it is hardly surprising that this type of agreement is mostly in use in Latin American countries 'where the nationalist sentiment concerning hydrocarbons is the strongest' (p.97). Others maintain that concessionary systems are not a suitable form of contract for the Middle East oil producers. These countries are influenced by Islamic law, the Shari'ah, which forbids foreign ownership of national resources. Furthermore, because fiscal terms are fixed upon signature of the contract between the government and contractor, contractual systems offer a more stable environment than the concessionary systems.

The main difference between the PSC and a service agreement lies in the mechanism used to remunerate the oil company. In a concessionary system, the oil company receives the net income after costs, tax and royalty. Under a PSC, the company gets cost recovery and a share of the remaining profit, whilst under a service contract it receives the cost recovery and a profit fee or remuneration until handover date.

Although the principles are the same under PSC and service contract, such a difference in remuneration generates further distinction in terms of duration of contract, cost-reduction incentives and impact of changes in oil price and reservoir characteristics.

PSCs can be long-term in nature but in service agreements the contractor

Table 3.4 Contractual systems: summary

Country	*Royalty*	*Income tax*	*Cost recovery*	*Investment credit*	*Bonus*	*DMO*	*Profit split*
Indonesia	FTP 20.0%	44.0%	—	15.5%	Yes	Yes	64%/36%
China	Sliding scale 0–12.5%	33.0%	62.5%	9.0%	—	—	X Factor
Iraq	—	—	50.0%	1.5 Remuneration index	Yes	—	—

involvement depends on the handover date, which in turn is affected mainly by capital expenditure and oil revenue. Generally speaking, service agreements are short-term, normally lasting for nine years, compared with up to 30 years under a PSC. As such, under a PSC, the contractor receives profit throughout the life of the contract, which is normally the life of the field, whereas under a service agreement the contractor cost recovery and profit remuneration end at the handover date.

As a consequence of the limit on cost recovery, contractors are normally encouraged to reduce their capital cost. However, in the service contract, the contractor has no incentive to reduce the long-term costs, since the field is likely to be under the control of the government. This can be considered as a major limitation of the service contract because a long-term partnership with a contractor may result in better overall field performance and much more value for the state than in the short-term approach. As such, service agreements are more suited to low-risk, short-term projects, but not to marginal oil fields.

Furthermore, in both types of contractual agreements, the contractor is largely exposed to reservoir and oil price risks. In the event of unsuccessful exploration, the contractor does not receive any compensation. Similarly, if the oil price declines then the share of revenue allowed for cost recovery decreases as well. However, under the service contract, unlike the PSC, the contractor does not benefit from any upside in reservoir or oil price, since it receives a pre-determined remuneration fee.

This suggests that the toughest fiscal terms from a company standpoint are likely to be found under contractual regimes while more lenient terms are expected under concessionary regimes. This is investigated in Chapter 6.

3.7 CHAPTER CONCLUSIONS

Across the oil producing world widely varied systems and techniques whereby governments acquire their share of national oil proceeds have developed, underpinned by a large variety of fiscal packages. The key determinants have been local conditions, especially those conditions relating to the chosen style of relationship between the governing authorities and the oil-extracting enterprises concerned. These in turn tend to be determined by the general state of political maturity of the state in question and by prevailing ideologies and political fashions.

It has been shown in particular how two broad categories of relationships have emerged over the years – the concessionary and the contractual – with several shades and varieties of each system lying in between.

An important and striking lesson to be drawn from a study of various systems and reforms is that ownership and control are not necessarily in close correlation. It has been shown that while concessionary systems, whereby governments release total or partial ownership, at least at the wellhead and sometimes in the ground, to private concerns, would seem to imply loss of control; this is not always in practice so. Conversely, where governments retain total ownership and allow operations only on a contractual basis, there is no guarantee that this will ensure full political control and accountability. The UK experience during the Thatcher privatisation period is especially relevant here.

A further conclusion is that although one might expect to find tougher terms in contractual arrangements this is not necessarily the case (as the following chapters will confirm). Concessionary arrangements can be just as tough and while two concessionary regimes may have similar structures the tax rates applied within them can lead to major differences of outcome; the UK and Norway regimes provide interesting contrasting approaches. This confirms the central point that approaches to the matter of sharing the oil wealth, as well as creating a favourable investment momentum and climate, can and do differ very considerably.

A broader concluding point is that politics and populism play a vital part in shaping these decisions. At root, all governments have to operate in a context of public concern that a country's resources should belong to that nation, and not be diverted into other pockets, whether private or foreign or both. Policy makers have to contend with a fundamental suspicion, in both advanced and developing societies where oil production is significant, that control over oil resources is about to be surrendered and that 'our oil and gas' must be tightly protected.

It is this which leads governments and their advisers not only to cling to contractual arrangements but even to resist within these systems, production sharing agreements which might lead companies to 'get away with' the oil revenues which people feel belong rightly to them. And it is this which explains why IOCs and their backers find that the superficial shape of fiscal packages and government/industry relations in oil-producing countries provides no certainty about the actual conditions that emerge in practice. Thus oil companies which initially shunned certain production sharing schemes have found that these, while denying actual ownership, can nevertheless provide satisfactory returns. *Pari passu*, oil companies attracted by concessionary arrangements have found, as this chapter has shown, that the 'easy' returns from concessionary schemes turn out to be less accessible than initially assumed.

In short, from the investor's and IOC's point of view there can be good and bad contractual arrangements, good and bad PSAs, good and bad concessionary systems and very good or very bad fiscal packages. Judgment has to be deeply informed by both experience and by foresight. Fiscal regimes are rarely static, particularly concessionary regimes. What might be considered an attractive regime when acreage is licensed can turn against the investors when developments come on stream, oil prices rise or government policy changes and vice versa. The UK regime has already been through several cycles of both extremes. Oil and gas projects last many decades from the acquisition of the first licence to decommissioning of the last field. Few fiscal regimes can expect to remain static over such long periods; investors need to recognise such risks along with the more project specific risks when deciding when and whether to invest.

The central dilemma, of course, confronting both governments and oil companies alike the world over, is that if returns to the investor are too jealously restricted then investment will not take place. It is this constant search for a balanced apportionment of rewards and benefits which colours the debate in countless Ministries of Finance and Energy, and around council and cabinet tables in many countries. Examples, ideas, models and innovations can be borrowed, swapped, copied and replicated between countries. But in the end, all face local conditions and local political and social pressures of which account have to be taken. Ignore these and the most perfect and tested regimes become uncompetitive, as governments have all too often found out to their cost. The lesson has to be constantly relearned.

4 The UK petroleum fiscal regime

The history and example of the UK: how oil taxation policy shaped the development of the North Sea province

4.1 POLITICAL BACKGROUND

In the construction and development of the UK's North Sea oil tax regime the prevailing political context of the period needs to be taken very much into account.

In the late 1960s and early 1970s the overwhelming view, shared by all UK political parties, was that the state had a major role to play in North Sea development and that the discovery and development of substantial oil and gas reserves would have major (and favourable) implications for security of national energy supplies. Heavy emphasis was also put on the job-creating potential of North Sea investment, with the strong likelihood, greatly welcome to Labour Members of Parliament representing Scottish constituencies, that the most favourable impact would be on Scotland's industrial workforce and make inroads into the heavy and persistent unemployment there.

As far as the state's role was concerned it has to be remembered that the first developments were occurring well before the era of Margaret Thatcher and the resurgence of belief in markets. Both the Labour and the Conservative parties politically accepted the view that large sections of the economy, notably the main utilities, should remain in state hands, as they had been since 1945. And both sides accepted that the trade unions, with their fundamentally corporatist and socialist views, had a central role in economic and industrial policy. It was therefore assumed as natural that when the UK began to emerge as a significant oil-producing country, the state would have a major stake in this 'new' industry as well. The British Labour governments of the late 1960s and 1970s at first went further. The instinct was to keep the entire development in state ownership, broadly on a contractual basis. Labour ministers were heavily influenced by Scandinavian socialism, which was believed to be a highly successful model at the time, and in particular by the emerging Norwegian approach to the management of oil and gas resources. The Energy Secretary of State, Mr Tony Benn, was a zealous and radical socialist who believed, almost to an idealistic extent, in worker ownership and state participation on behalf of the people. His Cabinet colleagues on the whole retained more realistic views and saw that a concessionary approach, mobilising the full resources of the great international oil companies, was probably the right and only way forward. It was against this background that the first proposals for North Sea oil taxation were put forward under a Labour Government in 1974, and subsequently embodied in legislation in the following year.

But this did not prevent furious rows continuing inside government during the 1970s period of Labour Government (1974–1979) about the degree to which the state should be involved, and the right form in which the new oil wealth should be shared. So intense were their quarrels that by the end of the 1970s Mr. Benn had refused to involve himself in further discussion with Government colleagues and refused to attend the relevant Cabinet meetings. In effect, it was explained by Energy Department officials – only half jokingly – to his Conservative successor in 1979, David Howell, that Tony Benn and his whole Department had made a unilateral declaration of independence so far as oil policy was concerned.

However, by then the main ideological battle had been lost and it had been accepted, to the dislike and dismay of the political Left, that private enterprise would continue to play the lead part in meeting the major new challenges of North Sea oil recovery and that the overall policy, including the tax system, should be shaped accordingly. The state's 'share' would be secured by a robust and demanding tax regime rather than by direct ownership, so favoured by Mr. Benn and the political Left. This was therefore the embryonic fiscal system which the new Government of Margaret Thatcher inherited in 1979.

The change of Government in the UK coincided with a period of extreme oil price volatility, with the fall of the Iranian Shah and disruption in Iranian oil production sending world oil prices rocketing. This in turn reinforced the view of the incoming Conservative administration in 1979, with its central focus on balanced budgets and limiting public borrowing, that a strong oil tax regime should be kept in place and indeed further tightened as oil prices rose. Rising oil revenues appeared to be a most welcome means of reconciling conflicting objectives in Conservative policy – the need to balance the budgetary books and the need to cushion, as far as possible, the heavy increase in transitional unemployment as market-based policies of modernisation were pushed through. Representations from the oil industry that expenditures were also rising, as the large costs emerged of developing North Sea platforms such as the giant Condeep structure, tended in a era of soaring crude prices to be brushed aside – at least by the Treasury which dictated tax policy almost regardless of Energy Department remonstrations and advice.

A second and parallel debate was also taking place throughout the 1970s on the security supply aspect. When the size of North Sea reserves first became apparent both politicians and the media saw this as salvation both in terms of improving the perennially bad UK balance of payments (and bolstering the sterling exchange rate after years of decline) and as a guarantor of vital oil supply security in place of heavy reliance on an ever-turbulent Middle East. It only gradually dawned on the UK policy-makers that the condition for attracting international investment into the North Sea had to be that the North Sea was an international province. This meant in effect that while investment could come from anywhere the resulting oil could be sold anywhere. There could be, and were, minor restrictions requiring oil to be physically landed on UK soil, but the idea that the UK market had a preferential position and that UK consumers would always have first access existed only in the minds of wishful thinkers at Westminster and in the media. The story is told of how the British Prime Minister at the time of the first OPEC oil shock in 1973, Edward Heath, summoned leading oil company executives to his country home and was amazed to learn from them that North Sea oil would continue to be sold on world oil markets rather than reserved for British consumers. Indeed it was pointed out to the bemused Prime Minister and his advisers that any sale of UKCS oil at less than the full market price to the highest bidders in escalating world markets would damage the government's revenues severely, besides being totally impractical and undermining all future investment confidence.

It was against this lively political background that British petroleum tax policy took shape throughout the seventies and early eighties.

The evolving system consisted of three main instruments namely royalty, PRT and CT. From the start, although the declared broad objectives were to balance tax revenue gains on the one hand, plus a welcome reinforcement to the balance of payments, with a suitable return to oil companies and their investments on the other hand, the undoubted bias was towards the revenue maximising side.

The UK government enjoyed its greatest intake of revenue from oil companies during the early 1980s, but it was under oil companies' pressure to ease the tax burden even at this point in time. This pressure continued until 2002, with the level of government take gradually falling from approximately 87 per cent in the 1980s to just 30 per cent in the mid 1990's. In April 2002, however, the UK government increased its take for the first time since 1983 through the imposition of a 10 per cent supplementary charge on the CT based income. Then, in 2005, in view of the significant increases in oil prices, the upwards shift in expectations of the medium term outlook for future oil prices and the dramatic increase in public spending, the UK government decided to increase the level of the supplementary charge by 10 per cent, with effect from 1 January 2006.

The major changes highlighted above are analysed in detail in this chapter. Section 2 studies the development of the fiscal regime between 1975 and 2005, including a brief description of the characteristics of the main tax instruments.[1] Section 3 focuses on the debate arising from the principal amendments. It further analyses the advantages and disadvantages of each of the tax instruments, taking into consideration the arguments raised in previous studies undertaken in this area. Section 4 discusses the major findings arising from this analysis and the conclusions derived. Section 5 includes the final remarks.

4.2 EVOLUTION OF THE UK NORTH SEA TAX SYSTEM

This section charts the evolution of the UK oil taxation since 1975. It proceeds by describing the five main evolutionary phases, starting with the originating legislation enacted in 1975, and the following amendments undertaken in 1983, 1993, 2002 and 2005. The section describes the principal tax instruments and highlights the main factors leading to the five major changes that affected the level of tax take and the structure of the system itself.

The section should be read against the background context – not always grasped – of internal Whitehall politics which gives the main authority in these and other tax fields firmly to the Treasury and Treasury Ministers. Faced with Treasury determination the 'line' or sponsoring departments – such as in this instance the then existing Department of Energy, latterly part of the Department of Trade and Industry (DTI)[2] – simply do not have the final say in taxation policy or tax levels.

4.2.1 Foundation of the regime

The July 1974 government White Paper,[3] set out two principal objectives with respect to the taxation of E&P activities on the UKCS. These were firstly to secure a fairer share of profits for the nation and secondly to assert greater public control. This was the White Paper and policy statement within which the basic structure of the current oil taxation system was established – subsequently legislated for in the Oil Taxation Act in 1975.[4] We look now in turn at the three key tax elements or instruments deployed – namely royalty, PRT and CT.

Royalty

In extractive industries, royalty is a payment to a landowner, the Crown, for the right, granted under the license, to extract oil and gas.[5]

In the UK, the royalty rate was fixed at 12.5 per cent on the gross revenues of each field with a deduction for conveying and treating costs. These costs represent the cost of bringing the petroleum ashore and its initial treatment. Royalty was based on a six-month period and was administered by the DTI rather than the Inland Revenue who have responsibility for the other tax instruments.

Petroleum Revenue Tax

PRT is a special petroleum profits tax. It is assessed on a field basis; hence a company with taxable losses in one field cannot offset them against profits in another field. This is because each field is treated separately under a 'ring fence' arrangement. As a result, all fields are treated equally irrespective of ownership. PRT is charged on a half-yearly basis, initially at a rate of 45 per cent, on the value of oil and gas produced. This broadly equates to receipts less the expenditure incurred in developing and operating the field. PRT was introduced to capture economic rent from the more profitable fields. Less profitable projects are shielded from the tax as a result of various allowances and reliefs. Three main reliefs are identified:

i. Uplift, which is an additional allowance of 75 per cent to capital expenditures (CAPEX), so companies will not start paying PRT until they have at least recovered 175 per cent of their CAPEX.
ii. Oil allowance, which allows one Mt of oil per annum to be exempt from PRT up to a cumulative maximum of ten Mt. As a result, PRT is unlikely to be payable on fields with reserves of less than 100 mmbbls. The oil allowance was introduced to help the development of marginal fields.
iii. Safeguard, which limits the PRT liability in any chargeable period to 80 per cent of the amount by which cumulative gross profit exceeds 15 per cent of cumulative expenditure. Safeguard was introduced to ensure that, while it applies, PRT – calculated after taking account of all other reliefs – does not reduce a participator's return on capital in any chargeable period to 15 per cent or less. As such, the safeguard limits PRT liability for a part of the field's life and allows fields to achieve a certain level of return on investment before they incur any PRT liability.

PRT is similar to RRT (analysed in Chapter Two). However, the two taxes differ in their respective treatment of expenditure carried forward for offset against future profits. RRT allows such expenditure to be carried forward in real terms, together with an interest mark up, while PRT compensates for the absence of this relief by allowing uplift to apply to most development expenditures[6]. Although there is no provision for a return allowance with the PRT, but the generous uplift is a surrogate. Furthermore, the safeguard relief is the equivalent to a 15 per cent return allowance under an RRT scheme.

Corporation Tax

CT was initially set at 52 per cent on company net profits – the same rate that applied to all of UK industry. Exploration costs were deemed fully deductible at the time incurred, i.e. expended, while development costs were made subject to various tax depreciation allowances. CT is the standard company tax on profits that applies to all companies operating in the UK. However, in normal CT applications a company can offset losses generated by one activity against income generated by its other activities. In the case of UKCS E&P activity, there is a ring fence that prohibits the use of losses from other activities to reduce the profits originating from within the UKCS ring fence. Conversely, losses and capital allowances inside the ring fence may not be set against income arising outside the ring fence.

4.2.2 Tightening of the system (1978–1982)

Following the increase in oil price in the mid 1970s, the UK Government implemented measures to increase the level of total tax take on UKCS activities. In 1978, it increased the PRT rate to 60 per cent, reduced the uplift allowance to 35 per cent and reduced the oil allowance from one Mt to 500,000 tonne per year, with a maximum allowance of 5 Mt. In 1980, the PRT rate was raised to 70 per cent, thereby increasing the combined marginal rate to some 87 per cent. Further, a new tax, Supplementary Petroleum Duty (SPD), was introduced.

Like Royalty, SPD was charged on a field by field basis by reference to 20 per cent of gross revenues less an oil allowance of one Mt. per annum. SPD was applied in the early production life of the field and was payable on monthly basis.

4.2.3 Abolition of royalty (1983)

In 1981/1982, the reduction in both oil prices and declining levels of development activity, combined with continuing industry pressure, led the UK Government to consider some adjustments to the fiscal regime. In 1983, for the first time, relaxations in the system were introduced, chiefly to encourage exploration and appraisal activity and to encourage the development of new fields. SPD was abolished and replaced by Advance Petroleum Revenue Tax (APRT). Like SPD, APRT was imposed on gross revenues less an allowance of one Mt per year. The rate applied was 20 per cent and payments were to be made on monthly basis. However, unlike SPD, APRT was not a new tax but rather an instrument for accelerating the payment of PRT. It consisted of an advance payment of PRT that would be offset against the actual PRT payments due later in the life of a field. The APRT was close to a gross royalty for rich fields. Additionally, the PRT rate was increased to 75 per cent. In the same year the government further amended the regime by abolishing royalty on fields receiving development consent after April 1982.

The oil allowance against PRT was restored to one Mt per year for a maximum of ten years. In addition, a cross-field allowance was introduced with respect to PRT, permitting up to ten per cent of the development costs of a new field to be offset against the PRT liabilities of another field. By the end of 1986, APRT was abolished and CT that applied on oil activity reduced to 35 per cent, though the desire to reduce the CT rate was driven by the broader requirements of UK Industry as a whole, not just North Sea considerations.

4.2.4 Abolition of Petroleum Revenue Tax (1993)

In 1993, the Chancellor of the Exchequer announced in his budget speech that 'as the North Sea has developed, the PRT regime has begun to look increasingly anachronistic . . . As profits in many existing fields attract a marginal tax rate of over 83 per cent, there is little incentive for companies to keep costs under control or for additional investment in existing fields'.[7] Consequently, PRT was reduced to 50 per cent on existing fields receiving development approval before April 1993 and abolished on all fields receiving development consent after that date.

4.2.5 Imposition of supplementary charge (2002)

In 1998, following the increase in oil prices in 1996/7, the UK Government proposed two alternative fiscal reforms. One was the application of a supplementary corporation tax on upstream activity profits. The other was the re-introduction of PRT on fields receiving development consent after March 1993. In the former case, a single tax would be applied for the majority of fields and the overall corporation tax would be 35–40 per cent, the highest since 1986. Under either option, the Government intended to abolish the 12.5 per cent royalty on production. Following a sharp fall in oil prices in 1998, these proposals were dropped.

However, after 1998 circumstances changed when oil prices exceeded $30 a barrel and North Sea production reached record levels. The discovery of the Buzzard oil field, which was the UK's biggest new oil find in almost a decade (*circa* 300 mmbbls), brought a positive outlook as regards the North Sea oil reserves.

In 2002, the UK Government introduced new changes to oil taxation in the UKCS. The changes were very close to one of the reform packages proposed in 1998. A 10 per cent supplementary charge on profits subject to CT was applied in addition to the normal 30 per cent rate, as a revenue raising measure. The charge was to be calculated on the same basis as normal CT, but there was no deduction for financing costs against the supplementary charge. Additionally, a 100 per cent capital investment allowance was introduced against both general CT and the supplementary charge, instead of the 25 per cent allowance per annum declining balance previously available. Furthermore, royalty was abolished on older fields that had received development consent before 1983, in an attempt to encourage fuller exploitation of reserves from those fields.[8]

4.2.6 Doubling the supplementary charge (2005)

In 2005, the UK Government doubled the supplementary charge to 20 per cent. The latter changes to the North Sea tax regime were introduced in order to 'maintain a balance between oil producers and consumers, by promoting investment and ensuring fairness to taxpayers in view of the recent significant increases in oil prices and the upwards shift in expectations of the medium term outlook for future oil prices'.[9]

The UK offshore oil and gas industry is the highest taxed industry in the UK. As of 2006, fields developed since March 1993 are taxed at 50 per cent, liable for both CT at 30 per cent plus the supplementary charge at 20 per cent. The marginal tax rate rises to 75 per cent on fields developed prior to 1993, which are also liable for PRT at 50 per cent.

4.3 CONTROVERSY SURROUNDING UK OIL TAXATION

Chapter Two concludes that it is difficult to design an ideal tax system and that each tax instrument when applied to oil activity has both advantages and disadvantages. Consequently, it is not surprising to find considerable debate surrounding the numerous main amendments to UK oil taxation policy. The remainder of this section summarizes the controversies relating to the structure of the fiscal regime in the UK. It studies the arguments for and against the main tax instruments, as discussed in previous works.

4.3.1 Royalty and the 1983 changes

The abolition of royalty on fields that received development consent after 1982 generated two opposing views, although the majority welcomed the changes.

Scholars like Moose (1982), Devereux and Morris (1983), Bond et al (1987), Kemp (1990), Nelsen (1991), Kemp and Stephens (1997) and Martin (1997) referred to the inappropriateness of imposing royalty and, in particular, its negative effect on the development of marginal fields. These authors argued that the 1975 fiscal system imposed such a high burden on marginal fields that if they were to be developed either crude oil prices would have to rise or the UK tax system would have to be modified to reduce the fiscal burden. The authors also emphasized the inappropriate revenue base of Royalty, making it an unsuitable method for taxing mineral exploitation. This was implicitly recognized by the UK Government when new fields were exempted from Royalty in 1983. The 1975 fiscal package is in general described as regressive in relation to economic rent, mainly because Royalty is regressive as regards profits, while the post 1983 package is usually described as wholly profit related and, as put by Kemp (1990, p. 621), 'constitutes a major structural improvement, which has improved the investment environment in the UK'.

The abolition of Royalty was an important step towards achieving neutrality of the regime. 'The application of PRT and CT only represented an entirely new approach by Government to the taxation of oil profits. It signalled that taxation would be used to secure a full share for the Exchequer of the substantial economic rent expected from UKCS oil production'.[10] Royalty is believed to generate a high fiscal risk since it is not fully profit-related and impacts more severely on less profitable fields, principally because costs are not allowed as deductions. A study by Martin (1997) showed that the abolition of Royalty was the main reason that led to the peak in oil production in 1984/1985. However, with respect to Martin's findings, one has to consider the lagged effect of taxation.

The abolition of Royalty was particularly welcomed by the oil industry. In 1991, Texaco's president argued that the changes would provide a substantial encouragement to exploration and development activities and create incentives for long-term investments.

Despite such statements, the abolition of Royalty was met with some criticisms. Some scholars argued that the abolition of Royalty, while maintaining PRT and CT, did not alter the fundamental deficiencies of the UKCS tax system. Mabro (1994) compared not charging a Royalty on oil to a situation where the government handed out buildings rent free to businesses and simply charged them corporate tax on their profits.[11] In a more general discussion, Raja (1999) described not imposing Royalty 'as senseless' because 'a resource is being extracted from a country without a charge' (p5), while Mommer (2001) argued that Royalty was the only instrument that made the UK fiscal regime a more proprietorial regime,[12] providing more control for the UK Government over oil activity. Wright (2003) maintained that using upstream taxes that guarantee at least some income whatever the oil price, as Royalties do, is a sensible strategy. In this way, 'the tax may be transformed into an accepted cost of production which ensures that the resource owner is unambiguously compensated for the depletion of an exhaustible resource' (p.22).

4.3.2 Petroleum Revenue Tax and the 1993 changes

As with the abolition of Royalty, the abolition of PRT on fields that received development consent after 1992 generated controversy. However, in this case the divergence in views was more pronounced. Many scholars favoured PRT as an instrument to capture economic rent on oil related activity and strongly criticized its abolition, unlike others who emphasized its limitations.

Among the first group, Zhang (1995) focused on the neutrality of PRT and argued that if the UK Government maintained its 1983 share of UKCS profits, revenues would have been almost three times their 1993 levels. Accordingly, the author concluded that the abolition of PRT in 1993 resulted from either a weakness in the UK Government planning or because of unseen distortions. Some authors maintained that PRT was efficient and almost neutral despite the high marginal rates of tax on oil revenues when all allowances were exhausted. They also argued that PRT was progressive in relation to variations in the oil price and development costs. According to Kemp et al. (1997, p.117) 'PRT could collect a share of economic rents from fields without necessarily endangering the viability of a development project . . . it is progressive on its impact on profits'.

In agreeing with such a view, Mommer (1999) argued that PRT was the main excess profit-collecting device in the UK, and its several reliefs 'ensure that PRT cannot, even accidentally, cut into the normal profits to which the companies are entitled' (p.15). Miller et al (1999) proposed that the UK Government should reimpose PRT on the exempt oil fields at the 50 per cent rate.

From an industry perspective, UKOOA[13] (1993) argued that the abolition of PRT reliefs could slow UKCS exploration and discourage investment. The association debated that such a change would, in particular, affect small companies as a consequence of the removal of cross-field allowance. This would also affect government revenues, since in the long term, reserves would shrink and there would be fewer developments and less construction, hence the UK Government would be the big loser. Taylor, of Esso UK PLC, argued that two opposing effects resulted from the changes in PRT. On the one hand, the reduction in PRT to 50 per cent on fields that received development consent before 1993 had a positive impact. On the other hand, the reduction of exploration expenditures and the loss of cross-field allowance led to a reduction in the development of new and small fields. But on balance, Taylor concluded that the overall impact was beneficial to the industry.

Among the group that addressed the limitations of PRT, two views can be distinguished. The first emphasized its problems but suggested some improvements, whereas the second advocated its complete removal.

Authors such as Devereux and Morris (1983), Bond et al (1987), Kemp (1990) and Kemp and Stephens (1997) related the main weakness of PRT to its imposition alongside Royalties and CT, both of which are considered as distortionary instruments. The authors described this characteristic as a serious deficiency of PRT. A second major weakness was attributed to the complicated structure of PRT, although in its original state it was a relatively simple tax. Rowland (1983) criticized the way the progressive aspect was applied to PRT. The author argued that PRT progressivity was attempted not by means of a suitable rate structure but by means of arbitrary allowances, which did not isolate the returns for those fields needing most protection. 'The allowances do not protect the returns on the fields most needing protection and the North Sea tax structure burdened the less profitable finds while giving relatively favourable tax treatment to the richer oil fields.'[14] Rowland and Hann (1986) even concluded that PRT had a regressive aspect in that its base did not grow in line with profits. The authors argued that progressivity should be automatic without changes being made, especially structural changes to the allowances. Bond et al (1987) maintained that the PRT allowances were intended to be of disproportionate assistance to relatively unprofitable fields but in practice this was not always the case. Robinson and Morgan (1978) and Robinson and Rowland (1978) concluded that PRT was in many ways a poor form of taxation and a poor source of revenues mainly because of the Safeguard; 'it is a complicated device and could be abandoned'.[15] In fact, according to the Inland Revenue (2000), some oil companies gained an unfair tax advantage by delaying their claims for operating expenditure relief while benefiting from the Safeguard provision. By deferring expenditure claims to a subsequent period, when Safeguard no longer applied, the deferred claim had a direct effect in reducing the PRT payable. This was contrary to the intent of Safeguard relief. Rutledge and Wright (2001) argued that the three main PRT reliefs – uplift, oil allowance and safeguard are 'equally important weaknesses' (p.5). The authors maintained that the uplift postponed PRT payment and the oil allowance was based on the assumption that small oil fields were necessarily less profitable, while the safeguard was the 'strangest provision', since it was based on the presumption that the amount of tax paid should not exceed 80 per cent of the excess of gross profits over the 15 per cent return on capital (p.6).

The UK government also expressed its view regarding the abolition of PRT. According to the then Chancellor of the Exchequer, PRT was an expensive tax that cost the Exchequer an estimated £200M in 1991 and 1992. Consequently, near term budget arithmetic was the main driver for reform from the government perspective. The impact of a complex array of reliefs (principally from exploration and appraisal) plus notable reinvestment in PRT fields (from the Piper Alpha redevelopment and investment in sub-sea safety systems across the North Sea) had caused the PRT tax yield to turn negative, a situation the government regarded as neither tolerable nor sustainable. Most probably, this policy reaction has implications for the long-term survival of PRT when the yield turns negative again in the future, once removal costs begin to grow substantially by the middle of the second decade of the twenty-first century.

Additionally, by allowing companies a larger share of the profits generated, the 1993 reforms were intended to reduce the apparent disincentives to cost cutting and future investment in existing fields. Kemp (1990) raised the issue that the uplift provision encouraged more capital-intensive exploitation methods than would a neutral scheme. The author argued that the interaction of this allowance with the Safeguard provision meant that gold-plating incentives could occur. Also, the study by Martin (1997) showed that the abolition of PRT was the main reason behind the 1995 peak in oil production of 2.49 mmbbl/d. This result underlined the non-neutral aspect of PRT (but again one has to consider the lagged effect of tax changes). Finally, Watkins (2001) concluded that the number of modifications to which PRT was subjected were 'a testimony to its clumsiness' (p.13).

4.3.3 Corporation Tax, Supplementary Tax and the 2002–2005 Amendments

CT has both advantages and disadvantages, as highlighted in Chapter 2, and there is also a divergence of opinion concerning its imposition. This section studies the debate surrounding the application of both CT on oil activity in the UKCS and the imposition of the 10 per cent Supplementary Tax (ST) in April 2002, and then the doubling of the charge in 2005, since the ST is computed on a similar base to CT.

Many scholars argued that a tax applied on total company profits from UKCS activities was an appropriate instrument, as companies could adjust their operations so as to improve their after-tax returns on high-cost projects, rather than dealing with single fields as is the case with PRT. Several authors also emphasized the neutral aspect of CT and even described the UK regime based solely on CT as an example of a highly neutral tax regime. Additionally, CT is considered as simple to administer – in fact it is the simplest way for the Government to raise revenues from E&P companies. From the UK government perspective, imposing an IT, such as CT combined with the ST, was intended to encourage long-term investment without providing better tax reliefs than those available to other industries and, as such, to prevent unwelcome repercussion effects.

Opposing such arguments authors like, Devereux and Morris (1983), Kemp (1990), Kemp and Stephens (1997), Rutledge and Wright (1998) argued that CT had an inappropriate tax base, which did not capture economic rent. The authors contended that the severity of the tax burden for a field depended on which companies were involved because capital allowances from one field could be used to offset tax liabilities on another. They also argued that CT was not directly related to economic rent, as it did not allow a normal return on investment as a cost. As such, these authors maintained that CT was non-neutral and could create distortions because it failed to distinguish between normal profit (i.e. the required return on capital invested) and pure profit or economic rent. Rowland and Hann (1986) underlined the non-progressive aspect of CT, and argued that it collected proportionately more from each field when prices were lower and that unprofitable fields received a greater CT burden on unit profits than did their more profitable counterparts. However, it is important to stress that the authors asserted that the regressive nature of CT was accentuated because PRT, a non-progressive tax, was itself a deduction against CT.

Rutledge and Wright (1998) emphasized the inability of CT to capture economic rent. Consequently, the authors concluded that imposing only CT on E&P activity did not generate a fair share of revenues for the government and that it made the UK fiscal regime the weakest in the world. Supporting such findings, Miller (2000) argued that with 30 per cent CT only, oil companies were not paying their fair share of taxes. According to him, before April 2002 the UK government revenues were far below the levels of the

1980s, where in 1984/85, they reached a peak of £12.2bn. Tax receipts subsequently declined with the fall in oil prices to a low of £1bn in 1991/92. Although the tax receipts recovered to £3.3bn in 1997/98, they dropped again to £1.6bn in 1998/99. Further, when companies' profits reached a peak of over £18bn in the mid-1980s, the UK government take was about £12bn (more than 60 per cent), but when in 1996/97 companies' profits reached another peak of about £16bn, the UK government revenues were less than £4bn, with companies paying only quarter of their gross profits in tax.

The industry response to the 2002 fiscal package was one of dismay and UKOOA lobbied hard to reverse the changes. Companies, such as BP and ExxonMobil, maintained that the changes to capital allowances and the abolition of Royalties were not expected to come anywhere near offsetting the ST. Leith (2002) argued that with hostile environments like that of the North Sea, the 2002 fiscal changes left companies feeling betrayed and raised concerns about when fiscal stability would be achieved.

Industry representatives argued that there was no room for additional taxes. According to UKOOA (2002), prices of between $14 to $18 a barrel were needed in the UKCS to make a return. This was because the majority of the large oil fields were now discovered and only small fields remained, which were more expensive to develop on a unit cost basis, hence less profitable. UKOOA (2002) maintained that the April 2002 changes could adversely affect smaller companies, jobs and investments, as well as generating an unstable environment in which companies must operate.

The 2005 changes generated even stronger reactions and criticism. The UK government expected to generate an additional £2bn from oil activity in 2006–2007 as a result of the increase in tax. However, six months after the increase in tax, estimates were revised and the government wrote off three-quarters of the £2bn originally expected revenues, in the light of the decreasing North Sea production. Then, in the space of further six months following the March 2006 budget the UK government further reduced the yield expectations from the North Sea by £2.8bn for the tax year 2007–8. This led to the criticism that an over reliance on North Sea tax revenues creates instability in the general tax regime as inherent volatility in oil revenues undermines budget arithmetic. This in turn creates the need for tax rises elsewhere in the economy if revenue forecasts prove over optimistic. The 2006 Oil and Gas UK Survey concluded that the UK government has underestimated the rise in costs in the North Sea and the decline in production in the province. Paradoxically, high oil and gas prices both contributed to and constrained activity in the oil and gas sector in 2005. While they have the effect of making a greater volume of reserves economically attractive to recover, they also put pressure on resources and increase capital development and exploration and appraisal costs. The issue of global competitiveness of the UKCS was also raised. According to Oil and Gas UK (2006), oil and gas activity in the UK became 16 per cent less attractive because of the increase in tax, which reduced the value of new exploration and development and negatively affected the international competitiveness of the UKCS.

Although HM Treasury promised that there would be no further tax changes for the life of the then parliament, to provide some stability for investors, the tax changes over a three year period, and the whole history of the UK fiscal regime, raised concerns about the instability of the system. The offer of stability for the life of the then parliament was described as offering only limited comfort for investors. Given that investments typically take up to two years to come on stream, investors may still consider that they are significantly exposed during the productive life of new developments. A study carried out by HM Treasury (2006) found that the majority of companies included in the study (29 of 37) believed that increases in taxation depress exploration activity. Lack of confidence in the future attractiveness of the fiscal regime was cited as the second most significant factor restricting exploration, following the global competition for limited funds. Peter Davies, for 17 years BP's chief economist, stated that the steep decline in North Sea production would be much slower if the fiscal regime were more benign.

Not surprisingly, however, the UK government brushed aside the arguments that higher taxation deterred activity in the North Sea, stating that the regime 'compares well internationally and promotes investment while ensuring fairness for British taxpayers from what is a national resource'.

4.4 THE UK CONTINENTAL SHELF FISCAL REGIME: ASSESSMENT OF THE MAIN TAX INSTRUMENTS

Earlier chapters have identified the major characteristics of the key tax elements in the UK regime. Here they are briefly recapitulated.

Royalty is a simple instrument to administer and it generates early revenues for the government. However, it is regressive, non-neutral and not targeted on economic rent. PRT is a special petroleum tax, targeted on economic rent. It allows a certain return before any tax is paid. The nature of its allowances and deductions ensure that it is progressive. Nevertheless, it is a complicated tax and tends to delay fiscal receipts. CT is simple and applies without exception to all industries in the UK. However, it is levied on a company basis and, similarly to PRT, it tends to delay fiscal revenues and may not be properly directed at rent. On balance, when the UK fiscal regime is assessed against the criteria of an ideal system as discussed in Chapter 2, the following observations are relevant.

Firstly, the UK fiscal regime lacks stability, as it has been subjected to frequent changes. This criticism has often been made in previous studies, as no other sector in the UK economy has been subject to such instability. Since 1975, more changes have been recorded due to tax legislation than price changes.[16] Robinson and Rowland (1978) argued that the government introduced several changes before the practical operation of the system could be observed. Such a weakness questions the effectiveness of the regime and its ability to cope effectively with different economic conditions, such as changing oil prices. Further, even though the regime was more risk-sharing in its initial structure, its various amendments increased political risk and reduced investor confidence.

From the UK government's perspective, the many adjustments made to the regime reflected the changes that were taking place on the UKCS, such as a decreasing field size distribution and quite sharp changes in the price of oil. In fact, when oil prices began to increase from 1973 to 1981, PRT was increased from 45 per cent to 60 per cent, and later to 70 per cent in 1980. When the oil price reached a peak in 1981, SPD was introduced. A relaxation of the system came about after the decline in oil price starting in 1983. Then when oil prices started to increase again at the outset of the twenty-first century, the UK government applied two tax changes, within four years, by increasing the tax rates.

Although some degree of flexibility would be appropriate to the regime so that it has the capability to adjust to changes in the external environment, ideally the scheme should be so devised that it applies without adjustment over a wide range of circumstances. Regime modifications should not be undertaken on a frequent basis, be they of a major or structural nature, nor undertaken without advanced warning. Investors add a risk premium when faced with greater fiscal instability. This makes investment in the UKCS less attractive, particularly when assessed against global competition. Furthermore, oil prices are volatile and it is almost impossible to track every change. This explains why several scholars have criticised the UK government for changing the regime in response to upward movements in crude oil prices. Rowland (1983) described such measures as 'an ill-conceived move based on a myopic view of how the oil industry operates, of the factors affecting the oil industry and of the burdens imposed by the cumbersome North Sea tax structure' (p.202). Nelsen (1991) argued that while it appeared that both the UK and Norway imposed a tax system in response to oil price changes, in practice it seemed that this was true only for Norway, while in the UK, however, the objective was often to increase the Treasury's take from the UKCS.

The second important conclusion that can be derived from the analysis of previous studies' arguments is that the UK fiscal regime is complicated and several authors consider such complications unnecessary. This is particularly true for PRT and the complex nature of the differing reliefs and allowances available.

Thirdly, it is argued that the regime lacks neutrality, as it can affect decisions like the development of marginal fields and early abandonment or reduction in exploration activity. Royalty, in particular, is described as being a typical non-neutral tax. In fact, after its abolition in 1983, exploration and appraisal expenditures rose from £816M in 1987 to £1,955M in 1991, and between 1989 and 1993 the UK had the largest number of new field wildcat wells drilled (516) in the world. This increase in activity was, in turn, accompanied by an increase in government revenues.

The abolition of PRT in 1993 was also found to have a similar positive effect on both levels of activity and tax revenues. Nevertheless, it is important to stress that PRT generates the largest share of revenues for the government compared with Royalty and CT. It produced almost £42bn for the Exchequer in 25 years between 1975 – when it was introduced – and 2000, compared with £23.2bn from CT and £20.2bn from Royalty.

The generation of revenues for the government leads to the fourth observation, also derived from the arguments raised in previous studies. It raises the issue of whether the UK government was receiving an appropriate share of revenues. Miller et al. (1999) argued that even the pre-1983 regime was not generating a fair share of revenues, the reason being that companies did not pay for licences to extract oil: these licences were and still are 'allocated free after a beauty contest' (p.1).

From these findings, it is clear that the fiscal regime applying to the UKCS suffers from several limitations that go back to its beginnings in 1975. The original regime was weakened by the many changes introduced in a relatively short space of time, adding further to the administrative burden. The House of Commons Select Committee on Energy (1982) highlighted such limitations and concluded that 'the tax system, at its current level of complexity and frequency of change, has now passed the point at which its impact can be said to be broadly neutral and a substantial risk exists that development is being discouraged.'[17]

4.5 A CHALLENGING SITUATION

Since 1975, the UKCS has undergone major changes. One fact that clearly emerges is the decline in the average size of fields during the 1990s, compared with the early development of the North Sea, as Figure 4.1 shows. A minority of fields account for the majority of aggregate reserves. From 2000, the largest five fields account for 37 per cent, the largest 10 for 52 per cent and the largest 20 for 71 per cent of the total reserves.[18] However, 29 of the UK major fields peaked prior to 1994. By 2000, they showed total oil production declines of more than 50 per cent from their maximum production levels.

To counteract the rapid decline of mature fields, new but smaller fields are being brought on-line at an increasing rate. From 1985 to 2006, the number of producing fields on the UKCS has increased three-fold. Although it took 25 years for the first 100 fields to be brought on-line it took only six years to bring the second 100. As might be expected however, the fields found during subsequent periods have become progressively smaller, with an average discovery size of 25 to 30 mmboe. That is very small compared to the larger UK fields, like Forties and Brent, with an average size above 2,400 mmboe. Although there is no official definition for fields' size, Table 4.1 illustrates the main classes adopted in previous studies, according to the size of recoverable reserves.[19]

Table 4.1 Fields' classification by size

Study by	*Very small*	*Small*	*Medium*	*Large*
Robinson and Morgan (1978)		100–250	250–350	>350
Kemp and Stephens (1997)	<100	100–250	250–500	>500
Sem and Ellerman (1998)		<100	100–400	>400
Watkins (2000)		<100	100–400	>400
Ruairidh (2003)	<100	100–200	200–400	>400

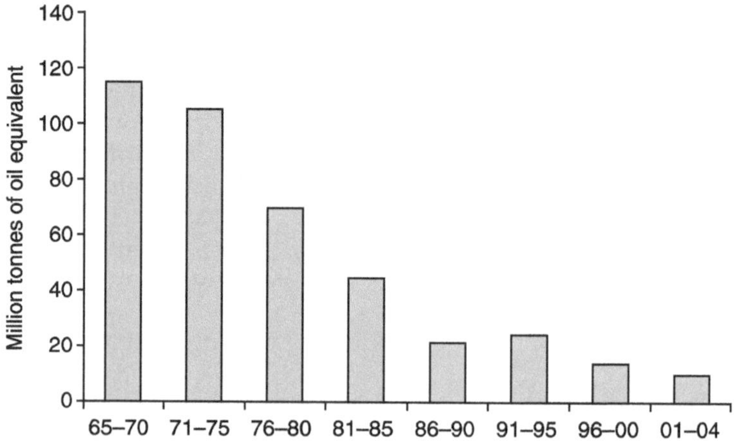

Figure 4.1 Average size of oil and gas fields.

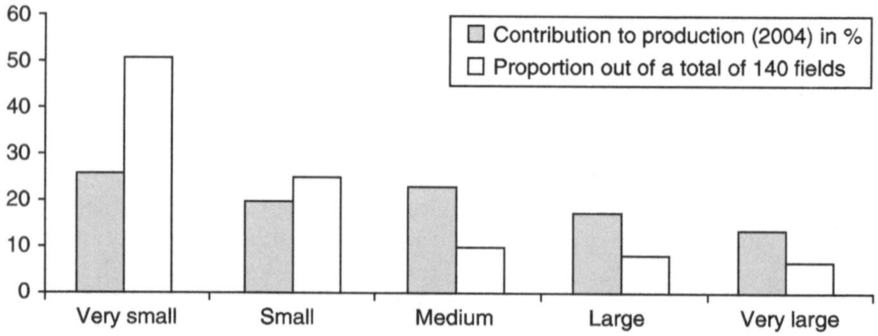

Figure 4.2 Distribution of fields by size and their contribution to total production.

Furthermore, many of the new smaller fields have lifetimes of 10 years or less. In an extreme example, Dauntless field was brought on-line in August 1997 and was terminated in April 1999. Figure 4.2 illustrates the distribution of fields by size, and the contribution of those fields to total production.

Clearly, the UKCS is a mature oil and gas province, which has been in production for nearly 40 years (as of 2008). However, this reality does not necessarily mean that 'North Sea oil, the precious resource that has contributed hundreds of billions of pounds to the UK economy, is now slipping into history'.[20] Other basins, such as the Gulf of Mexico, have undergone similar evolutions and seen activity actually increase, a few years after they were declared a dead sea.

A study carried out by UKOOA and WoodMackenzie in 2004 showed that there were still substantial opportunities to be accessed if the UK was to remain internationally competitive and able to sustain investment. If successful the UK could still be producing the equivalent of 65 per cent of its total oil requirements in 2020 and delay decommissioning by 10–15 years, making a major contribution to the UK's security of energy supply. In stark contrast, if the UK becomes less attractive to new investment, then the UKCS will only provide the equivalent of 15 per cent of total UK oil demand by 2020. Consequently, the UKCS can either face a rapid decline, hence exposing the UK to an increasing dependence on oil imports, or production can be sustained for a longer period of time, hence extending the benefits to consumers, companies and government alike.

Another aspect of the UKCS that can act as a constraint on UK government fiscal policy is the relative international competitiveness of the province. In 2002, it ranked 19th globally in terms of the average commercial discovery size. But since 1998, the scale of discoveries in other parts of the world, notably Kazakhstan, Angola, Brazil and Nigeria, have been an order of magnitude higher than the average discovery size in the UKCS. Additionally, the exploration and development costs in these regions are typically much lower than in the hostile and technically challenging UKCS environment. With $10 a barrel operating costs (and rising) in the UK North Sea compared with $5 in Angola and $6 in Gulf of Mexico, it is going to be harder to continue to attract investment in competition with the larger and more commercially attractive opportunities available elsewhere in the world.

As put by the UK Government Energy White Paper, published in 2007, production could fall from 3 mmboe a day in 2007 to around 1 mmboe a day by 2020. However, if a high level of investment is maintained, the rate of decline could be slowed. This would deliver significantly higher production (an extra 0.6 mmboe a day from 2020 to 2030) and consequently greater recovery of the UK's remaining oil and gas reserves (4 bnboe extra production by 2030). The challenge is to maintain the competitiveness of the UKCS as it becomes increasingly mature. The future of the UKCS and the North Sea as a whole depends on a combination of factors. The petroleum fiscal regime is a major determinant.

4.6 SUMMARY AND CONCLUSION

The UK petroleum tax regime has evolved over a period of more than thirty years and was first established in conditions very different from those of today, both industrial and political. As has been shown, the prevailing mood at the time of the first North Sea developments (in the late 1960s and early 1970s) was that the state should not only share heavily in the wealth so providentially discovered in British waters but that the state should also play a central part in the development and production of the new fields.

Subsequent debate and changes of political fashion modified this first enthusiasm as the global nature of the oil industry began to be appreciated by UK governments and the overriding need to develop the UKCS as an attractive and fully international province began to be accepted. Even so, the first petroleum tax package, introduced in 1975, was a 'tough' one, generating a marginal tax rate of 87 per cent and being based on the triple regime of Royalty, PRT and CT. Under the then Labour administration the principle of state participation was also given a central place, with 50 per cent of all oil produced on the UKCS being automatically reserved for BNOC, the government's new state oil company created for the purpose.

Although, over the years, since the 1970s the regime has been subjected to numerous shifts and alterations, it has remained a highly demanding one – a fact which is fully explained by the dominance of the UK Treasury in formulating North Sea taxation and the relatively secondary role of other Whitehall departments, such as Energy and later Trade and Industry, in the tax policy process.

Ironically, this constant tinkering with the tax regime, designed to maximize revenues from the North Sea to a hungry Exchequer and at the same time to maintain good incentives for further investment and development, has fallen short in both respects. As has been shown, the revenue flows in 2007 fell short of estimates while the qualities required of a tax regime which encourages investment in evolving conditions, as the province has matured, have not been evident. On the contrary, the regime has not only proved a lower generator of revenues than intended but has been dogged by numerous fiscal inadequacies, including lack of neutrality, lack of simplicity and lack of stability – all combining to make the UKCS progressively less attractive to the oil companies, especially as new opportunities elsewhere in the world have opened up.

Nonetheless, and despite the setbacks, the UKCS remains rich in opportunities, and these have been enlarged by the rapid advance of oil development and recovery technology, as well as by the substantial crude oil price rises of recent years. Exploration and development costs have therefore been contained, the understanding of the geological nature of the province has been significantly deepened – an advantage coming with maturity – and in the background there has remained the priceless advantage of rock solid political stability – in contrast to the unreliability of many other oil producing countries.

It should however be noted that the bond of trust between the oil industry and the government was all along relatively fragile. This was not so much to do with fears of extreme political instability as with a general scepticism amongst oil companies as to whether the government could deliver on its promises of creating a stable and helpful tax regime for the industry. An important lesson emerges here from the British experience – that if oil industry investment is to proceed on the large and long-term scale required then there has to be not merely a general and underlying assumption that broad political stability and responsibility will prevail, but also that the government can be trusted to maintain its overall balance between taking its fair share of revenues and yet leaving good incentives and returns in place for the oil industry and its backers. If governments are unable to deliver fiscal stability for political and constitutional reasons then oil companies will simply factor this risk into the investment appraisal process. In effect the additional fiscal risk will be required to be remunerated via a higher return to investors. Therefore unstable fiscal regimes will in the long run result in a lower level of government take than if more stability was on offer.

The history and example of the UK petroleum tax experience, covered in this chapter, provides an essential background both to an assessment of other oil tax regimes already in place round the world, and to the establishment of new, or modernised, regimes in major oil-producing countries. The example of Iraq comes very much to mind.

A detailed evaluation of the UK fiscal regime, in its various changing forms, and its precise impact on North Sea fields confirms that the North Sea oil and gas story is by no means over. Indeed, viewed in conjunction with Norwegian North Sea prospects, with growing High North possibilities and with the rising costs and inherent instabilities of traditional Middle East oil sources, it may well be that these northern regions have an even more significant role to play in world energy supplies. Finding the best and most incentivising fiscal regime to respond to this prospect becomes an evermore important priority.

5 The economics of petroleum projects

Measuring costs, returns and profitability for petroleum projects: how differing tax regimes affect the calculations and outcomes

5.1 INTRODUCTION

This chapter addresses the main parameters that affect the economics of a petroleum project. These are often misunderstood by governments (and even more so by the media and the general public). From outside the industry there is a problem of comprehension of the sheer scale of the costs and the extent of risks involved in all the various phases related to the exploration, appraisal development, production and abandonment of an oil field. The aim here is to show not only how difficult it is for policy-makers to focus on the range of diverse circumstances which occur during the full activity cycle in the life of an oilfield, but how complicated in consequence the computation of taxation can be. Inevitably, although modern administrations contain many bright and knowledgeable minds, one is left wondering whether governments can be aware of these complications and whether they can understand them fully.

Indeed, in the early 1970s in the UK, as the North Sea gradually opened up, the Minister then in charge of the delicate task of devising a brand new oil tax regime, Mr. Edmund Dell, openly admitted that when formulating the required tax structure neither he nor his advisers were fully aware of the likely production cost profile in the North Sea province. In particular, they did not know, and perhaps could not know, the probable range of costs likely to be encountered in the unique conditions of the North Sea. Only gradually, and after crucial policy decisions on the oil tax regime had been discussed and settled, did it begin to be recognised that the tax structure had to take account both of a wide range of unknowns and of the long sequential process of immense size and complexity which precedes the moment when oil finally becomes on stream. In the UK case, these unknowns eventually had to embrace such substantial leaps in technology and in costs as the construction of Condeep platforms off the West coast of Scotland – some of the largest structures ever created by man – and their installation in some of the most hostile environmental conditions ever faced, even by the most experienced oil operatives and companies.

We go on in this chapter to demonstrate how, although some countries have evolved similar-looking systems and structures for taxing their oil industries, the computation of their tax rules can make a significant difference. For instance, a tax structure of 30 per cent CT and 50 per cent PRT in the UK has a different impact on profitability than a tax structure of 28 per cent CIT and 50 per cent SPT in Norway. That is why judging and assessing a tax regime merely by reference to the type or the headline tax rates is too narrow a process, and why there is a need to go much further than simply noting rates if a reliable overall evaluation is to be conducted.

The chapter also explains how to compute a cash flow from an oil project and how to evaluate its profitability, under both a concessionary and a contractual regime. Six countries are used as examples. Deriving the cash flow model allows a better understanding of the functioning and interaction of the different tax instruments of a petroleum fiscal regime. It shows how the principal tax instruments and their different reliefs work, interact and impact on both oil field profitability and government revenues.

Petroleum fiscal regimes are based on very complex rules. The basics are straightforward enough. First, revenues less costs are calculated so as to produce the pre-tax cash flow. Second, a tax rate is applied to determine the total tax take, which is then deducted from the pre-tax cash flow in order to arrive at post tax profitability in a given period. But then the complications begin. An in-depth understanding of the different tax rules is essential in reaching any meaningful understanding or conclusion. As will be shown later, this is especially the case when, for example, loss carry forwards are involved at the early stages of an oil field's life.

The various phases of a petroleum field life cycle are our starting point. We then develop the profitability measure of a petroleum project, and explain in detail how profitability is calculated under the six international petroleum fiscal regimes covered in Chapter 3. A study of the financial evaluation technique to measure the economic profit of an oil project is also examined.

5.2 PETROLEUM FIELD LIFE CYCLE

5.2.1 Six phases

A full understanding of sharing the oil wealth and the taxation problems of oil and gas cannot be achieved without at least a basic appreciation of the physical nature of oil operations.

There are six phases in the life of an offshore oil field. These are as follows:

The acquisition of a license or concession

The search for oil begins when the government announces its intention to offer oil companies the right to prospect in a part of its territorial waters.

Exploration

At this phase, seismic surveys are undertaken to identify the prospect. Once technical data is obtained and analyzed, the decision is taken whether to proceed further. If the conditions are right to continue with the project, the next stage is to drill an exploration well. If the well proves dry the exploration costs of the dry hole are written-off, whereas if oil is found the company proceeds to the testing phase.

Oil exploration can cost tens or hundreds of millions of dollars. The actual costs depend on such factors as the location of possible oil reserves (i.e. near land or in deep water), how large the oil field is expected to be, how detailed the exploration information must be, and the type and structure of the rock below the ground. It is not easy to determine a typical cost of such activities. The exploration phase also involves high risk. Until a hole is drilled, the existence of oil or gas is theoretical; 'dry' holes are common even in established production areas. Early explorers relied on looking at surface rock formations for clues about the rocks below – a hit and miss approach. Now geophysical surveys help pin-point likely traps – seismic survey is the most common method. Promising prospects are then drilled and results used to delineate the reservoir and design the extraction scheme. But even with modern technologies there is a high risk of a dry well – only one in ten exploration wells finds oil, and only one in four of those finds proves commercial. To be commercially viable, a well must be able to produce enough oil or gas to justify the costs of drilling and placing it on production. Since exploration activity is high risk and expensive to undertake, firms are anxious to ensure, that wherever they drill or explore, there will be a reasonable probability of success.[1]

Appraisal, development and production phases follow successful exploration.

Appraisal

Following a discovery, it is necessary to appraise the reservoir and ascertain its characteristics (size, structure and quality), thereby reducing technical uncertainty. If exploratory wells establish the presence of producible quantities of oil or gas, development wells are drilled to define the size and extent of the field. In development drilling the odds for success are higher; perhaps six or seven successful wells for every ten drilled. But the element of risk is still present: there may not be enough oil or gas to be commercially attractive; or the technology required to produce oil or gas may be too expensive.

Once data has been obtained and interpreted, the decision to develop the discovery must be taken. This decision depends on numerous factors, including an estimate of the future oil price at the time the project would be expected to come on stream.

Development

If the field is commercially viable, the next stage is the development phase. A decision is taken as regards the development technology to be employed in exploiting the reserves of the field in the most efficient way. In many countries, a detailed development plan has to be submitted to the government for approval before construction proceeds.[2]

Production

Once the first production wells are drilled the production phase begins and the project comes 'on stream'. A number of production wells are drilled to access as high a proportion of the field reserves as possible. The natural pressure within the reservoirs forces the oil up the wellbore, allowing it to be delivered to an offshore production facility on the sea surface or to a production facility onshore. It is only when production starts that both operating revenues and operating costs occur. The costs occurring before the production stage are generally regarded as capital expenditures. In general, about 25 per cent of the oil can be recovered from a typical reservoir by natural means or primary recovery techniques. Enhanced-recovery techniques allow production of more oil from many reservoirs.

Abandonment phase

This is the final stage in the cycle, where the field is no longer profitable and is decommissioned. Production levels decline as a field becomes depleted. The point is reached where production levels fall to a level which ceases to cover operating costs (economic cut off). Abandonment or decommissioning costs are the cost associated with abandoning a well or production facility. Such costs usually cover the plugging of wells, removal of well equipment, production tanks and associated installations. Decommissioning of oil and gas production facilities at the end of their producing lives, particularly in an offshore environment, represents perhaps the second most financially material event in the exploration and production business cycle, after installation of the facilities themselves. The cost of decommissioning facilities in the UKCS has been estimated to exceed $10bn.[3]

5.2.2 Implications

An internationally competitive oil tax regime recognises the unique characteristics of the oil industry.

Oil and gas projects are by nature long-term, with much of the investment and costs being incurred upfront. In some areas like the North Sea, an oil field life cycle tends to be longer than in most other areas of the world both because of the nature of the environment and the scale of the risks and costs involved. The exploration and appraisal stages, in particular, can last many years. There is also a significant time lag, often of many years, from the initial discovery of oil or gas reserves to the time of first production. Exploration and development activities have often taken ten years or more and even then it may take another twenty or thirty years to produce all recoverable reserves. Accordingly, there may be substantial delays before oil companies begin to obtain a return from their investments; hence current years' earnings are often meaningless in relation to costs.

Moreover, the oil industry differs from other industries because of the uncertainty inherent in oil and gas exploration and production activities. Relative to most other industries, the oil industry is characterised by high risk. This risk is present at all stages of the project's life cycle, including the exploration, development and production stages. Risks can be political, exploratory (chance of failure), technical (reserves and cost estimation), economic (oil and gas prices), or commercial (fiscal risk). For most industries, when investment is made, it is known what the increase in output from that investment should be. There is much more uncertainty in expenditures incurred to explore, appraise and develop oil and gas fields. Large investments are necessary before it is known whether the returns will be large or small.

The oil industry is also capital intensive. Substantial amounts must be spent annually on exploration to discover sufficient oil to replace the oil that is currently consumed. Furthermore, unlike other businesses, an oil project has a finite life because its reserves are depletable. This means that the company has a limited number of years over which to realise a competitive rate of return on its investment.

Making important decisions in the petroleum industry requires incorporation of major uncertainties, long time horizons, multiple alternatives, and complex value issues into the decision. Exploration and production of oil and gas is a high-risk venture. During the exploration phase, major uncertainties are related to volumes in place and economics. Geologic concepts are uncertain with respect to structure and reservoir characteristics. But there are also other uncertainties affecting economic evaluations. These relate to costs, probability of finding and producing economically viable reservoirs, and oil price. In fact, the economics of an oil or gas project determine whether the project will go ahead. Exploration decisions do not necessarily require future development and production. Rather, any discovery is evaluated on its own merit.

It is important for any government to consider these realities when structuring its fiscal regime. Governments tend to underestimate the complexity of oil and gas activity and the costs and risks related to this industry. For instance, while governments regard an increase in oil price as an increase in oil companies' profits, hence consider it as a basis for an increase in taxation, they tend not to foresee the parallel rise in costs. Higher oil prices can encourage greater activity, but because there is a limited pool of rigs available worldwide, when demand for rigs increases, the cost of hiring those rigs will increase as well.

5.3 NET CASH FLOW FROM AN OIL FIELD

In the following section, the Net Cash Flow (NCF) of an oil field is computed under the six fiscal regimes that were described in Chapter 3, and which include the UK, Norwegian, Australian, Indonesian, Chinese and Iraqi regimes. This analysis is also helpful to understand the differences between various structures. For illustrations, see Appendices A–C.

5.3.1 Net Cash Flow under a concessionary regime

At a given period t, the profitability of an oil field is given by its NCF after tax or post tax as in the following:

$$NCF_t = R_t - C_t - T_t \tag{5.1}$$

Where:

- R_t is the gross revenue generated at period t; $R_t = P_t Q_t$, where P_t is the price of oil and Q_t is the output produced at period t.
- The total cost, C_t, incorporates two main costs namely; the Capital Expenditures, CAPEX, or CE_t and the Operating Expenditures, OPEX or OE_t.
- T_t is the total tax paid at period t. Under a concessionary system, the total tax take includes Royalty, SPT and IT.

The total tax paid varies with the tax structure that applies. The following section explains how the total government take varies from one structure to another. The section develops the NCF under the three concessionary regimes analysed in Chapter 3, namely the UK, Australia and Norway.

The section that follows looks at the UK petroleum fiscal regime in detail. But it may reasonably be asked why the focus is so heavily on UK experience? The UK tax system is, after all, very complicated and for that reason is certainly not the ideal model to replicate. Other regimes have evolved which appear simpler. For instance, Norway adopts a similar general structure to the UK but computing the tax take is much easier and more straightforward. As Robinson and Morgan (1978) describe it: 'Tax systems are rarely simple but the legislation covering the taxation of UK North Sea oil (the Oil Taxation Act, 1975) is quite extraordinarily complex' (p.93). Also, the late famous tax expert, Campbell Watkins, expressed his frustration with respect to the complexity of the UK petroleum fiscal regime, especially PRT, by the following: 'one realises that the system was designed by a lunatic, one who couldn't stop tinkering – like Ranieri, formerly the Chelsea manager.'

The underlying reasons for the notable complexity of the UK's petroleum tax law lie in the nature of the country's legislative process. Because of the absolute supremacy of Parliament, there has to be watertight legislative authority for every aspect of taxation and the absolute assurance that it is in full conformity with the rule of law and can withstand robust challenges in the Courts. Hence the extraordinary detail in every line of draft Parliamentary Bills dealing with these matters. All possible contingencies have to be legislated for and, as far as possible, all parties treated with an even hand. The system has to be designed to be proof against accusations of discrimination in favour of, or against, one class or group and another, or one individual concern and another. The inevitable result is a tortuous and labyrinthine tax law, not necessarily to be copied but certainly to be learnt from – both in relation to its virtues, which do exist, and to its flaws, from which other tax policy-makers can usefully profit.

So for these reasons, while other regimes are described in detail in the Appendices, we use the UK experience and example as the anvil on which to hammer out more general lessons about the construction and pitfalls of petroleum tax systems.

NCF under the UK system[4]

The post-tax Net Cash Flow that applies to fields that received development approval after 1993 is expressed as:

$$NCF_t = R_t - OE_t - CE_t - CT_t \tag{5.2}$$

where CT is assumed to incorporate the ST imposed in 2002.

However, as demonstrated in Chapter 4, currently (as of 2007) two fiscal structures apply to oil and gas activity. The former one with CT and ST only that applies on fields that received development consent after 1993. The second structure includes, in addition to CT and ST, PRT that applies to fields that received development consent before 1993. Consequently, the post-tax *NCF* of fields that received development before 1993 is expressed as:

$$NCF_t = R_t - OE_t - CE_t - PRT_t - CT_t \tag{5.3}$$

But prior to the abolishing of Royalty in 2002 for all fields, the post-tax *NCF* of oil fields that received development approval before 1983 is expressed as:

$$NCF_t = R_t - ROY_t - OE_t - CE_t - PRT_t - CT_t \tag{5.4}$$

Royalty

In April 2002, the UK government decided to abolish Royalty on all fields. This decision was made effective in December 2002. Prior to that year, Royalty applied on fields that received development approval before April 1982, at a rate of 12.5 per cent and charged on half yearly periods. The rate was imposed on the gross revenue with deductions for conveying and treating costs. These costs include the cost of getting the oil from the wellhead to the point of sale but exclude the exploration and drilling costs. They comprise:

- 70 per cent of the capital costs of the platform depreciated (on a straight-line basis) over eight years (or 16 chargeable periods) or the life of the field, whichever is the shorter.
- Approximately 60 per cent of total platform operating costs.
- 100 per cent of the costs of transportation.

Given the conveying and treating costs, the effective Royalty rate is likely to be between 9 and 12 per cent of gross revenues.[5] The Royalty take is given as:

$$ROY_t = t_r R_t \tag{5.5}$$

The post-Royalty revenue becomes:

$$P_t Q_t - t_r(P_t Q_t) = (1 - t_r) P_t Q_t \tag{5.6}$$

Royalty is an allowable cost for both PRT and CT in the case of a field paying all three.

Petroleum Revenue Tax – PRT

PRT is assessed on a six-month period at a rate of 50 per cent on 'assessable profit' for fields that gained development approval before 16 March 1993. This rate was changed five times between 1975 and 1993, as Table 5.1 shows.

Under the PRT rules, a ring fence exists around the field where only expenditure incurred on the oil field can be set against the income from the field and not against the profits from another field.[6] The assessable or taxable profit is the gross revenue less a series of deductions, principly Royalty, Opex and Capex, uplift, losses brought forward and oil allowance. Although Safeguard relief applies, it is not given as a deduction but is calculated

Table 5.1 Evolution of PRT rate

Period	*PRT rate*
1975–1978	45%
1979	60%
1980–1982	70%
1983–1993	75%
1993 Onwards	50%

separately. Opex and Capex are fully deductible in the year in which the expenditure is incurred.[7] Certain types of costs, principally financial costs, are excluded.

Capex benefits from an additional relief known as uplift or supplement, at a rate of 35 per cent.[8] As such, 135 per cent of Capex is deductible from gross revenue, reducing the assessable profit by the following amount:

$$CE_t + up_t CE_t = CE_t(1 + up_t) \tag{5.7}$$

Where up_t is the uplift rate on capital expenditure in period t.

No PRT is paid until the accumulated Capex and uplift has been written off. However, uplift on Capex is granted only up to payback period, K, which is defined as the first period in which cumulative cash flow becomes positive. In other words, the payback period is the point where the cumulative incomings exceed cumulative outgoings, (outgoings being defined as including not only capital expenditure but also the uplift). As such, the payback period, K, can be found as the minimum value of K for which the following relationship is satisfied:

$$\sum_{t=1}^{K}(R_t - ROY_t - OE_t) > \sum_{t=1}^{K} CE_t(1 + up_t) \tag{5.8}$$

After the payback period, no uplift is granted and Capex in subsequent periods although not qualifying for uplift continues to be allowed as a deduction.

Losses are carried forward and set against profits in future chargeable periods. However, when production has ceased, losses (such as abandonment costs) can be carried back against earlier period's profits, working backward until the loss is exhausted.[9]

Where there is still a profit, after the deduction of expenditures and losses, oil allowance is given. This relief exempts a fixed amount of production from each field from PRT until such time as the total oil allowance for the field is fully utilized.

Oil allowance is a deduction from profits equal to the value of 250,000 tonnes of oil for each six-month period up to a cumulative maximum of 5 Mt,[10] multiplied by the relevant price of each period. If production does not reach 250,000 tonnes in a chargeable period, that part of the oil allowance is not lost but is available in later chargeable periods, but always with the limitation of 250,000 tonnes per chargeable period and 5 Mt overall.

Any profit remaining for the period after the deduction of expenditures, losses and oil allowance is liable to PRT. Consequently, the assessable profit for PRT, to which the PRT rate will apply, is given by:

$$\pi_{pt} = R_t - ROY_t - OE_t - CE_t(1 + up_t) - Loss_{t-1} - OA_t \tag{5.9}$$

Where:

- π_{pt} is the PRT assessable profit
- $Loss_{t-1}$ is the loss carried forward from Period $t-1$ for PRT purpose[11]
- OA_t is the oil allowance in period t

As such, the mainstream PRT take is defined as:

$$PRT_t = t_p\pi_{pt} = t_p\{R_t - ROY_t - OE_t - CE_t(1 + up_t) - Loss_{t-1} - OA_t\} \tag{5.10}$$

Where:

- PRT_r is the mainstream PRT in period t
- t_p is the PRT rate

At this stage, the safeguard relief rules are applied.

This is a form of tapering relief, i.e. an upper limit, under which an oil field will never pay more than the safeguard liability. As such, in certain cases, safeguard can further reduce the amount of PRT chargeable, thereby allowing a field to achieve a minimum level of return on investment before it incurs any PRT liability. The safeguard applies as follows.

Firstly, an 'adjusted profit', π_a is calculated and which is the gross revenue less Royalty and operating costs.

$$\pi_a = R_t - ROY_t - OE_t \tag{5.11}$$

Secondly, this profit is compared to the accumulated CAPEX (without the uplift), $\sum_{n=1}^{t} CE$, called the Safeguard Base.

Then,

- If $\pi_a < 15\%$ of $\sum_{n=1}^{t} CE$, no PRT is paid.

- If $\pi_a \geq 15\%$ of $\sum_{n=1}^{t} CE$, PRT is compared to the Safeguard limit, which is 80% of ($\pi_a - 15\%$ of $\sum_{n=1}^{t} CE$), and the company pays whichever is the smaller amount. As such, when the Safeguard limit is lower than the PRT liability, the Safeguard reduces the amount of PRT chargeable.

Safeguard applies over only a limited period of time, which is the number of chargeable periods up until the field has reached payback plus half of that number of periods. Therefore, S, the period in which the Safeguard provision ends, is given by:

$$S = 1.5K \tag{5.12}$$

Corporation tax

Unlike PRT, CT applies on a company rather than a field basis. An oil company is subject to the standard CT rules that apply to all companies operating in the UK but, in addition, is subject to the ring fence rules. UK E&P activities are treated as distinct from all other activities carried out by the company and profits from these activities are referred to as 'ring fence' profits. In order to prevent tax leakage, only losses incurred within the ring fence are allowed as a deduction from ring fence profits. The main CT rate applies at 30 per cent. This rate was changed several times between 1975 and 2007 as Table 5.2 shows.

The assessable profit for CT is calculated after deduction of Royalty, Opex, capital allowances (depreciation), together with any losses brought forward from previous years, interest costs, as well as any PRT payable.

The principal capital allowances are the First Year Allowance (FYA) and the Writing Down Allowance (WDA) which cannot both be claimed in the same year. The FYA represents an immediate relief; its rate has varied over time:

- Prior to 14 March 1984, FYA rate 100 per cent
- 14 March 1984–31 March 1985, FYA rate 75 per cent
- 1 April 1985–31 March 1986, FYA rate 50 per cent
- After that date, FYA ceased to apply.

If FYA is claimed, the expenditure remaining, the residual balance, will qualify for a WDA in the following period. If 100 per cent FYA is due, the residual value is zero. Prior to April 2002, WDA applied at a rate of 25 per cent on the undepreciated pool of expenditure brought forward from the previous years. However, after April 2002, a 100 per cent capital allowance was applied instead of the 25 per cent rate.

Table 5.2 Evolution of CT rate

Period	*CT rate*
1975–1983	52%
1983–1984	50%
1984–1985	45%
1985–1986	40%
1986–1990	35%
1990–1991	34%
1991–1997	33%
1997–1998	31%
1999–2007	30%

Any losses, which are inevitable in an activity involving a long lead-time between development and the generation of positive cash flows, are carried forward and set against future profits in other chargeable periods.

When production has ceased, a claim is made to carry back the loss (abandonment costs) against earlier profits, working backward until it is exhausted.

The assessable profit for CT is defined as:

$$\pi_{ct} = R_t - ROY_t - OE_t - PRT_t - CA_t - Lossc_{t-1} \tag{5.13}$$

And the CT take will be:

$$CT_t = t_c \pi_{ct} \tag{5.14}$$

Where:

- π_{ct} is the CT assessable profit
- $Lossc_{t-1}$ is the loss carried forward from period $t - 1$, for CT purpose
- t_c is the CT rate
- CT_t is the Corporation Tax in period t

In the 2002 budget, the UK Government imposed ST at a rate of 10 per cent and in 2005 the tax was doubled. This tax is applied to the same tax base as CT, the only difference being that there was no deduction for financing costs.[12] Nevertheless, since finance costs are not incorporated in the calculation of CT in this chapter, the ST and CT will be calculated on the same tax base. As such, it can be assumed that given a ST rate of 20 per cent the applicable CT rate will be 50 per cent.

The assessable profit for ST is as follows:

$$\pi_{st} = R_t - ROY_t - OE_t - PRT_t - CA_t - Lossc_{t-1} \tag{5.15}$$

And the ST take is:

$$ST_t = t_s\pi_{st} \qquad (5.16)$$

Where:

- ST_t is the Supplementary Tax in period t
- t_s is the Supplementary Tax rate in period t

Post tax net cash flow

The post-tax NCF of an oil field, under the 1975 tax structure in the UK, i.e. where Royalty, PRT and CT apply in a particular period, t, can be expressed as follows[13]:

$$NCF_t = R_t - ROY_t - OE_t - CE_t - PRT_t - CT_t \qquad (5.17)$$

Where:

- The post-Royalty revenue is given by:

$$(1 - t_r)R_t \qquad (5.18)$$

- The post-PRT profit is given by:

$$(1 - t_r)R_t - OE_t - CE_t - t_p\{R_t - ROY_t - OE_t - CE_t(1 + up_t) - Loss_{t-1} - OA_t\} \qquad (5.17)$$

- The post-CT profit (including the ST), or the net post-tax cash flow, is given by:

$$(1 - t_r)R_t - OE_t - CE_t - t_p\{R_t - ROY_t - OE_t - CE_t(1 + up_t) - Loss_{t-1} - OA_t\} - t_c\{R_t - ROY_t - OE_t - PRT_t - CA_t - Loss_{t-1}\} \qquad (5.19)$$

NCF under the Australian petroleum fiscal regime[14]

The Australian petroleum fiscal regime combines PRRT and CIT. Under this regime, the post-tax NCF at period t, NCF_t, can be expressed in the following equation:

$$NCF_t - R_t - OE_t - CE_t - PRRT_t - CIT_t \qquad (5.20)$$

where:

- $PRRT_t$ in period t.

$$PRRT_t = t_{ap}\{R_t - OE_t - (CE_t + up_{at})\}$$

With:

- t_{ap} is the PRRT rate
- up_{at} is the uplift rate
- CIT_t is the CIT in period t

$$CIT_t = t_{ac}(R_t - OE_t - D_{at} - PRRT_t) \quad (5.21)$$

With:

- t_{ac} is the CIT rate
- D_{ac} is the depreciation

PRRT is deductible for CIT purposes.

NCF under the Norwegian petroleum regime[15]

The Norwegian petroleum regime incorporates an SPT and a CIT. The post tax NCF at period t can be illustrated in the following equation:

$$NCF_t = R_t - OE_t - CE_t - SPT_t - CIT_{nt} \quad (5.22)$$

where:

$$SPT_t = t_{ns}(R_t - OE_t - D_{nt} - up_{nt}) \quad (5.23)$$

and,

$$CIT_{nt} = t_{nci}(R_t - OE_t - D_{nt}) \quad (5.24)$$

with:

- SPT_t is SPT in period t (not deductible for CIT purposes)
- t_{ns} is the SPT rate
- up_{nt} is the 5 per cent uplift for six years
- t_{nci} is the CIT rate
- D_{ns} is the depreciation

5.3.2 NCF under contractual based systems

Determining the NCF under contractual systems is not as straightforward as under concessionary systems. Several stages must be determined; these are the following:

First, Net Revenue is determined. This is the Gross Revenue less Royalty, if applicable.

Second, cost oil is calculated. This includes broadly the operating expenditures, depreciation of capital expenditures and any investment credit and uplift. Investment credit applies only to facilities such as platforms, pipelines and processing equipment, while uplift applies to all capital costs.

Third, the costs available for recovery are then compared to the limit imposed on revenue, in order to determine the level of costs allowed for deduction at a particular period. For instance, if the cost recovery limit is 80 per cent in a given period the maximum cost that can be deducted is 80 per cent of revenue. If costs exceed that limit, the difference between the actual value of costs and the allowed value is carried forward to a future period.

The following stage differs between a PSC and a Service contract. In a PSC, the difference between net revenue and cost oil determines the profit oil that will be shared between the contractor and the government, depending on the split rate. As such, the contractor's share can be expressed as in the following:

$$\text{Contractor profit oil} = \text{Net revenue} - \text{cost recovery} - \text{government share} \quad (5.25)$$

Finally, the contractor profit oil can be subject to IT. In this case, the contractor profit oil can be considered as the taxable income under a concessionary system. In general, Investment credits and uplifts are cost recoverable but not deductible for calculation of IT. The opposite is true for bonuses, which are not cost recoverable but are tax deductible.

Consequently, the contractor entitlement can be calculated as follows:

- Cost Recovery
- *plus* Investment credits
- *plus* Contractor share of profit oil
- *less* DMO
- *less* Government tax
- *less* Royalty (if applicable)

(5.26)

Government total share can be expressed as the sum of:

- Royalty (if applicable)
- Share of profit oil
- Bonus

- DMO
- Tax

In a service contract, the contractor entitlement includes its cost recovery (normally plus interest) and an agreed rate of return, as the remuneration fee. This sum covering cost recovery, interest and the rate of return is paid over a certain number of months in equal instalments. Once the contractor receives all its payment, (the 'handover date'), the foreign contractor hands over facilities to the government (or the national company) and as such it is no longer involved in the project. Consequently, up to the handover date, the contractor entitlement can be expressed as in the following:

- Cost Recovery
- *plus* Investment Credits
- *plus* Remuneration Fee
- *less* DMO
- *less* Government Tax
- *less* Royalty (if applicable)

(5.27)

The government share in this case is any remaining profitability of the oil field, once the contractor receives the remuneration for its service.

The Indonesian petroleum fiscal regime[16]

The contractor NCF at a given period t under the Indonesian PSC can be illustrated by the following equation[17]:

$$\text{Contractor NCF} = \text{Total revenue} - \text{OPEX} - \text{CAPEX} - \text{Government FTP} - \text{DMO} - \text{Government profit oil} - \text{Bonus} - \text{IT} \quad (5.28)$$

Where:

- FTP is the First Tranche Petroleum. It requires that 20 per cent of the production to be shared at 64/36 per cent in favour of the government before cost recovery. Hence it acts like a Royalty and it can be computed in the following way:
  - Total FTP = 20% × Revenue (5.29)
  - Government Share of FTP = 64% × Total FTP (5.30)
  - Contractor Share of FTP = 36% × Total FTP (5.31)

- DMO is given by:

  - Revenue × 75% × 25% × 36% (5.32)

  (After 60 months of production (i.e. 5 years), the contractor sells 25 per cent of its share of oil (36 per cent) to national oil company at 25 per cent of the market price (Price differential of 75 per cent).
- Government Profit Oil is the government share of Profit Oil and it is given by:

  64% × Total Profit Oil (5.33)

  (hence contractor's share of profit oil is 36% × Total Profit Oil)

Where:

- Total profit oil = Total revenue – Total FTP – Cost recovery allowed (5.34)
- Total cost recovery = OPEX + Intangible CAPEX + Depreciation + Investment credits (5.35)
- Cost recovery limit = 80% × Total revenue (5.36)

- Any cost recovery, which exceeds the limit is carried forward to the following period.
- Cost recovery allowed = Minimum of cost recovery limit and total cost recovery, taking into account cost carried forward.
- Bonus varies with daily production[18]

  - IT = Tax rate × Taxable income (5.37)

  where:

  - Taxable income = Contractor total profit + Investment credits – DMO – Bonus (5.38)
  - Contractor total profit = Contractor profit oil + Contractor share of FTP (5.39)

In this case,

Total Government take = Government share of FTP + DMO + Bonus + IT (5.40)

The Chinese petroleum fiscal regime[19]

The contractor NCF at a given period *t* under the Chinese PSC can be illustrated by the following equation[20]:

Contractor NCF = Net revenue – OPEX – Depreciation – Government share of profit oil – IT (5.41)

Where:

- Net Revenue = Total Revenue – Royalty – VAT (5.42)

- Royalty is calculated on a sliding scale basis.[21]

- VAT is 5% of Total Revenue (5.43)

- Depreciation is 100 per cent of CAPEX as spent. Any unrecovered balance is carried forward to the following period and is compounded at a 9 per cent interest rate.
- Government share of profit oil (per cent) is determined by the X Factor, depending on annual production.[22]

- Government share of profit oil = Government share in percentage × Total profit oil (5.44)
- Contractor share of profit oil = Total profit oil – Government share (5.45)
- Total profit oil = Net revenues – Cost recovery (5.46)
- Cost recovery = OPEX – Depreciation (5.47)
- Cost recovery limit = 62.5% × Total revenue (5.48)

- Any cost recovery, which exceeds the limit, is carried forward to the following period.
- Cost recovery allowed = Minimum of cost recovery limit and Total cost recovery, taking into account Cost carried forward.

- IT = 33% × Taxable income (5.49)
- Taxable income = Net revenue – OPEX – Depreciation – Government share of profit oil (5.50)

In this case,

Total Government take = Royalty + VAT + Government Share of profit oil + IT (5.51)

The Iraqi petroleum fiscal regime[23]

The contractor's NCF under the Iraqi regime can be illustrated by the following equation[24]:

NCF = Total income – Total costs (5.52)

Where:

- Total Income = Contractor Remuneration + 8 Quarters CAPEX + Cost Recovery Allowed (5.53)
- Total Costs = OPEX + CAPEX (5.54)

- Contractor remuneration is calculated using the following steps:

  - Cumulative CAPEX = Cumulative CAPEX until field reaches handover date.
  - Remuneration Index is assumed to be 1.5.
  - Expected cumulative CAPEX = Maximum of cumulative CAPEX to handover date.

  - Overall remuneration = Remuneration Index × expected cumulative CAPEX (5.55)
  - Contractor remuneration = 10% × revenue (5.56)
  - Balance to be recovered = Overall remuneration – Cumulative remuneration (5.57)

  - 8 Quarters after Handover (i.e. 2 years) means that the balance to be recovered at Handover will be recovered in 8 quarters, by equal instalments.

- Cost recovery:

  - Cost recovery limit = 50% × Revenue (5.58)
  - Net income = Total costs – Cost recovery limit (5.59)
  - Cumulative net income$_t$ = Net income$_t$ + Cumulative income$_{t-1}$ (5.60)

  - Cost recovery allowed = Minimum between total costs and cost recovery limit

  - Cost unrecovered = Cost recovery allowed – Total costs (5.61)
  - Cumulative cost unrecovered$_t$ = Cost unrecovered$_t$ + Cumulative unrecovered$_{t-1}$ (5.62)

- When all costs are recovered (i.e. Cumulative unrecovered = 0), the field reaches handover date.

Finally,

$$\text{Government take during contract} = \text{Revenue} - \text{Total costs} - \text{Contractor NCF} \quad (5.63)$$

5.4 MEASURING ECONOMIC PROFITABILITY

The previous section of this chapter explained how to calculate the NCF in petroleum activity under different fiscal regimes. However, NCF is calculated for a given period of time. To value their projects, oil companies estimate the after tax present value of their total expected net cash flows discounted for both time and risk. This method is called Discounted Cash Flow (DCF), and it has been for several decades in the energy industry, the most common form of project evaluation. The DCF technique has also been (and still is) the most commonly used method in evaluating expected future cash flow. A study done by Siew in 2001 found that 99 per cent of oil companies use this technique. Furthermore, the majority of economic studies[25] utilize this traditional technique to evaluate the profitability of an oil field[26].

Under the DCF technique, the investment's evaluation is usually done in three steps:

1 First, the analyst estimates the net cash flows that will occur at each time period in a particular scenario.
2 Second, the cash flows are discounted using a certain discount rate, incorporating a risk premium (See below).
3 Finally, the DCFs are added to form the project value, also called the Net Present Value (NPV).

The NPV measures the economic profit of an investment and is calculated by discounting the stream of revenues generated by the investment (cash inflows) less the present value cost of the investment (cash outflows). It is this assessment of present value of cash inflows and outflows that underlines the value of an investment. An NPV of zero means that the project's cash flows are just sufficient to repay the invested capital and to provide the required rate of return on that capital. If a project has a positive NPV, then it generates a return that is greater than is needed to pay for funds provided by investors, hence it should be accepted. If a project has a negative NPV, it is generally rejected as it does not increase the firm's value. Finally, in the case of two mutually exclusive projects, the project with the highest NPV will be usually selected. As such, when assessing the performance of an investment, the economic profit, measured by NPV, is the key variable of interest.

In addition to NPV, there are other applications of DCF and other project evaluation methods, but there is a general agreement that the NPV is the best single measure of profitability.[27] Furthermore, several studies consider NPV to be the measure of the economic rent generated from petroleum extraction activity. Rowland and Hann (1987, p.4) argue that

> 'the economic worth of a licence to produce oil from a tract of the UKCS may be measured by the present value of the flow of the future revenues from that tract's production less the present value of associated future costs, where the costs include monetary items such as equipment as well as non-monetary items such as exposure to risks. The difference between these two amounts, the net present value (NPV), is the economic rent of that tract. It may be positive, negative or zero. If it is positive, it implies that the licensee is enjoying profits in excess of those necessary to induce the production of petroleum (pure profits)'
>
> Rowland and Hann, 1987 p.4

There are two main advantages in using the DCF method. Firstly, it is quick and relatively easy to understand and apply. Secondly, it is a cash flow based technique, which takes into account the time value of money.[28]

DCF estimates the profitability of a project by calculating the Net Present Value, NPV, which is expressed in the following:

$$NPV = \sum_{t=1}^{n} NCF_t \times DF \tag{5.74}$$

The discrete discount factor, DF, is given by the following expression:

$$DF = \frac{1}{(1+r)^t} \tag{5.65}$$

While continuous discounting is given by the following:

$$DF = \lim_{t \to \infty} \frac{1}{(1+r)^t} = e^{-rt} \tag{5.66}$$

Where r is the discount rate.

If there is no uncertainty, cash flows are discounted for time only, and the discount rate would be the risk-free interest rate. If there is uncertainty, cash flows are discounted for both time and risk, and the discount rate is the risk-free interest rate plus a risk premium. There is likely to be a range of discount rates employed by investors depending on the overall cost of capital and the risk premium relating to specific projects.

In some cases, a probability distribution for different scenarios is constructed. In this case, the Expected Net Present Value, ENPV, or the Expected Monetary Value (EMV) can be used as a measure of the overall profitability of the project. This is applied, in particular, at the exploration and appraisal phases of an oil field. Several scenarios are set, each with different probabilities of occurrence (e.g. chance of geological success, production costs, price variation, etc). For each scenario, NPV is calculated. By multiplying each NPV by its associated probability and then summing for all scenarios, one can determine the EMV of a given event.[29]

Finally, total government take in percentage is then determined as:

$$\frac{\text{Government Take}}{\text{Pre-tax NPV}} \tag{5.67}$$

5.5 SUMMARY AND CONCLUSION

Two key messages emerge from this chapter. The first is that the petroleum industry is special in its nature, its size, its risks and uncertainties and the diversity of its operational phase and sequences. The second is that the shaping of a fiscal system suitable for this industry, and for the twin objectives of securing a 'fair share' for the state whilst maintaining good incentives for investment and development, is a task of almost unparalleled complexity.

As the text has illustrated, the extraction of mineral oil falls into six distinct upstream phases. This of course is aside from the mid-stream transmission, processing and refining of crude oil and the downstream distribution and marketing operations, all in themselves both complex and challenging. The six upstream phases are:

- the procurement of licensed territory (land or sea – based) for the rights to explore;
- the exploration process;
- the appraisal of finds for the purpose of deciding what to invest and what are the commercial prospects;
- the development phase;
- actual production and bringing oil on stream; and
- the eventual decommissioning and abandonment (particularly relevant in the case of very large offshore surface installations).

Not only are prolonged time periods involved in each of these phases but the capital investment demands are vast and the uncertainties at each stage very high. Failure to discover oil, or to find it in commercially recoverable volumes and conditions, is frequent. Calculations of commercial viability, as have been explained, are themselves heavily influenced by a whole variety of circumstances, ranging from the geological and environmental, through to the fiscal, legal and political conditions surrounding oil industry activity in any one province or jurisdiction. The prevailing world crude oil price, along with judgments about its future evolution, are also a crucial variable where strong nerves are required to take a long term view beyond short term price volatility, which may well be intense, as past experience confirms.

As to the design of appropriate tax regimes it has been shown in this chapter how difficult the differing existing regimes are to evaluate and how misleading simple conclusions from visible tax rates can be. The display and explanation of the calculations necessary to establish potential net cash flow for any individual oil company projects and operations provides further vivid confirmation of this point.

The unpredictability of potential cost structures at every phase, even in preparing to bid for licences, let alone in the large capital expenditure involved at later stages, especially in novel offshore developments, is a central problem in trying to establish workable tax regimes. As a later chapter shows, the absence of adequate cost data can lead, and has led, the formulators of petroleum tax regimes into major difficulties with considerable distorting effects on the industry.

Finally, it is notable that even countries which appear to have exceptionally tough and insensitive fiscal regimes can in practice continue to attract oil company interest and investment. This is because, as survey work confirms, prospectivity rules.[30] The promise of major oil finds brings hungry oil investing enterprises into any relevant region. Likely fiscal terms, relations with the ruling authorities and general political, legal and social prospects then come into play. In Chapter 8 we shall examine some of the key underlying forces and influences which shape these wider conditions, and which add to the cauldron of risks and uncertainties which, above all, characterise the modern development and growth of the oil business and its relationship, primarily through fiscal systems, with governments the world over.

6 Regimes and outcomes

Profitability and government revenues; how outcomes can vary under different tax structures in differing conditions and over different time periods

6.1 THE EXERCISE EXPLAINED

This chapter takes the form of a hypothesis and a demonstration. It allows the reader to see quantitatively how different tax structures, if and when applied within one country (in this case the UK), and how different tax regimes when applied in selected oil producing countries round the world (the chosen examples being Norway, Australia, Indonesia, China and Iraq), would affect petroleum fields' profitability and government's revenues.

In the previous chapter, tax models for all six of these countries were selected for analysis. This chapter uses these models to calculate and compute the profitability of a sample of oil fields under a variety of regimes and conditions and the fiscal revenues which governments would hypothetically obtain from the activity in those fields.

The assessment in each case takes into full consideration the interests of both government authorities and oil industry concerns prevailing at the relevant point of time. It looks – in the case of the UK – at the way in which the successive tax regimes over the period 1975–2006 would have applied and worked, had they been kept in place unchanged. It also takes account of the fiscal impact on different fields, the size factor (very small, small, medium and large), as well as variations in the oil price (low and high). These latter two variables in particular have a decisive impact on the computations. For example, in the case of field size a low tax take on small fields can have as similar an impact as a high tax take on large fields. The prospectivity of an oil and gas province (i.e. the estimated size of the field) has a direct effect on investment decisions. For instance, oil in many small fields that were discovered on the UK Continental Shelf (UKCS) in the 1980s was left in the ground because investors were not interested in developing those fields – they simply were not commercial. Fiscal regimes and rates therefore need to be designed in ways that respect the geological prospect of an oil and gas province.

As for the movement of crude oil prices, this too has a major influence on the outcome and in practice the big changes in oil price levels in the first years of the twenty-first century have of course already transformed the international energy scene. After reaching very low levels in the 1990s (their lowest level was recorded at $10 per barrel in 1998), prices started to rise to almost reach $80 per barrel in 2007 and $100 in 2008 in nominal terms. Higher oil prices make investment in smaller fields more attractive, but they also encourage governments to take action to increase their fiscal take as happened in the UK back in 2002 and 2005 in particular. In other countries, governments rushed to change their fiscal terms. Venezuela and Russia are striking examples of this policy reaction to rising crude prices.

The hypothetical examples and calculations in this chapter have been carried out in the light of all these factors. We look first of all at the whole UK experience through time and assess in sequence the impact of each of the major tax structures that have applied since 1975 until 2006, thus seeing what would have happened both to field profitability and the UK government's revenues, had they been kept in place unaltered. The second part of the analysis compares the impact of various tax regimes in six countries on profitability and revenues.

The aim of these examples is to illuminate further how different tax structures and regimes actually work out in practice (not always in ways intended or expected), how their impacts compare and how sometimes quite different regimes can nevertheless lead to surprisingly similar outcomes. For example, similar results emerge for both the Norwegian and Indonesian regimes, even though the former operates under a concessionary system, where oil ownership at the wellhead is passed to the operating company or entity, while the latter is a strictly contractual one where the oil is government-owned both in the ground and at the point of production. This of course raises again the interesting question as to whether it really matters who owns the oil – an issue raised in Chapter 3 and to which we return in detail in Chapter 8.

Any analysis of this kind requires some assumptions. These are outlined in Section 2. Section 3 carries out the analysis on the UKCS. Section 4 expands the analysis to the international comparison. Final remarks are presented in Section 5. Only four of the twenty five selected UK fields are used for illustration in the main text of this chapter (Argyll, a very small field, Arbroath, a small field, Tern, a medium field and Schiehallion, a large field). Detailed results on the 25 selected fields, and the outcomes which result from the various models, are set out for the assiduous reader in Appendix D.

6.2 ASSUMPTIONS

Fields

Different sizes of fields generate different levels of profitability. In relative terms, small and medium fields do not generate the same levels of economic rent as large fields. Consequently, different tax instruments have a varying impact on field profitability in so far as 'one size does not fit all', and given the individual characteristics of each oil field, such as water depth, size, costs and life, which are specific to each field.

To illustrate this variable impact, a sample of oil fields is selected and classified according to the size of their recoverable reserves into very small, small, medium, large and very large categories, as in Table 6.1. This classification is the result of a comparison of size division from major sources, as Table 3.1 in Chapter 3 illustrates.

A sample of 25 oil fields is selected for investigation on the basis of their providing a representative sample of post 1993 (pre-2004) producing oil fields in the UK North Sea.[1] The use of real data affords the study a more authoritative status. Smith and McCardle (1999) argue that the use of a model field can oversimplify the problems analysed, because in reality there are many complications such as uncertain production rates, development costs and construction lags.

For the purpose of this exercise, quota sampling is used to ensure that unit subgroups are represented in the sample in approximately the same proportions as they are represented in the population. The data set includes 10 very small, nine small, four medium and two large fields.[2] No very large fields are incorporated in the analysis because there has been no UK discovery of this size for the last 20 years. Further, the very large fields that are in production are currently in their final stages of decline.

Oil fields are grouped by size because the main factor determining the variable effects of the differing tax packages is oil field size. This partly explains why the UK government for example reduced its take from approximately 87 per cent in the early 1980s to 40 per cent in 2002, as the number of small

Table 6.1 Field size

Field size	*Recoverable reserves (mmbbl)*
Very small	<100
Small	100–200
Medium	200–400
Large	400–500
Very large	>500

fields increased relative to the larger accumulations.[3] However, other factors come into play – namely oil field profitability and productive life expectancy.

In order to avoid unnecessary complications, the exercise carried out in this chapter takes as its basic operating premise a single company which operates and owns a single oil field. If there are several companies investing in an oil field, each will own a percentage and the tax base will apply on the individual company, not the overall profitability, of the field.[4] As justified by Robinson and Morgan (1978, p.113), 'the outside observer cannot know in detail the tax position of the companies'. At the end, the profitability of an oil field, which is greatly influenced by taxation, is a key determinant of the attractiveness of an oil province.

Tax scenarios

Field profitability and government revenues are evaluated under two main sets of tax scenarios:

1 The first set of tax scenarios illustrate the main fiscal packages that applied to the UKCS over the period 1975–2006. In total, eight tax scenarios were considered. These include:

Table 6.2 Tax scenarios

Scenarios	*Package (%)*				*Marginal Rate (%)*	*Period*	*Application*
	Roy	*CT*	*ST*	*PRT*			
UK_{75}	12.5	52	0	70	87	1975	on fields that received development consent before 83
UK_{83}	0.0	33	0	75	83	1983	on fields that received development consent after 83
UK_{93a}	0.0	30	0	0	30	1993	on fields that received development consent after 93
UK_{93b}	0.0	30	0	50	65	1993	on fields that received development consent before 93
UK_{02a}	0.0	30	10	0	40	2002	on fields that received development consent after 93
UK_{02b}	0.0	30	10	50	70	2002	on fields that received development consent before 93
UK_{05a}	0.0	30	20	0	50	2005	on fields that received development consent after 93
UK_{05b}	0.0	30	20	50	75	2005	on fields that received development consent before 93

2 The second set of tax scenarios is concerned with international comparisons. Five are used to illustrate the regimes that were described in Chapters 3 and 5, namely; Norwegian, Australian, Indonesian, Chinese and Iraqi regimes. These in turn are compared to the eight UK tax scenarios. The latter is done in order to illustrate how the structure of a regime varies and compares to other regimes round the world over time. For a summary of these scenarios, see Table 3.4 in Chapter 3.
3 An additional scenario is considered. This is the base pre-tax scenario where no tax applies.

Oil prices

Oil fields' profitability and government revenues are further evaluated under two price scenarios:

1 A low oil price scenario, where a \$19.5/barrel Brent price is assumed in the base year (2000). This value represents the average oil price achieved in the 1990s. It also represents the low case scenario assumed by the E I A (2006) in its oil price expectations for 2020.
2 A high oil price scenario, taking into consideration the average annual Brent prices achieved in 2000–2005 (\$28.5 in 2000, \$24.4 in 2001, \$25 in 2002, \$28.8 in 2003, \$38.7 in 2004 and \$54.3 in 2005).[5]

These two scenarios are considered because on the one hand, the increase in oil price triggered the increase in taxation on oil activity in several petroleum provinces like the UK and Venezuela, and on the other hand, oil companies in general do not base their investment decisions on assumptions of \$60/barrel but far less, although in response to the recent increase in oil prices, companies have raised the prices they use to evaluate new investment opportunities.

Additional assumptions

The analysis is undertaken in nominal terms and subsequently deflated. All figures are expressed in £million and in real terms, assuming a constant annual inflation rate of 2.5 per cent as from 2000. The inflation rate used represents the UK Retail Price Index and the five years average US deflator (Bank of England, 2006). k_t is the inflation factor, where $k_t = k_{t-1}\exp(k)$, with $k_0 = 1$ and k the constant annual inflation rate of 2.5 per cent. Furthermore, a constant exchange rate of US\$1.6 to the pound sterling is used and which represents the five years average exchange rate (2000–2005) (Barclays Bank, 2006).

For discounting purposes, the nominal risk-free rate, i, is assumed to be 4.5 per cent, as this approximates to the average nominal risk free rate in 2002 as given by the UK Debt Management Office (2003). The discount rate, r, is assumed to be 10 per cent in real terms, as has been applied in the majority of published studies, to mirror the industry's discount rate.[6]

6.3 RESULTS AND ANALYSIS

It is not surprising to see that the profitability of each field has decreased under all tax scenarios, and that it is higher under high oil price scenario than low oil price scenario, as Figure 6.1 shows. Under the high oil price scenario, most, if not all, fields (except one) have an NPV higher than £300 million. The story is different under the low oil price scenario, where a significant decrease in fields' profitability is noted; seven fields have profitability below £200 million. Under this scenario, several fields suffer from a decrease in profitability to below £30 million. Much lower government revenues are obtained under the low price scenario.

The following sections concentrate on the results from the analysis carried out on the UK tax scenarios, and then on the international regimes. The principal emphasis of the discussion is on comparing the effects of different tax packages on different field sizes.

6.3.1 The UK case

i. Impact of different tax structures on oil fields' profitability

Figures 6.2–6.5 illustrate the results of the four selected fields under different tax structures.

Under Scenario UK_{75} where 12.5 per cent Royalty applies alongside 72 per cent PRT and 50 per cent CT, hence a marginal rate of 87 per cent, there is a significant reduction in profitability for all fields, particularly very small and small fields. In fact, the largest decrease in profitability of all fields occurs under this scenario. Such a low level of profitability can discourage field development and may lead to early abandonment. This outcome is mainly

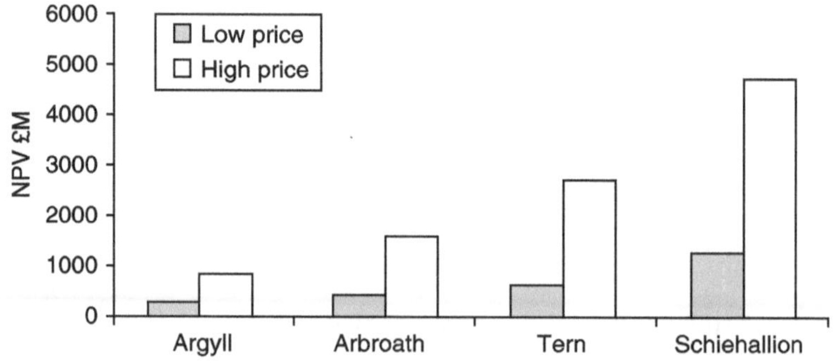

Figure 6.1 Pre-tax NPV.

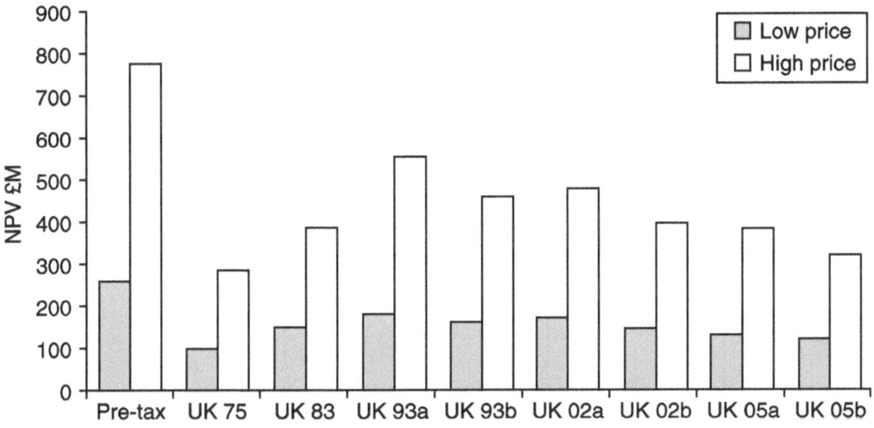

Figure 6.2 Argyll field: NPV under different tax scenarios.

due to the imposition of Royalty, which is not only a regressive tax but also not profit related. Royalty draws cash from a field as soon as production commences, irrespective of field profitability.

For instance, in the case of one field, Royalty occurs three years before CT and six years before PRT while in the case of another field Royalty is due two years before CT but eight years before PRT.

When Scenario UK_{75} is compared with Scenarios UK_{83} and UK_{05b}, where marginal tax rates are respectively 83 and 75 per cent, one can see that the decrease in the profitability of smaller fields is not as pronounced. Under both scenarios UK_{83} and UK_{05b}, no Royalty applies and the tax structure is based on PRT and CT. But smaller fields are usually protected against the payment of PRT, given various reliefs, in particular the oil allowance. This is why even if the marginal tax rate is 83 or 75 per cent, many smaller fields in fact pay between 30 and 50 per cent effective marginal rate.

Similarly, when considering the scenarios where CT and ST apply (namely Scenarios UK_{02a} and UK_{05a}) and the scenarios where PRT applies alongside CT and ST (namely Scenarios UK_{02b} and UK_{05b}), it is expected to see that the higher tax rates lead to a more substantial decrease in profitability of various oil fields. But this is not the case when considering smaller fields, as the imposition of PRT does not have any impact on those fields' profitability.

For medium and larger fields (and some of the small fields that are in a PRT paying position), a more consistent pattern can be noted, as the general rule that higher marginal tax rates lead to bigger decrease in fields' profitability is sustained. In general, the highest profitability is noted under the lowest marginal tax rate of 30 per cent in the case of Scenario UK_{93a} where 30 per cent CT applies, while the lowest profitability is recorded under the highest marginal tax rate of 87 per cent in the case of Scenario UK_{75}. Furthermore, for these fields, the abolition of Royalty increases the PRT take

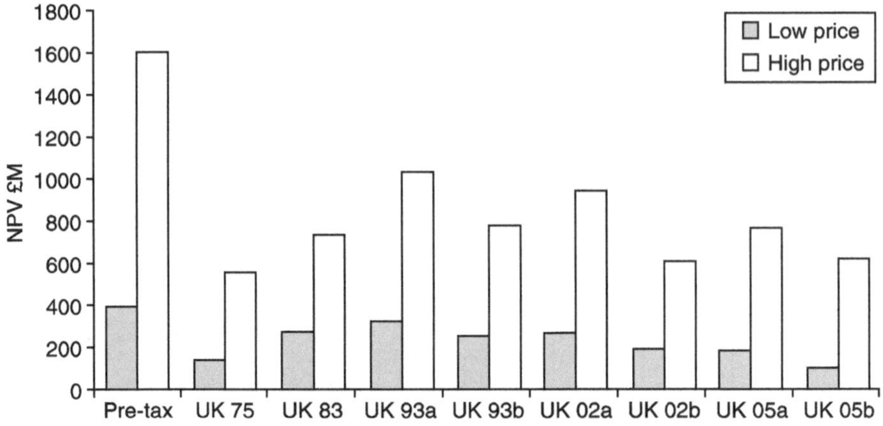

Figure 6.3 Arbroath field: NPV under different tax scenarios.

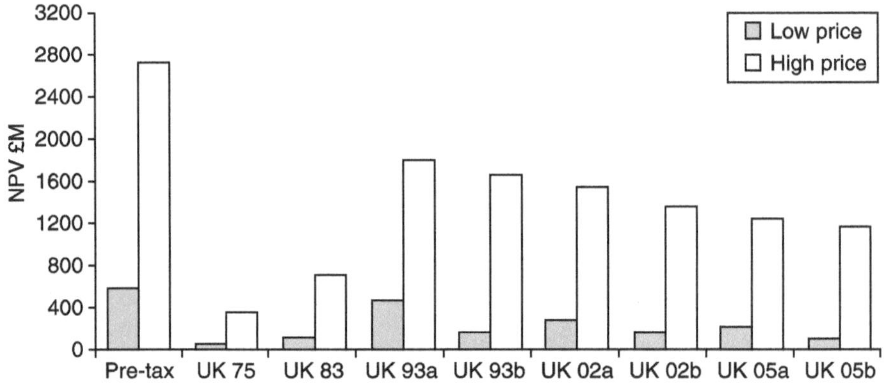

Figure 6.4 Tern field: NPV under different tax scenarios.

because Royalty is allowed for deduction from the PRT taxable income. In other words, when Royalty was abolished, the taxable income subject to PRT became higher as Royalty was no longer deductible.

ii. Impact of different tax structures on government revenues

In terms of government revenues, the lowest fiscal take is generated under Scenario UK_{93a} where 30 per cent CT applies. This applies to all fields, as illustrated in Figures 6.6–6.9. However, for smaller fields the same observation can be made under Scenario UK_{93b} where 50 per cent PRT and 30 per cent CT apply (65 per cent marginal tax rate), as those fields are protected against the payment of PRT. The largest fiscal take is noted under the original fiscal structure back in 1975, illustrated by Scenario UK_{75} where the marginal tax rate is 87 per cent.

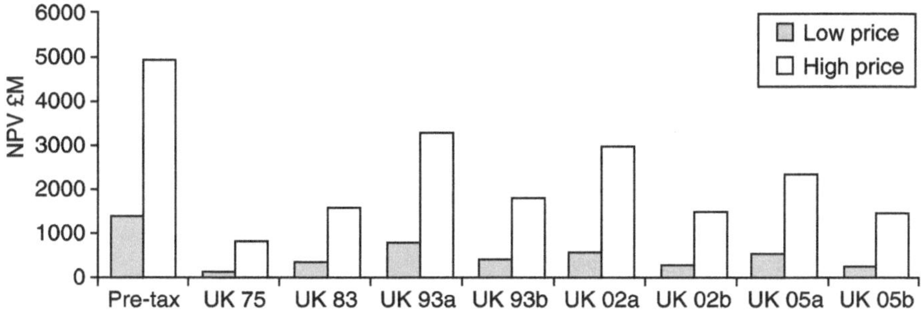

Figure 6.5 Schiehallion field: NPV under different tax scenarios.

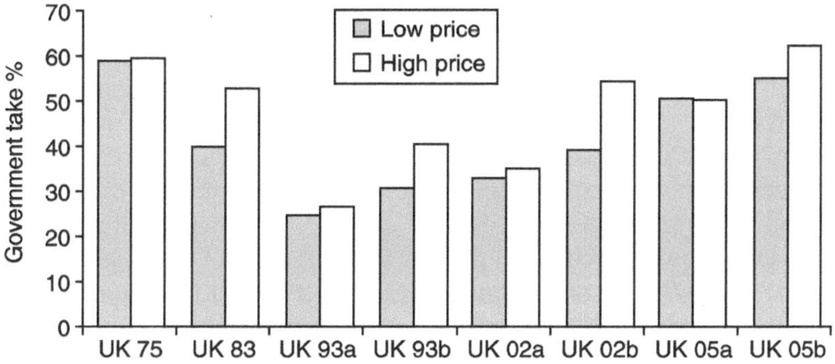

Figure 6.6 Argyll field: government take under different tax scenarios.

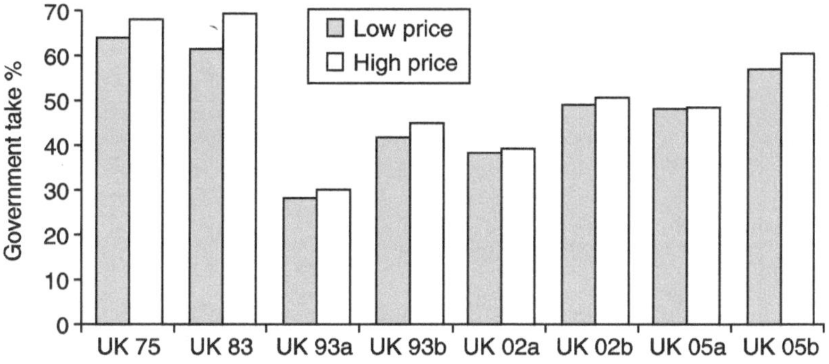

Figure 6.7 Arbroath field: government take under different tax scenarios.

In all the tax scenarios where PRT applies, the major source of government take comes from the larger fields. While the abolition of PRT does not induce a significant reduction in government revenue in the case of small and very small fields, in the case of medium and large fields the revenues are almost halved.

In terms of government take, expressed as a percentage of the pre-tax NPV of a field, the following can be noted. Where PRT applies and in the case of very small and small fields, the effective marginal tax rate is much lower than the imposed rate. For instance, under Scenario UK_{93b} (30 per cent CT and 50 per cent PRT) where the marginal tax rate is supposed to be 65 per cent, the effective tax rate barely reaches 42 per cent for very small fields, while the rate varies between 30 and 56 per cent for small fields under both high and low price scenarios. For larger fields, the rate is higher; it varies between 53 and 55 per cent for medium fields and around 60 per cent for large fields. As such, the outcome is very similar to imposing 30 per cent CT with 10 per cent ST (UK_{02a}) and even 30 per cent CT with 20 per cent ST (UK_{05a}), with respective marginal tax rate of 40 and 50 per cent. Similarly, imposing 50 per cent PRT with 30 per cent CT and 10 per cent ST (UK_{02b}, 70 per cent marginal tax rate), the effective marginal tax rate varies between 40 and 55 per cent on very small fields, 38 and 50 per cent on small fields, 54 and 60 per cent on medium fields and reaches 60 per cent in the case of larger fields. Again the outcome is not very different from the scenarios where CT and ST only apply.

The effective tax rates are higher under a combination of 50 per cent PRT, 30 per cent CT and 20 per cent ST (UK_{05b}, 75 per cent marginal tax rate), where the tax rate varies between 50 and 60 per cent on very small and small fields, and 60 to 69 per cent on medium fields. The full marginal tax rate is obtained in the case of one large field only – Schiehallion – under the low price scenario – where the effective marginal tax rate reaches 75 per cent. No striking differences are noted in the marginal tax rates under the two selected price scenarios, especially where CT and ST apply, while in general small differences occur where PRT applies. This outcome can be attributed to the neutral aspect of the fiscal packages.

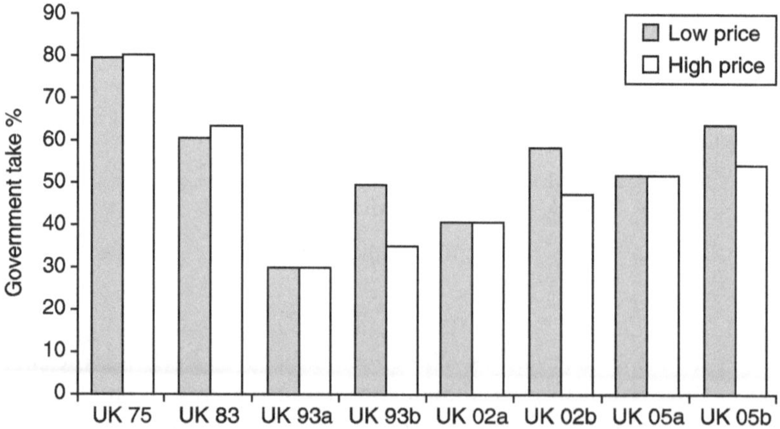

Figure 6.8 Tern field: government take under different tax scenarios.

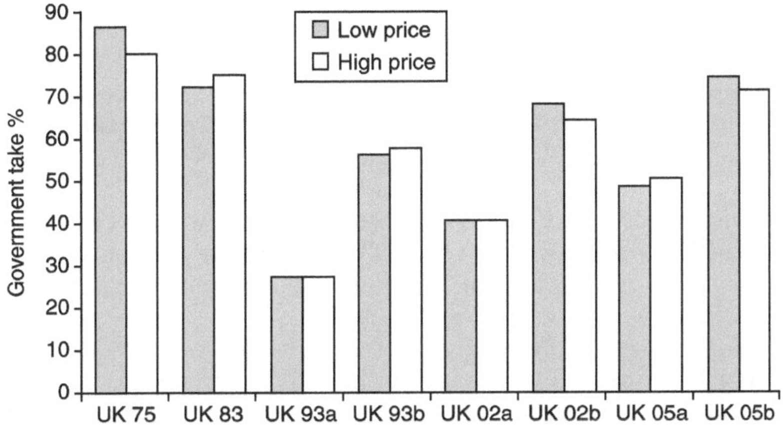

Figure 6.9 Schiehallion field: government take under different tax scenarios.

Discussion

The most severe fiscal package in terms of government take on profitability is the one that applied to oil activity before 1983, based on the combination of Royalty, PRT and CT. This is the only scenario that rendered several fields unprofitable, especially under a low price scenario. Royalty is a regressive tax instrument, and in a mature province like the North Sea it is unlikely to be a suitable tax instrument. From the analysis carried in the sections above, it can be concluded that maintaining the pre-1983 structure would have resulted in many fields being abandoned or undeveloped. This can explain the limited reaction to the abolition of Royalty in 1983 on fields that received development consent after that year, and then on all fields in 2002.

One can also understand the controversy created by the 1993 changes which involved abolishing PRT on fields that received development consent after that year. Similarly, when the UK government decided back in 2002 to impose 10 per cent Supplementary Charge instead of re-introducing PRT several questions arose from such a decision.

As the previous section shows, PRT is better adapted to the size of oil fields than ST. It generates a higher profitability and lower revenues to the government in the case of smaller fields than in the case of larger fields, as compared to the packages where CT and ST apply. PRT has such an impact on smaller fields principally as a result of the oil allowance, which exempts a fixed amount of production from each field from PRT until the total oil allowance for the field is fully utilized. The oil allowance is the most important relief for smaller fields. The effects of the other PRT reliefs, namely the uplift and safeguard, depend mainly on the value of CAPEX as well as the payback period. As the larger fields tend to have a longer payback period and larger CAPEX spend than the smaller ones, the uplift and safeguard reliefs are of greater significance. But the oil allowance is also important for the larger fields, which have the capacity to maximise all of the available allowance because of their high levels production. Additionally, the oil allowance is worth more at higher oil prices.

More importantly, the fiscal scenarios where PRT applies automatically capture the increased profitability resulting from oil price increases, without the need to alter the PRT rate. This shows that PRT adjusts more flexibly to changes in oil price than CT or ST. Consequently, one wonders why the UK government firstly abolished PRT in 1993 and secondly did not consider re-introducing PRT as a mechanism to capture higher revenues from oil activity in the UKCS.

The reason can possibly be that PRT suffers from two major problems; firstly, its limited capability to generate high fiscal revenues in the case of smaller fields or a low oil price and secondly its complicated structure; in fact, PRT is the most complex tax instrument to compute as compared to Royalty and CT. The UK government action in 1993 was driven in part by the need to raise revenues and stem the losses from PRT mainly due to exploration subsidies. In the period 1991–93 it was discovered that the PRT yield had been virtually eliminated by the expenditure on exploration and certain large investments in large PRT paying fields. When the government removed the exploration allowance against PRT, revenues were immediately restored. Furthermore, the reintroduction of PRT would have presented many practical and administrative problems, which probably explains why the UK Government did not pursue this option. Specifically the large number of fields developed since 1993 (when PRT was abolished) would have been brought back into PRT, necessitating retroactive PRT field determinations (ring fence coordinates) and the creation of a virtual PRT economic history, which would have produced inevitable complexity in respect of transition rules.

In the late 1970s and early 1980s, the UK government leaned towards generating high revenues from the oil industry, whereas from 1983 to 2002, the emphasis was on encouraging new developments and increasing production. From 2002 to 2006, once again, the focus has been on capturing larger revenues from the oil and gas industry given the upsurge in oil price, as well as the need to fund substantial public expenditure.

But as has been discussed in the previous chapters, higher tax rates do not necessarily mean higher revenues, and higher oil prices do not necessarily mean higher profits. This is in particular true in the case of the UKCS where production is in decline, hence putting upwards pressure on costs. In fact, high oil prices can both contribute to and constrain activity in the oil and gas sector. While they had the effect of making a greater volume of reserves economically attractive to recover, they also put pressure on resources and increased capital development and exploration and appraisal costs. As such, in a mature province, where production is declining, higher oil prices can be seen as a compensation for rising costs instead of an incentive for the government to raise taxes.

The UK fiscal regime suffers from technical deficiencies, not least the inability of a fiscal package based on CT and ST to adjust automatically to changes in the oil price without structural changes being made. Furthermore, the complexity resulting from the application of two different packages in the UKCS – 50 per cent for new fields since 1993 but 75 per cent on many older fields developed before 1993 – distorts decision making and tends to divert investment away from the 75 per cent regime towards the 50 per cent regime. But it is those investments which are needed to sustain the production from older, larger fields and prolong the life of the province.

The UK Government could consider the following two options. The first is to abolish ST and introduce PRT at a 50 per cent rate. However, in addition to the administrative burden, such a step would lead to lower fiscal revenues generated if there is a decrease in oil price and a reduction in the output of larger fields. Furthermore, because the UKCS is a mature province with the majority of fields falling into the small and very small categories, PRT is unlikely to generate high fiscal revenues, given its generous reliefs. Abolishing any one of those reliefs would have a discriminating effect with respect to fields' size. PRT can also lead to an inefficient allocation of expenditures as a result of its various reliefs and can actually give rise to investment disincentives in larger fields.

This leads to the second option, which is to abolish PRT on all fields and apply a higher ST rate. This would simplify the tax regime and treat all fields and all basin investment on the same basis, as well as possibly generating higher revenues. From the industry's perspective, PRT abolition would be controversial as it would be divisive; some companies pay substantial PRT, others pay none. The losers would complain and the winners would keep quiet. However, the Treasury ruled out such as change in a position paper published in March 2007.

On balance, if changes are inevitable and in order to sustain production from the UKCS as long as possible, the UK Government could consider abolishing PRT on those fields that received development consent before 1993 and maintain the stability of a regime based solely on CT. This is particularly important given that production in the UKCS increasingly depends on smaller, high costs fields, that future oil prices are almost impossible to predict and that in a mature province like the UKCS economic rents are likely to decrease. Inevitably as production continues to decline and unit extraction costs rise, tax capacity will be squeezed out of the basin and fiscal policy will need to respond swiftly to sustain competitiveness. In time both PRT and ST might be removed returning the basin to the same tax regime as applies to the rest of UK industry. This is nothing new and prevailed in the period 1993–2002 when 30 per cent CT applied on fields that received development consent after 1993. The success of such a fiscal policy is clear from the statistics; a period of rapid production growth, sustained investment and rising tax receipts in an environment of oil prices averaging below $20/bbl.

In fact, in countries like the UK and the USA, where the oil industry is not the backbone of the economy but many other sectors are equally or more profitable and make a bigger contribution to GDP and where oil and gas production is in decline, applying only the general CT to the oil industry would make a good deal of sense, especially given the generally positive attitude towards capitalism.

6.3.2 International comparison

This section compares the impact of the six petroleum fiscal regimes on different field size, cost structure, and government revenue, and under different price scenarios. Those regimes are: UK, Norwegian, Australian, Indonesian, Chinese and Iraqi. The study focuses on determining the ways those countries attempt to achieve the balance between maintaining the attractiveness of their oil province to international investors while generating a *satisfactory* share of revenue for their governments. The analysis also focuses on the change in the international competitiveness of the UK fiscal regime from an investor standpoint from 1975 until 2006. The comparison is done under the same assumptions as in the previous section, except that only the low oil price scenario is considered for reasons of simplification.

Fields profitability under various fiscal packages

Figures 6.10–6.13 illustrate the profitability of the four selected fields under the six selected regimes (note that for the UK, the regime as of 2005 has two structures as discussed in earlier sections). The figures also incorporate the historical packages that applied in the UK over the period 1975–2006, as analysed in the previous section. This allows the reader to compare how the international competitiveness of the regime varied over that time period.

For all fields, the highest level of profitability is noted under the fiscal package that applied in the UK with 30 per cent CT only (Scenario UK_{93a}).

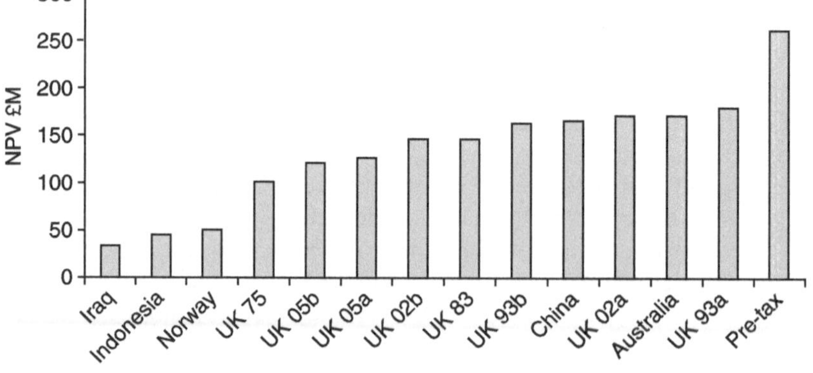

Figure 6.10 Argyll field: NPV under different tax regimes.

This can explain why the Van Meurs Associates (1999) study, which compares the extent to which a regime is favourable relative to other regimes from an investor standpoint, gave the UK a profitability ranking of 10. That means that there are only nine other countries that have petroleum regimes more favourable to the international investor. The increase in tax take in subsequent years, coupled with declining production and increased costs, reduced the international competitiveness of the UKCS from an investor's standpoint. According to Oil and Gas UK (2006), the 2005 fiscal changes (doubling of ST) made oil and gas activity in the UK 16 per cent less attractive, as the increase in tax reduced value of new exploration and development, which in turn reduced the global competitiveness of the UK.

As Figures 6.10–6.13 show, the 2005 tax changes in the UK have a greater impact on the international competitiveness of the regime in the case of fields that are still in a PRT paying position than those that do not. That puts the regime in terms of its impact on oil fields' profitability close to the 1975 structure that applied in the UK and more importantly close to the Iraqi, Indonesian and Norwegian regimes. Yet, the UKCS province does not provide the opportunities in terms of finds and size of fields as those provinces do or as the UKCS province provided 30 years ago.

In general, there is consistency in results for the four fields selected. Lower profitability is recorded under the Iraqi, Indonesian, Norwegian, UK (2005 structure with PRT paying fields, and 1975 and 1983 structures). Higher profitability is noted under the other UK structures, the Chinese and Australian regimes, although the impact of the Australian regime becomes more pronounced as the fields become larger.

Although the UK 1975 tax structure (Scenario UK_{75}) includes Royalty, the taxable base for Royalty differs from the Chinese regime. Whilst there is a fixed rate of gross revenue, (12.5 per cent in the UK), in China it is on a sliding scale of production, varying with the annual production and further exempting the first tranche of production of 20,000 bbl/d from the payment

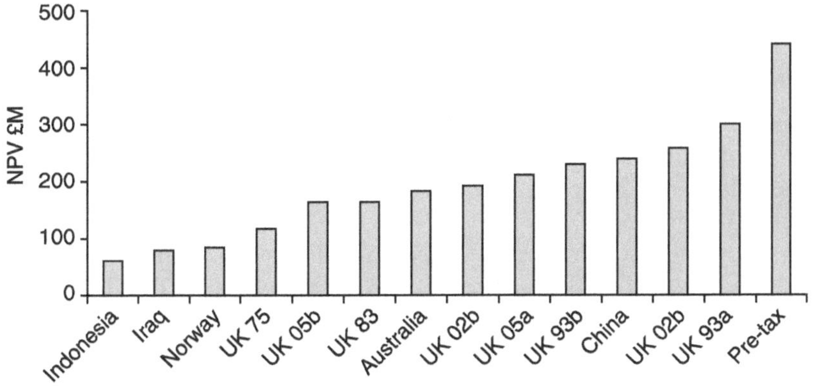

Figure 6.11 Arbroath field: NPV under different tax regimes.

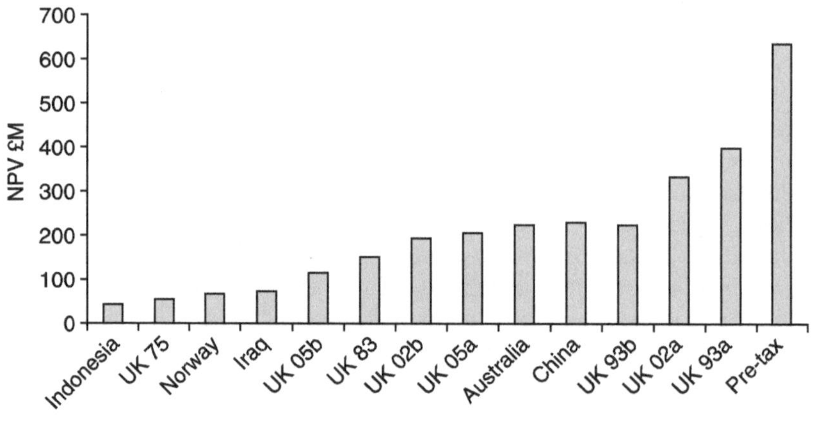

Figure 6.12 Tern field: NPV under different tax regimes.

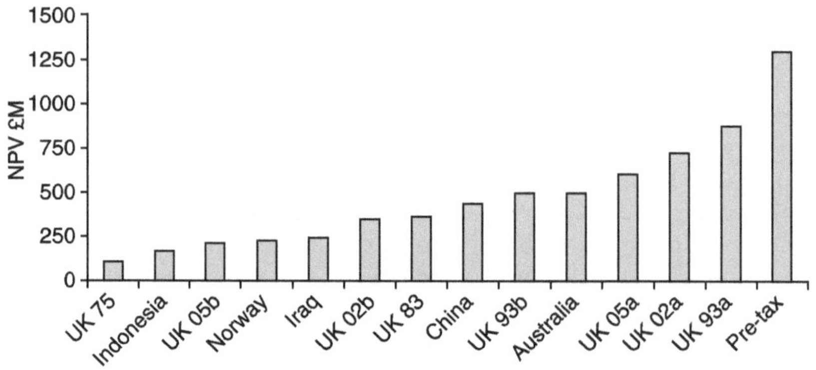

Figure 6.13 Schiehallion field: NPV under different tax regimes.

of the tax. This makes the Chinese Royalty more progressive than the UK Royalty.

Government revenue under different fiscal packages

Figures 6.14–6.17 illustrate the effective marginal tax take from each field under the different fiscal packages. The rates are compared with the world average rate of 65 per cent, as determined by Johnston (2002) in a study covering 133 regimes.

The lowest takes within the UK, as compared to other regimes, are recorded under Scenario UK_{93a} (30 per cent CT), UK_{02a} (30 per cent CT and 10 per cent ST), UK_{05a} (30 per cent CT and 20 per cent ST – except for the very small field), and UK_{93b} (30 per cent CT and 50 per cent PRT). Those structures, in addition to the Chinese and Australian regimes, have a lower than world average marginal tax rate. For the very small fields, all the tax structures that

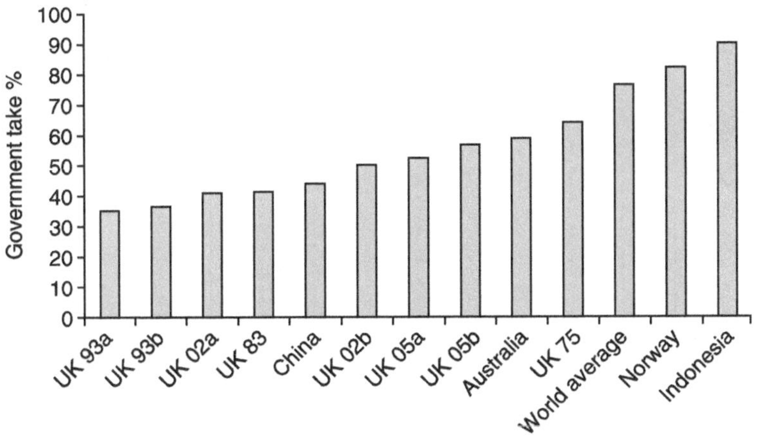

Figure 6.14 Argyll field: government take under different regimes.

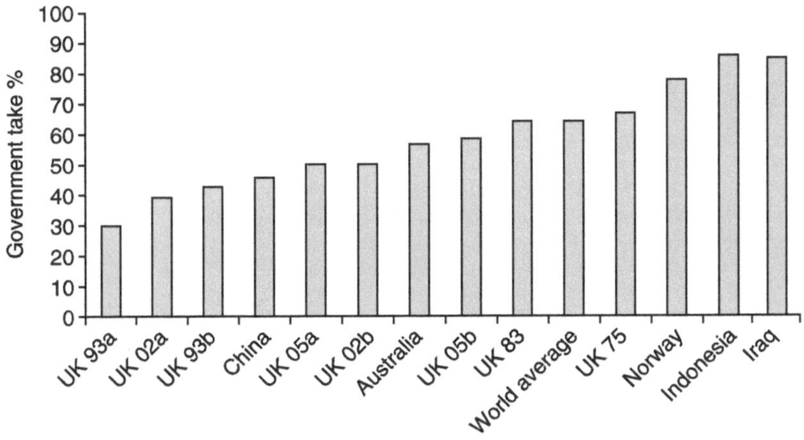

Figure 6.15 Arbroath field: government take under different regimes.

applied in the UK have a marginal tax rate lower than the world average. This outcome does not show the same consistency among the other fields, especially large fields.

In Norway, the government adopted several measures to relax its petroleum fiscal regime, among others the abolition of Royalty. Still, the Norwegian fiscal regime has one of the highest tax takes, especially when compared with the other two concessionary regimes. This can be due to the fact that the SPT is not allowed as a deduction for CIT, in contrast to both the UK and Australia.

The Indonesian and Iraqi regimes, as well as the 1975 tax structure that applied in the UK, also have two of the highest marginal tax rates. The Iraqi

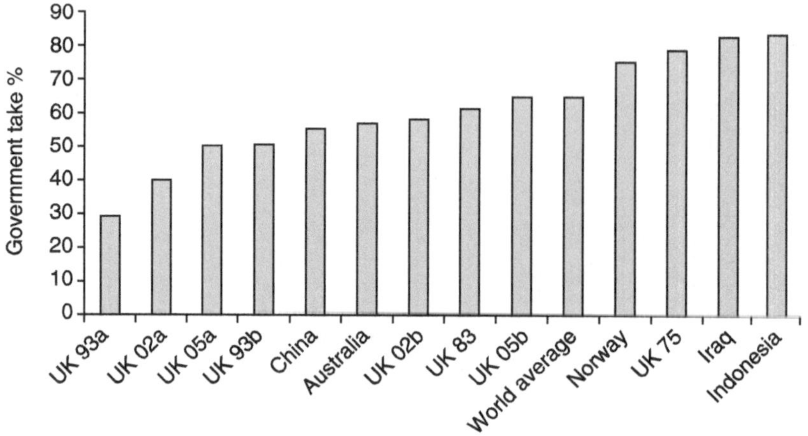

Figure 6.16 Tern field: government take under different regimes.

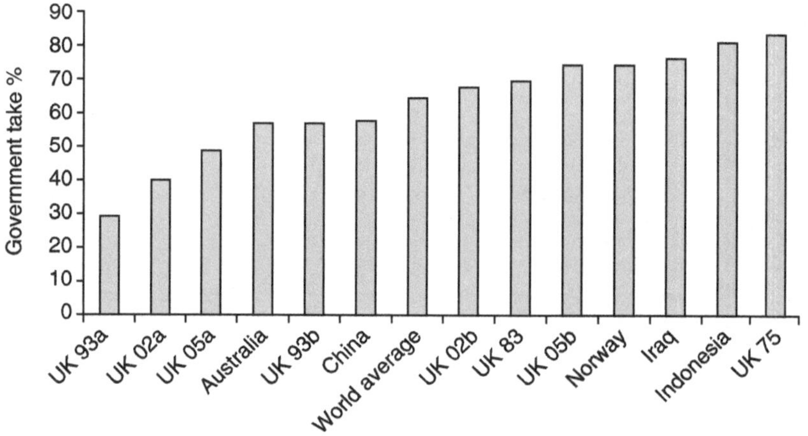

Figure 6.17 Schiehallion field: government take under different regimes.

regime take is higher on smaller fields, whilst the result is reversed for the Indonesian regime and the UK 1975 tax structure, which both in fact have the highest marginal tax rate on large fields.

A proportional regime indicates that the same percentage tax take occurs in fields of quite different profitability. As such, the UK tax structures that are based on income tax only (CT and ST), as well as Norway, Australia and to a lesser extent Indonesia, can be described as proportional. But when the percentage take increases with the field size and profitability, the system can be described as progressive. Consequently, all the other UK scenarios – those incorporating PRT – in addition to the Chinese tax regime can be described as progressive. Iraq, however, can be considered as a regressive system, with the effective tax rate declining with the field size.

Discussion

Although tough fiscal terms are expected to be found under contractual regimes, the analysis above indicates that concessionary systems like the Norwegian can be even tougher, while some PSCs, as in China, can lead to similar conclusions as other concessionary regimes. As such, economically speaking, the type of contracts and the entitlements to ownership are of rather legal and political significance only.

While the Indonesian regime is based on PSC and the Iraqi is based on buyback contract, both regimes provide similar economic outcomes. Yet the Iraqi regime is unlikely to be suitable for smaller fields, where the tax take can reach 90 per cent. The high level of government take is even more discernible if the total field life is considered, and rather than just the period of the contracts' duration (i.e. up to the handover date), as assumed elsewhere in this book.

Additionally, it would be misleading to describe a regime with low tax rates as weak and a regime with high tax rates as strong. Much depends on the objectives of government policy. A country may have a low tax take for a number of reasons, namely, high costs, small volumes, high geological risk, basin maturity, the need to attract more investment to compensate for perceptions of high fiscal risk and the belief in a low tax environment for business in general. Consequently, one would expect that in a competitive world, areas with the least favourable geology, highest development and operating costs and lowest wellhead prices would offer lenient terms. Although the average government take worldwide is around 65 per cent, this rate can be seen as high or low depending on the geological potential. 'For countries with better-than-average potential (and low cost), the government take is closer to 80 per cent. However, better-than-average geological potential is rarely sufficient to sustain such a high government take'.[7]

The UK, Australian and Chinese regimes are more 'lenient' than the other selected regimes for the following main reason – the prospectivity of their oil province is rather modest while exploration and development costs are rather high compared to the Norwegian, Indonesian and, most importantly, Iraqi provinces. Also countries with a high degree of state ownership and control (such as Norway) can sustain a higher take than those with little or no state involvement. For the former the high tax flows from one pocket of the state to another and makes less difference to investment decisions.

Compared with Australia and Norway, the UK offers the most generous reliefs, particularly with respect to PRT and the swift amortisation of CAPEX, the treatment of abandonment costs and the deduction of PRT from the CT taxable base. In the UK, no project pays any tax until payback is reached and pre and post tax are the same. This is a uniquely favourable arrangement. Australia implements a similar structure to the post-1983/pre-1993 UK regime, but it limits its reliefs to uplift, while abandonment costs are not allowed for deduction. Norway offers 30 per cent uplift on CAPEX, and allows interest expense against all taxes as well as a certain deduction of abandonment cost, but the SPT is not deductible from the Income Tax base, rendering the total tax take more significant compared with the other two countries. Additionally, the international competitiveness of the UK tax regime has changed over time, and the 2005 changes have an adverse effect on the competitiveness of the regime, especially when the 20 per cent supplementary charge is combined with 50 per cent PRT.

Norway has fiscal takes very close to the countries under contractual regimes, but the Norwegian regime is significantly simpler than the other two concessionary systems, while in the UK, the computation of the fiscal take is the most complicated. Furthermore, Norway still provides significant potential. Despite more than 30 years of activity, the Norwegian side of the North Sea still has considerable oil and gas deposits to develop, and the province is less mature than the UK side. Norway's oil and gas potential as a whole comes not only from the North Sea, but also from the Norwegian and the Barents Seas, which are less explored than the Norwegian side of the North Sea.

Norway also allows itself to set high tax rates, not only because it offers bigger opportunities than the UK or Australia, but also because much of its oil and gas resources are owned and controlled by the State (mainly through Statoil and Hydro). Private oil companies tend to be caught in the middle as their operations depend on Statoil's decisions, and Statoil, being a state owned company does not complain about the high tax rates.

China offers the most lenient terms among the contractual arrangements, particularly in the case of the smaller fields, given the progressive aspect of both its sliding scale Royalty and the negotiable profit split.

In Indonesia, different fiscal elements apply to ensure the government receives a significant share of revenue, particularly from the larger fields. For instance, although no Royalty or cost recovery limit applies, the 20 per cent FTP acts like a Royalty. Additionally, bonus and DMO apply and they are linked to the annual production. However, the main limitation of this regime is that government share varies with production rather than with profitability. This is good news for the IOCs but not for the government.

As for Iraq, again the Van Meurs study ranks the Iraqi buyback at level 312, indicating that the regime is one of the least favourable for investors, despite its large reserves and low cost of production. The ranking definitely worsens if political instability is taken into consideration. Put bluntly, IOCs hate buyback contracts, where government take can reach even 100 per cent. In some Gulf countries, some IOCs have been making $1 per barrel for 30 years, regardless of oil price levels. Still, those companies accept the buyback terms as a loss leader; they want to be present in oil rich countries; they want to establish strong relationship with host governments, hoping that one day the contract terms and regimes will change and they will be able to get a better deal. However, such an attitude can be disadvantageous from the government's perspective, as buybacks may not attract the same level of capital and investment as is the case with other regimes. Companies also worry about how much technology they will bring to the host country when they are not able to leverage it.

PSCs and service agreements with a high fixed profit/production split rate in favour of the government do not seem suitable for the development of small marginal fields, given the limit on cost recovery. Furthermore, exploration is conducted at the contractor's own risk, with no reimbursement where it is unsuccessful. Service contracts can be more rigid than PSCs given their short duration and the fixed remuneration fee. This may be of advantage for the oil company especially at times of low prices but not in periods of high prices.

Finally, an additional dimension should be considered when evaluating the fiscal regime, and incorporated into the analysis above – namely the industry's structure and the type of players in the oil and gas province.

In the UK, the remaining reserves to be exploited are smaller and more technically challenging than those developed in the past. As such, they compare unfavourably with the global portfolio of the oil majors, who dominated the province for more than 30 years. The UK no longer provides the scale of development that can make a significant incremental contribution to a super major. The renewed interest in the province comes from a new breed of operators, who are the small independent E&P players. Companies such as Apache, Venture Production, Talisman Energy, Perenco, Paladin Resources, CNR, ATP, Petra, and EnCana, can contribute significantly to enhancing the level of activity in the UK North Sea. They are more focused on developing and creating value from small fields, while the majors are trapped on the treadmill of replacing corporate production and are forced to search for large volumes often at the expense of value. Mature and smaller fields are more economically viable for the smaller companies since they have less overhead costs in comparison to the majors. The independents are in general more aggressive in bringing discoveries and developments to production quickly and seeking out additional opportunities to maximise volumes, using different ways of working to extract the remaining reserves.

The tax regime should take into consideration the structure and dynamic of the oil and gas industry. Returning to the UK situation, the fiscal changes made in the first decade of the twenty-first century do not support the new breed of players. As the supplementary charge does not include a deduction for financial expenses, it can place a burden particularly on smaller UKCS E&P companies who are the new generation of investors.

6.4 SUMMARY AND CONCLUSION

Fiscal instruments and structures in many varieties are available to policy makers as they seek to achieve the necessary but elusive balance between attracting investment with the promise of good returns, and securing a reasonable share of economic rent for the state. The exercise undertaken in this chapter has shown the diversity of ways in which the authorities in six major oil-producing countries have attempted to reconcile these two conflicting objectives.

Countries need to ensure that their regimes are enduringly competitive. Regimes should be capable of evolution, so as to reflect changing opportunities and new conditions. No fiscal regime should be carved in stone. Had the UK maintained its fiscal structure that applied in 1975, many fields would not have been developed. Against that, it has to be said that over-frequent alterations to the regime are not desirable, especially if they are made in response to various short-term changes in oil prices.

Changes in oil price inevitably alter government attitudes with respect to the balance between generating revenues and maintaining investment attractiveness. The changes in oil price so far in the twenty-first century have generated various responses in different oil producing countries. In some countries, like the UK, the government made legislative changes, there being no automatic response built into the system to the increase in oil price. This freedom to make tax changes by law is more common in concessionary regimes. In PSC and service agreements tax rates are held constant during the contract. In contrast, in concessionary regimes amendments are possible at anytime (the fiscal regime was changed twice in the UK, within a period of three years).

In other countries, no intervention is required as the regime responds automatically to oil price movements (as in Azerbaijan or Angola). But in countries like Venezuela and Russia, the trend has been towards resources nationalism. In many oil-producing countries, oil companies have found themselves facing outright hostility, with fresh obstacles in the way of accessing reserves. In Russia, Shell and BP have both found themselves subject to increasingly demanding reviews of performance and general conduct – reaching to the point where contracts granted on one set of terms are then revoked when failing to meet new standards and performance criteria that may have had no mention in the original deals. However, sometimes, it is the IOCs themselves that trigger such reactions. As competition for oil and gas resources intensifies, they bid extensively for blocks and accept very onerous fiscal terms to get the acreage or bid large signature bonuses simply to secure the acreage. The Chinese national oil companies provide a typical example in their race for oil especially in Africa. Had the conditions been different – for example, a weaker oil price – the scene would be different.

As has been explained higher oil prices may seem to some to be the obvious justification for raising tax rates. But this is not necessarily so. Higher crude oil prices can mean increased costs. A clear implication from this chapter is that in mature provinces like the UK, adjustments to the fiscal regime should be considered carefully, as they can easily have a lasting impact on the life span of the province and the attractiveness of the province for investment. The oil industry, like any other industry, has to attract capital, encourage investors and deliver returns to shareholders. High petroleum taxes can only be sustained if justified by the rents. Investors are unforgiving; they will not tolerate low or inadequate returns, they will simply invest elsewhere, leaving IOCs with inadequate capital to invest, and thereby having to put a constraint on supply. The important role of capital markets is often ignored in this debate. Investors clearly will not tolerate lower returns from the oil industry just because a host nation determines the rent must be high to meet ideological requirements, divorced from the economic realities of the basin.

The analysis carried out in this chapter further shows that each fiscal system has its advantages and disadvantages. Accordingly, it is impossible to categorise fiscal regimes as good or bad, because each regime is applied under specific circumstances. While contractual arrangements are imposed to ensure a higher degree of government control, such structures are unlikely to be applied in liberal economic environments such as the UK. Additionally, it can be very restrictive to judge about the performance of a regime simply by looking at the formal and visible pattern of arrangements between the state and the companies, or by nominal tax rates. Several factors, such as fiscal reliefs and the process of calculating the tax base, can lead to significant differences among fiscal packages, while the same results can be achieved with different structures and regimes.

The chapter likewise emphasises the argument raised in Chapter 2 that clearly there is no one ideal fiscal regime suitable for all petroleum projects in all countries. No two PSCs are the same, and harmonisation of mineral levies across the countries is a distant prospect. In the very telling words of Helliwell (1982), 'generalisation about anything as complex as taxation can be dangerous.'

7 Other financial evaluation techniques

Some alternative ways of measuring the profitability of oil projects and the potential tax impact

7.1 INTRODUCTION: A CHOICE OF METHODS

The previous chapter took the reader through a quantitative and detailed analysis of oil projects using conventional accounting tools. Here we move on and look at other more controversial, but potentially valuable, techniques for measuring project outcomes which could, if carefully applied, provide both more accurate and precise figures for company decision-makers and investors and at the same time give the tax authorities a better basis on which to assess the effects of different tax policies and the likely yield.

The choice of the financial evaluation technique is of particular significance for both companies and government. Both parties have an interest in choosing the best financial tools, given the very large sums at stake and given what has been described as the archetypal uncertainty inherent in oil developments. To assess the taxation impact, an appropriate evaluation technique must be adopted. An inappropriate technique can result in a misleading figure both as regards profitability and taxable capacity.

There has been a longstanding debate about the best methodology in this area – as in other areas of accountancy – and some authoritative voices have been heard in favour of moving away from familiar DCF calculations. For example, Bjerkedal (2000, p.4) contends that, under some evaluation techniques, 'a tax system can appear less attractive, even though it is not . . . in this case very severe conclusions can be drawn and companies can make wrong statements, based on incorrect computation methods in evaluating project economics'. Similarly, Emhjellen and Alaouze (2001) argue that changing the valuation method may affect an oil company's investment decision on new projects because the ranking of projects will vary under different valuation methods. In a blunter assessment, and while attempting to explain the reason that led to the decline in the value of oil companies over the last 15 years, Siew (2001) asserts that oil companies have made incorrect investment decisions based on faulty project appraisal methods.

For several decades in the energy industry, the most common form of project evaluation has been the DCF technique. However, over the last few years, there has been an increasing interest in the use of more useful and more modern evaluation techniques, such as MAP developed by Jacoby and Laughton (1991) and ROT. These techniques were developed to overcome some of the weaknesses of DCF, and can be considered as evolved versions of the traditional technique. They can allow a more efficient valuation of risk, hence an improved investment decision making by oil companies compared with the commonly applied DCF.[1]

As noted in Chapter 5, the DCF method is used by 99 per cent of oil companies, and the majority of previous studies[2] utilized this traditional technique to evaluate the profitability of an oil field, the main advantage of the DCF technique being its simplicity. Nevertheless, despite this strong loyalty to the old ways an evaluation of after tax profitability of an oil field under both the old DCF method and more modern techniques can therefore be beneficial. It is useful to see if the more modern techniques yield up a significant difference from the traditional method and therefore whether, despite the extra complexity, they justify departure into unfamiliar and undoubtedly more complicated new areas.

The remainder of this chapter is organized as follows. Section 2 analyses and compares the concepts of the traditional DCF and MAP. Section 3 compares DCF with ROT. To illustrate the differences between the methods, a number of examples are set out and followed through used. Section 4 presents the conclusions of this chapter.

7.2 DISCOUNTED CASH FLOW VERSUS MODERN ASSET PRICING

7.2.1 Concepts and computational steps

As shown in Chapter 5, under DCF, the project[3] evaluation is usually done in three steps:

- The analyst estimates the project net cash flows that will occur at each time period in a particular scenario.
- The project cash flows are discounted using a certain discount rate, incorporating a risk premium.[4]
- The discounted cash flows are added to form the project value, also called the Net Present Value (NPV).[5]

This method is a cash-flow based technique, which takes into account the time value of money, and most importantly, it is quick and relatively easy to understand and calculate.

However, scholars like Jacoby and Laughton (1992), who recommended the MAP model as a substitute to DCF, argue that there are several problems in following the DCF method, mainly:

- 'The discounting in the DCF is only vaguely related to the uncertainty in the cash flows' (Jacoby and Laughton, 1992, p.9). The use of uniform discounting in the DCF method is based on the 'false' premise that the risks inherent within different components of the project cash-flow are of the same magnitude. This is of particular significance when using the assumption that the main uncertainty results from oil price.
- Under DCF, the discount rate is constant and therefore it does not take into consideration the resolution of uncertainty over time. As such, the future cash flows can be discounted excessively and this can lead to a tendency to throw capital at any project alternative that will accelerate the receipt of revenues. Consequently, DCF can introduce bias against long-term decision-making.
- DCF analysis depends critically on the choice of a project discount rate. However, many organizations do not understand the very complex issues that lie behind the chosen rate. DCF method sometimes treats risk in an *ad hoc* matter through some combination of subjective choices of discount rates.
- The focus of the DCF analysis is on a 'now or never' investment decision. It does not allow future management flexibility, which can add value to an investment. Consequently, DCF can undervalue projects.[6]

Given those limitations, in 1991, Jacoby and Laughton introduced an alternative to DCF for the evaluation of petroleum projects. They called the new technique MAP, which is based on the Derivative Asset Pricing theory, (DAPT), (explained in Section 7.2.2). The DAPT was developed over the last three decades hence it is not a new approach. However the theory is applied in the pricing of complex financial instruments, whereas MAP expands the model for the evaluation of petroleum projects, where the technique is still in its infancy.

MAP is based on the following two major ideas:

- Firstly, a project can be valued by considering the cash that it consumes and generates. Cash flow is a commodity and can be valued according to the two characteristics that are important to people who trade in it. These characteristics are time and risk. The DCF method recognizes this idea in the use of discount rates that combine a risk free rate (valuation for time) and a risk premium (valuation of risk).

Valuation for time

People prefer to receive cash sooner rather than later. A dollar received now is more valuable than a dollar received five years from now because of the investment possibilities that are available for today's dollar. Therefore, there is a time discount in the valuation of the claim to a cash flow. The longer the time to the receipt of the cash that an asset provides, the lower the value of the asset.

Valuation for risk

For a risk free cash flow there is no discount for risk since there is no risk involved. As such there is only discounting for time. The time discount rate is derived from the risk free cash value, which in turn can be expressed in terms of the risk-free interest rate. However, when cash flows are uncertain there needs to be a discount for risk in addition to discount for time. As put by Salahor (1998), most people have an aversion to uncertainty in their level of welfare. If they have a choice, most people would prefer to reduce uncertainty in their lives by investing their current wealth in assets that would provide extra cash in future situations where they would otherwise be poor, rather in situations where they would otherwise be rich. In the former case, assets will have higher value than those in the latter, as there will be a mark-up for risk of the expected payoff.

When the existence of uncertainty directly influences financial market prices it is called 'priced risk'[7] and requires non-zero risk discounting, but when it does not have any direct influence it is called 'unpriced risk',[8] which does not require risk discounting. An oil project faces uncertainty as regards the price of oil, which is normally a priced risk, as well as project-specific technical and geological determinants as regards the volume of oil to be produced, which is normally a non-priced risk.

- The second idea is the 'principle of value consistency' or the 'no-arbitrage principle', which states that if two assets have the same cash flow outcomes they have the same price. The special form of this principle is the 'principle of value additivity, which allows division of the cash flows of a project into parts with different risk characteristics for evaluation and then addition of the value of the parts to get the value of the whole project.

Under the MAP technique, the analyst performs the equivalent of the first two steps in the DCF evaluation process but in the reverse order, as described below:

- The analyst discounts the uncertain project cash flow determinants using appropriate discounting structures for each determinant.

- The input valuations are filtered through the project structure to find the cash flow values.
- These values are added to form the total project value.

In this case, MAP is believed to overcome the limitations of DCF in the following ways:

- The DCF technique recognizes the first idea behind MAP regarding the use of a discount rate that combines both a risk-free rate (valuation of time) and a risk premium (valuation of risk). However, with DCF, the effect of uncertainty is determined by the risk premium in the discount rate which is the same for the different components of the cash flow. With MAP, however, the risk adjustment applies only on the risky components of the cash flow. So, instead of applying a uniform project discount rate, under MAP discounting is done at the level of the cash flow components. As such, MAP can provide a company with a 'framework for determining the differentiated effects on asset values of the diverse combinations of uncertainties to which its different assets are exposed' (Laughton, 2002, p.12). Discounting individual project determinants, as MAP does, involves fewer considerations than directly discounting project cash flow. For instance, discounting the price of a barrel of oil to be received 10 years from now is simpler than discounting the set of cash flows for a producing field.

  In principle, MAP can give more appropriate value estimates than DCF because it discounts revenues and costs using a discount rate that reflects the riskiness of each of the cash flow components. The following simple example demonstrates the difference in profitability between using DCF and MAP to evaluate a project.

  Although the difference in the profitability of the project under the two methods is small, for oil companies, however, with billion dollar multi-period projects, the possible valuation and decision errors may be substantial.

Table 7.1 DCF versus MAP

Project	*Expected CF Year 1*	*DCF NCF discounted @10%*	*MAP*		
Cost	–100		Discounted @6%	A	–£94.34
Revenue	400		Discounted @12%	B	£357.14
NCF	300				
Profitability		£272.73	Total (A + B)		£262.80

- Under MAP, the discounting of value for risk is determined by how uncertainty is resolved over time. Unlike DCF, where discounting is done at a constant rate, under MAP uncertainty is resolved as new information arrives over the course of time. Furthermore, the use of a constant discount rate throughout the life of a project is based on the assumption that oil price grows at a constant rate over time. MAP, however, can more readily exploit a sophisticated dynamic model of oil prices as compared with the DCF technique.[9]
- Choosing an appropriate discount rate is very complex under DCF. With MAP, the discount rate is not given as a direct input into the evaluation as is the case with DCF, but is allowed to arise jointly from the discounting of the project's determinants and from the project structure.
- MAP incorporates flexibility in decision making, allowing the company to change the timing of its investment. However, when flexibility is taken into consideration, MAP is referred to as ROT. This concept is discussed in detail in Section 7.3.

7.2.2 Modern Asset Pricing discounting

Chapter 6 explained the discounting method used in DCF to compute the NPV. This section demonstrates how discounting under MAP is derived and the extent to which it differs from DCF discounting. The following includes an explanation of the Derivative Asset Pricing theory, on which MAP is based, the valuation of risky assets and the commonly used oil price models.

The Derivative Asset Pricing Theory

MAP is based on the DAPT that is at the core of most financial analyses in the options, futures and securities markets. Derivatives are financial instruments that derive their values from the prices of other assets. Their principal function is to serve as tools for managing exposure to the risks associated with the underlying asset. When the magnitude of the cash flow associated with an asset (the derivative asset) is determined by the value of other assets, (called the underlying asset), then the value of the derivative asset can be calculated from the values of the underlying assets. This is accomplished by creating a trading strategy in portfolios of the underlying assets designed to replicate the cash flows; hence the value of the derivative asset.

The no-arbitrage principle makes such a valuation possible as different assets with the same cash flow consequences have the same price. If the relationship between the future traded price of a risky asset and the future cash flow from a risky project is known, then a portfolio with the same expected pay-off as the project can be created by investing in the traded risky asset and in the risk free asset.

The valuation of risky assets

A project can be thought of as a portfolio of claims to individual cash flows. In this case, one can focus first on the single cash flows and value each individually. Then, once each individual cash flow is valued, the project can be valued by summing the individual cash flow values.

Jacoby and Laughton (1992) provide a practical method for the evaluation of oil projects based on derivative asset pricing. The authors assume that oil price is the only uncertain variable, hence uncertainty of the project cash flow is determined only by reference to the uncertainty of the price of a barrel of oil. Therefore, the only uncertainty in value may be modelled through uncertain future oil prices.

Oil price can be modelled through the use of forward contracts, which are one of the most common types of derivatives. A forward contract obliges one party in the contract to buy, and the other party to sell, some asset at a specified price on some specified date (maturity date). It permits buyers and sellers of the asset to eliminate the uncertainty about the future price at which the asset will be exchanged. The fixed amount that is paid to obtain the forward contract is called the forward price or the certainty equivalent of the uncertain amount.

Each future oil price, P_t, can be formulated as the terminal value of the forward contract. In other words, each oil forward contract is a claim to a single cash flow at maturity, where the cash flow amount is P_t. Hence, to get the certain P_t, investors pay today the forward price, which reflects both time and risk preferences. As such, the underlying value of the derivative asset valuation depends on the current expectation of the output price claims, here oil price.

Let $V_0(P_t)$ be the current value of the claim to be received at time t and $E_0(P_t)$ the current expectation of the oil price evaluated at time zero. $V_0(P_t)$ is then given by:

$$V_0(P_t) = E_0(P_t)e^{-\mu t} \tag{7.1}$$

The future expected rate of return, μ, on the underlying risky asset is the sum of two terms, the risk free rate and a risk premium. The risk free rate is the return for time and it is assumed to be constant. The risk premium is taken to be proportional to the amount of volatility of oil price expectations at time t. This proportionality constant, also termed the price of risk, is assumed positive and constant over time so that there is risk discounting in the valuation of the output price claim. The price of risk can be identified as the risk due to oil market uncertainty. The future expected rate of return is then expressed as in the following:

$$\mu = i + \phi\sigma \tag{7.2}$$

Where:

- i is the risk free rate
- ϕ is the price of risk
- σ is the volatility of oil price expectations.

The current value of the claim becomes:

$$V_0(P_t) = E_0(P_t)e^{(-\phi\sigma t)}\, e^{(-it)} \tag{7.3}$$

The first discount factor $e^{-\phi\sigma t}$ is the discount factor for risk.[10] It is referred to in the remainder of the analysis as the Risk Discount Factor, RDF. This risk adjustment converts the forward price of oil into a certain equivalent price of oil. The second factor e^{-it} is the discount factor for time and it is referred to hereafter as the Time Discount Factor, (TDF), where i is the nominal risk-free rate.

Modelling oil price volatility

Determining oil price volatility is an important aspect of MAP since it has a significant impact on computing the RDF. It also constitutes a major difference between MAP and DCF, with respect to the assumption regarding the evolution of future oil price. The constant discounting in DCF is based on the assumption that oil price uncertainty grows at a constant rate over time, whereas with MAP, uncertainty is assumed to be resolved over time. MAP uses a stochastic process, more precisely a mean reversion model, to illustrate the behaviour of future oil prices.

A stochastic process is defined as 'a variable that evolves over time in a way that is at least in part random' (Dixit and Pindyck, 1994, p.60). A stochastic process, therefore, involves time and randomness. The most common stochastic processes used in modelling uncertainty related to oil projects are the Geometric Brownian Motion (GBM) with drift and the Mean Reverting Processes (MRPs).[11]

1 GBM: This popular and simple model is the most often used stochastic process in financial economics theory. It is also known as the 'random walk model'. The GBM presumes that the forecasted uncertainty is constant therefore shocks to the market have permanent effects. That is why the model is also called the permanent shock price model.

For an oil price that follows a GBM, the stochastic equation for its variation with time t is given by:

$$dP_t = \alpha P_t dt + \sigma P_t dz \tag{7.4}$$

Or:

$$\frac{dP_t}{P_t} = \alpha dt + \sigma dz \qquad (7.5)$$

Where:

- dz is the increment of Wiener process; E[dz] = 0. Var [dz] = dt
- α is the constant drift variable or the expected growth.
- σ is the annual standard deviation of $\frac{dP}{P_t}$. It illustrates the volatility of price, the random variation term or the deviation from the expected rate, hence the term of uncertainty.

2 Mean Reversion Model (MRM): This model presumes that the forecasted uncertainty declines over time so that the effects of shocks decay because of long term equilibrating forces. Prices in this model tend to revert to a prior trend after being shocked (Bradley, 1998). As applied to the petroleum industry the idea is that if the price is too far (above or below) a certain long-run equilibrium level P' market forces will act to reduce (if P >> P') or increase (if P << P') the oil production or exploration activity. This creates a reverting force that is similar to a spring, as strong as P is far from the equilibrium level P'.

If oil prices follow a mean reversion process, they have the following characteristics:

$$dP / P = \lambda(P' - P)dt + \sigma dz \qquad (7.6)$$

Where:

- λ is the speed of reversion or the mean reversion factor of oil prices, associated with a half life, HL. It is given by:

$$\lambda = \frac{\log 2}{HL} \qquad (7.7)$$

  When λ tends to zero, P_t becomes a simple Brownian motion and variance tends to $\sigma^2 t$.[12]
- P′ is the normal level or long-run equilibrium level of P. Hence, P' is the long-run mean price to which the price will tend to revert

For the GBM model, every change in the oil price is a permanent change in the long-run price drift. As such, the amount of uncertainty and its associated risk discounting continues to grow at a constant rate with respect to time. In contrast, mean-reversion assumes the opposite. Every price oscillation is simply a temporary deviation from the predictable long-run equilibrium level. Consequently, the reversion force effect does not permit, even in the distant future, extreme values for P. Hence, in the reverting model, there is uncertainty only in the very short term and the forecasted uncertainty is halved for each year that is added to the term of the forecast and the total amount of oil price uncertainty dissolves in the long term. Under conditions of oil price mean reversion, as forecast uncertainty reduces over time, the systematic risk discount also decreases to reflect this.

Baker et al (1998) present evidence of mean reversion. Pindyck (2001) argued that the mean-reversion model was better for oil prices after studying the long run evolution of the oil prices, using 127 years of data. According to Dias (2001), the mean-reversion model is more consistent with the futures market, with econometric tests and even with micro-economic theory.

As one of the concepts behind MAP is that uncertainty is resolved over time, it is based on the assumption that oil prices follow a mean reversion process. This can be seen as one of the main advantages of MAP over DCF.

MAP Net Present Value

The net present value calculated under MAP is called certainty equivalent to distinguish it from the NPV calculated under DCF. The after-tax project certainty equivalent, NPV_e, is given by:

$$NPV_e = \Sigma R_{et} - \Sigma C_{et} - \Sigma T_{et} \quad (7.8)$$

Where ΣR_{et} is the sum of the present values of the expected revenue cashflow, ΣC_{et} is the sum of the present values of the expected cost cashflow and ΣT_{et} is the sum of the present values of the expected tax cashflow.

R_{et} is the present value of the expected revenue cash flows at time t, hence the revenue certainty equivalent. It is given by:

$$R_e = Q_t \times V_0(P_t) \quad (7.9)$$

Replacing $V_0(P_t)$ by its value derived from equation (7.3), Revenue certainty equivalent becomes:

$$R_e = Q_t \times E(P_t) \times RDF_t \times TDF_t \quad (7.10)$$

Where:

$$TDF_t = \exp(-it) \quad (7.11)$$

and,

$$\mathrm{RDF_t} = \exp(-\varphi\sigma(1 - \exp(-\lambda t))/\lambda) \quad (7.12)$$ [13]

C_{et} is the certainty equivalent of the expected total costs cashflow at time t, and it is given by:

$$C_e = C_t \times TDF_t \tag{7.14}$$

$(R_{et} - C_{et})$ is the value of the pre-tax cashflow at time t.

T_e is the present value of the total tax cashflow at time t. Its computation is similar to the method used in Chapters 5 and 6, for example, but taking into consideration both the revenue certainty equivalent and the cost certainty equivalent.

7.2.3 DCF and MAP comparison: practical examples[14]

Table 7.2 presents the pre-tax NPV of the 25 oil fields selected for analysis in this book under the DCF and MAP techniques in order to highlight any differences between the two methods. The analysis is carried out under the same assumptions as those highlighted in the previous chapter. The additional assumptions used and which are mainly related to MAP, are summarised as follows:

- σ, the annual volatility of oil price was reported in the literature as typically in the range of 15 and 25 per cent per annum.[15] In this chapter, it is assumed equal to 20 per cent.
- λ, the speed of reversion of oil prices, is associated with a half life, HL, of 5 years (hence $\lambda = 0.139$).[16]
- ϕ, the price of risk, is considered 0.3503 in annual terms.[17]

The discounting methods produce different project NPVs. The difference is particularly significant for larger, long-term projects, like Tern, Alba and Schiehallion. As the fields become larger, with relatively longer productive life duration, the difference between the two methods becomes more pronounced. Under DCF, because the discounting is constant, long term projects can be under-valued compared with MAP, where given the mean reversion model, the risk discount rate declines from a short-term rate toward zero in the long term. As such, revenues are highly discounted in the long term and DCF compared with MAP results in lower values.

The quantitative differences in the two methods are mainly due to the decline in revenue discounting over the project duration under MAP. This reverse decline supports the criticism that Jacoby and Laughton (1992) make of the DCF method, highlighting in particular the inherent bias of the method against long term projects.[18]

The length of the field's productive life is not, however, the only factor affecting the difference in results between DCF and MAP. Both the distribution of revenues and costs play an important role. For instance, in the case of

Table 7.2 Oil field profitability under DCF and MAP–pre-tax scenario

Pre-tax scenario	*DCF (£M)*	*$MAP (£M)*	*Difference (£M)*	*Difference*	*Life (from production start-up)*
Fields	*1*	*2*	*(2–1)*	*(%)*	
Very small					
Argyll	258.93	318.1	59.2	23%	17
Arkwright	68.19	92.2	24.0	35%	18
Birch	45.49	55.8	10.3	23%	19
Blake	239.28	280.1	40.8	17%	12
Kappa	149.2	137.6	−11.6	−8%	10
Highlander	306.59	370.9	64.3	21%	27
Janice	139.91	170.6	30.7	22%	11
Tiffani	−249.45	−301.0	−51.6	21%	16
Thelma	194.22	252.8	58.6	30%	11
Toni	157.28	234.1	76.8	49%	16
Small					
Arbroath	436.38	651.3	214.9	49%	24
Auk	866.71	604.4	−262.3	−30%	36
Balmoral	108.45	199.9	91.5	84%	21
Beatrice	108.27	143.8	35.5	33%	24
Heather	129.83	208.1	78.3	60%	32
Leadon	486.5	677.2	190.7	39%	14
Montrose	217.47	272.2	54.7	25%	40
Osprey	233.6	329.2	95.6	41%	19
Scapa	347.77	511.5	163.7	47%	35
Medium					
Captain	440.46	643.8	203.3	46%	33
Clair	364.31	758.7	394.4	108%	28
Maureen	403.74	455.0	51.3	13%	16
Tern	621.64	1097.1	475.5	76%	25
Large					
Alba	885.92	1501.3	615.4	69%	24
Schiehallion	1302.05	2092.8	790.8	61%	25

Montrose, a small field but with a 40 years life, the difference between MAP and DCF is less pronounced than in the case of the other fields with long life. This is a consequence of the fact that annual revenues from this field are very modest.

In terms of the impact of the distribution of costs, with MAP, costs are discounted at a lower rate than DCF. Therefore, in the case of high cost fields, particularly those with substantial CAPEX, NPVs calculated using MAP are likely to be lower compared with those using the DCF method. Furthermore, the longer the period in which CAPEX occurs the lower the MAP NPV is likely to be.

Consequently, it can be said that the shorter (longer) the life of a field, and the smaller (larger) the field, the narrower (the wider) the difference is between the NPVs calculated under the DCF method versus those derived under MAP. However, it is difficult to generalise, as other factors such as the distribution of both revenues and costs over time needs to be considered.

One would also expect the tax take to be lower with MAP evaluation because taxation applies on the discounted revenues and costs. This further affects the timing of some reliefs, such as the PRT oil allowance in the UK, since its value depends on annual production and revenue. This concurs with the findings of Bjerkedal (2000), who argues that the taxes can be over-estimated in any project where a discounting rate above the risk free rate is used.

7.2.4 Conclusion on MAP

DCF and MAP produced different project NPVs. The difference is particularly significant for larger, long-term projects. This is mainly due to the DCF method's use of a high constant discount rate, which tends to undervalue long term projects, whereas in the case of MAP the risk discounting tends to decline over time, given the mean reversion model. As such, DCF can undervalue profitability while at the same time over-estimate the impact of taxation. Therefore, MAP can provide a more useful evaluation than its DCF counterpart.

In principle, the MAP method is more correct than DCF because it discounts revenues and costs using discount rates which reflect the risks inherent in each of these components. MAP discounts revenue using a discount factor that includes components such as oil price volatility, financial risk, mean reversion of oil prices and time. Additionally, MAP can more readily exploit a sophisticated dynamic model of oil prices as compared with the DCF technique.

7.3 DISCOUNTED CASH FLOW AND REAL OPTIONS THEORY

This section considers another technique that is sometimes suggested as a more accurate alternative to DCF. The technique, called Real Options Theory (ROT), takes into consideration an important aspect in investment decision making which is flexibility.

7.3.1 An additional dimension

When economic conditions are not favourable, companies are able to delay their investment decisions to a more profitable period, when faced with an uncertain situation. They can also choose to wait for more information to reduce the uncertainty and then proceed with the investment. The change in investment timing can in turn affect the timing of fiscal receipts. Governments normally aim to collect a part of the fiscal take at the early stage of an oil field life. If the development of an oil field is delayed, the fiscal receipts from that project are delayed as well. A good example of this occurred in the development of the huge Kashagan field in Kazakhstan, where a heavy delay in the development schedule (over two years) also meant that the hoped-for revenues to provide associated infrastructure for the field were also delayed, thus creating near deadlock. Accordingly, both oil companies' and government interests can be affected by a change in the development timing.

The ability to affect the timing of investment introduces a new aspect to the analysis, which is flexibility in decision-making. 'Flexibility is the degree to which a project is able to adjust to changes in different parameters'.[19] It can add value to a project, hence the need for an evaluation technique that captures it and allows a useful evaluation of field profitability as well as the appropriate impact of taxation on that profitability.

It is often argued that one of the main limitations of DCF technique is that it does not consider the timing of investment or production, as applied in its simplistic form. As such, DCF is unable to capture flexibility in decision-making since it is a static approach based on a 'now or never' decision, and because DCF does not make provision for flexibility, it can undervalue oil projects.

The application of a more useful technique, more precisely, ROT, for the valuation of petroleum projects is gaining interest in the academic literature.[20] An increasing number of organizations in the upstream petroleum industry have been experimenting with the use of the real options technique, which is becoming a significant focus of attention and comment in the energy industry.

ROT was originally developed for the appraisal of financial derivatives. The most common types of derivatives are forward contracts and financial options. An analogy exists between financial options and real investments, such as petroleum projects. It was this similarity that led to the adoption of ROT for the valuation of such projects.[21] Because ROT is based on the concept of 'wait and see' in decision-making, it provides management with certain degree of flexibility, which in turn produces an option value. 'The option value is the value of making a future decision after the outcome of an uncertain variable is known and therefore avoiding the risk of a poor outcome'.[22]

Ignoring the option value can lead to a significant underestimation of a project's value, in this case an oil reserve. By treating an undeveloped oil reserve as an option, its value can be determined correctly. Additionally, ROT can be considered as an expansion of MAP, but applied in situations where the management of future flexibility is analysed concurrently. As such, ROT also benefits from the major advantages of the MAP approach, namely, separate discounting of the individual cash flow components and the incorporation of a more rigorous oil price model.

Although a number of studies have addressed the subject of investment timing in the oil industry and the application of ROT to evaluate petroleum projects, only limited attempts have been made to evaluate the effects of taxation on timing. Among those attempts, Zhang (1997) applied ROT to evaluate the neutrality of PRT in the UK, but his analysis was limited to PRT without considering other combinations of tax instruments. It is interesting to analyse the extent to which taxation impacts investment timing. The analysis done in this section focuses on the impact of tax on an oil field development and tries to identify whether taxation enhances or deters a real option value, or whether it has any effect on the delaying of the decision to develop a field. An analysis of this kind allows identification of any related investment distortions and the addressing of the neutrality of the regime.[23]

The following sections develop the basic concepts of ROT, highlighting the limitations of DCF with respect to the value of waiting. We also review the concepts of financial options and their analogy to real options, and then proceed with the evaluation of different fiscal scenarios using ROT.

7.3.2 Discounted Cash Flow: 'now or never' concept

This section develops a simple two-period example to illustrate the 'now or never' concept using the simplistic form of DCF technique. The example highlights the limitations of DCF in considering any increase in the project value, in the case where the investor chooses to wait for new information to arrive and for better economic conditions before undertaking his investment.

Assuming an oil project with an instant investment, $I = \$160$, producing 10 barrels of oil per period, with zero operating cost. The current price of a barrel of oil is $P_0 = \$20$, but in year 1, there is q=0.5 probability that the price will be \$25, and $(1 - q)$ probability that it will be \$15. After that, the price will stay at the new level. Using discrete DCF discounting, with a 10 per cent discount rate, the NPV of this project is equal to:

$$\text{NPV} = -160 + 200/(1.1) = \$21.8 \qquad (7.15)$$

Under the DCF approach, since the project NPV is positive, one should invest now. However, such a conclusion is not necessarily correct because it ignores the opportunity cost of investing now instead of waiting and keeping open the possibility of not investing should the price fall. For instance, if instead of investing now investors decide to wait and invest next year, the NPV in each price scenario is given as in the following:

–NPV_h (High Price Scenario): $NPV_h = (-160/1.1) + (250/1.1) = \$81$

$-NPV_l$ (Low Price Scenario): $NPV_l = (-160/1.1) + (150/1.1) = -\$9$

And the expected NPV in year 1, *ENPV*, is given by:

$$ENPV = 0.5\ NPV_h + 0.5\ NPV_l = \$36.4$$

This result indicates that it would be correct to delay the investment by one year. Since companies have the option to delay their investments, it is assumed that they will go ahead only if prices are high, as such earning NPV_h of $81 on their investment.

In this case, delaying the investment to year one allowed the company to earn an extra $60 (81.8–21.8) on its project. This difference between the profitability from investing in year one and the profitability of investing today can be regarded as the value of waiting. However, this value is not incorporated in the DCF technique, which assumes an inability to initiate actions to take advantage of changes in prices. In this case, companies are faced with a strict choice; either to invest now or to abandon the project.

The lack of flexibility in DCF is one of the major limitations of this technique, leading Dentskevich (1991) to conclude that DCF tends to misvalue investments. This is particularly true in situations of high uncertainty where management can respond flexibly to new information. In the DCF technique, a high level of risk is normally reflected in a high discount rate, which in turn reduces the value of a project. However, 'that would grossly underestimate the value of the project, as it completely ignores the flexibility that a company has regarding when to develop the project.'[24]

Authors like Lund (2001) argue that flexibility can increase the value of a project by almost 95 per cent, while Pike and Neale (1996) maintain that the 'true' NPV from a project should be expressed as the sum of the NPV of the basic project and the NPV of waiting. This can explain the reason why companies frequently defer wealth creating projects or accept uneconomic projects. Ekern (1998) argues that a traditionally calculated positive NPV is neither a necessary nor a sufficient condition for a project to be profitable.

7.3.3 Real Options Theory: basic concepts

ROT was developed to overcome the limitation of DCF in terms of incorporating flexibility in project evaluation. The options evaluation technique was originally applied in the pricing of complex financial instruments, but the origin of the term 'real options' can be attributed to Myers (1977) who first identified the similarity between real assets and financial options. This analogy led to the development of options technique for the valuation of real projects.

This section reviews the basic concepts of ROT and analyses financial options, addressing their similarity with real investments and more precisely with the development of an oil field.

Irreversibility and timing

The DCF technique is based on what is sometimes called 'questionable assumptions'. Firstly, it assumes that investments are reversible (i.e. they can be undone and expenditures recovered should market conditions turn unfavourable). Secondly, if investments are irreversible they are a now-or-never proposition, that is, if the firm does not undertake the investment now it will lose the opportunity forever. Although it is possible that some types of projects can fall into these categories, several do not. These assumptions can undermine the robustness of the DCF approach.

When a firm makes an irreversible investment it gives up the possibility of waiting for new information that might affect the desirability or timing of the expenditure. This lost value is an opportunity cost that must be included as part of the cost of the investment and investment rules that ignore this can be significantly in error. In order to incorporate the opportunity cost into the evaluation of a project, both irreversibility and timing are required. Irreversibility refers to the fact that once investment is taken, some costs cannot be recovered if the investor changes his mind. Timing refers to the ability to delay investment as an alternative to investing today, until new information arrives.

While the DCF rule compares investing today with never investing, a more useful comparison can be to examine a range of possibilities; investing today, or waiting longer and perhaps investing next year, or waiting longer and perhaps investing in two years and so on. This ability to delay an irreversible investment can profoundly affect the decision to invest.

Irreversibility and timing constitute the key assumptions in ROT. They provide a company with the opportunity or option to invest. Because this option can be valuable, it is somewhat inappropriate to ignore it from the evaluation of project's profitability, particularly when analysing the effect of taxation on that profitability.

The opportunity to invest is similar to holding a financial call option. Therefore, to understand the way flexibility is incorporated into the evaluation, the next section develops the concept of financial call options and expands the analysis to real projects, such as to the development of oil fields in the UK North Sea.

Financial options

Options in real investments originate from the idea of financial options. Like forward oil contracts, financial options are the most common derivatives and are used to manage exposure to the risks associated with the underlying asset.[25] A financial option is 'a contractual arrangement giving the owner the right, but not the obligation to buy (call option) or sell (put option) the underlying asset, at a given price, at some time in the future'.[26] The fixed price specified in an option contract is called the exercise or strike price, E, and the date after which an option can no longer be exercised is called the expiration or maturity date, T_M.

Financial options are widely used in the financial community, where it is possible to buy options on all kinds of assets such as shares, bonds, foreign currency and commodities. The rest of this section focuses on options over shares. Furthermore, there are two types of options – an American type, which can be exercised at any time up to and including the expiration date and a European option, which can only be exercised on the expiration date.

This chapter considers the American call option, because in the upstream oil industry, several real options are of American nature. For example, purchasing an oil lease normally gives the oil company the right but not the obligation to develop the field should commercial oil be discovered. It is most likely that such an option can be exercised at any time during the life of the lease.

For illustrative purpose, assume an American call option that expires in three months time. Its underlying price, which is the closing price on the current date, is 120. The strike price is 115 and the last price at which the option was traded was seven. The hypothetical value of an option if it were to expire immediately is called its intrinsic value. Therefore, if the American option considered in this example is expiring immediately, it would be worth the difference between its underlying price (120) and its striking price (115), as such if exercised immediately the intrinsic value of the call is five. However, the option price is seven, therefore exceeding its intrinsic value by two. This difference is called the option's time value,[27] also called the option premium.

Let F be the option value, which is the sum of its intrinsic value (stock price, S_T, less the exercise price, E) and its time value. As the expiration date of the option approaches, the time value decreases but at expiration the option is worth its intrinsic value. Figure 7.1 illustrates the call option payoff that depicts the relation between the value of the option (measured on the vertical axis) and the price of the underlying asset (on the horizontal axis). It is this payoff that affects investment-timing, in the following way:

- If the exercise price, E, is higher than the stock price, S_T, the option is *out-of-the money* or worthless ($F = 0$), and investors would not take the option, so as not lose money since exercising the option today would yield a negative net payoff. In this case, the intrinsic value of the option is zero, since it cannot be negative.
- If E is equal to S_T, the option is *at-the-money* and exercising the option today would yield a zero payoff ($F = 0$).
- If E is lower than S_T, the option is *in-the-money* and exercising the option today would yield a positive net payoff ($F = (S_T - I) + \mathit{Time\ Value}$). However, the fact that the option is in-the-money does not necessarily mean that investors should exercise the option. Investors should wait until the option is *deep-in-the-money* to invest, where there is no value for waiting,

or the value of waiting is too low compared with the intrinsic value ($F = S_T - I$).

In Figure 7.1, the dotted line represents the actual option value as a function of the stock price, while the lower limit shows that the value of the option equals the payoff if exercised immediately. It also shows that the option value never falls below this payoff, hence at expiration, the value of the call can be expressed as max ($S_T - E$, 0).

Analogy between financial options and oil projects

The analogy between financial and real options is the basis for using ROT in the valuation of corporate investments. The common element for using this theory in the evaluation of real projects is that the future is uncertain, and in an uncertain environment having the flexibility to decide what to do after some of that uncertainty is resolved definitely has value. Options pricing theory provides the means for assessing that value. Investment opportunities are options–rights but not an obligation to take some action in the future. As such, an irreversible investment opportunity can be compared to a financial call option. The holder of the call option has the right, for a specified period, to pay the exercise price and to receive, in return, the asset, for example a share that has some value. Similarly, a company with an investment opportunity has the option to spend money now or in the future (the exercise price) in return of an asset of some value (the entitlement to the stream of profits from the project). This flexibility may have value and should be reflected in the appraisal of a project.

The earlier applications of ROT are in evaluating exhaustible resources, namely petroleum projects, which require long term planning horizons. 'Nowhere is the idea of investments as options better illustrated than in the context of decisions to exploit deposits of natural resources'.[28] Given the

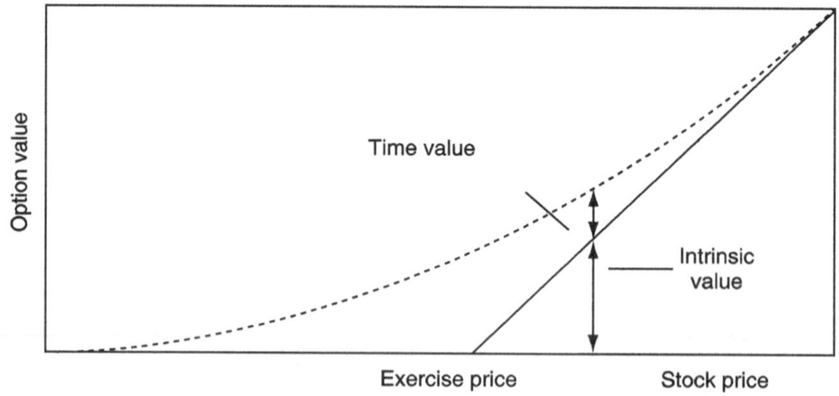

Figure 7.1 Call option pay-off diagram.

technical and economic uncertainties in oil projects, the application of ROT for the evaluation of such projects can be of particular significance.

The classical model of Paddock, Siegel and Smith (1988) is one of the earliest and most popular models to evaluate oil reserves using option-pricing techniques. An undeveloped reserve is an option; it gives the owner the right to invest in development of the reserve, immediately or later, depending on market conditions. By valuing this option, the value of the reserve can be determined as well as the optimum point at which it should be developed. Developing the oil reserve is like exercising a call option, and the exercise price is the cost of development. Oil activity is rich in real options, which if managed optimally enhance the value of the portfolio of projects and real assets in general for the oil company. An oil company has various options, such as the option to explore, to appraise, to develop, to produce and to abandon.[29]

In the exploration phase, the firm has the option to drill the well or to wait. If it decides to explore and does discover an oil reserve, the company has the option to invest in the appraisal phase to ascertain the geological characteristics of the field. If the appraisal is undertaken, then it has the option of committing a large investment in development of the reserve or to wait. If the field is developed, then it has the option to produce or to wait. If it produces and economic conditions turn unprofitable, the company has the option to abandon.

The focus of the analysis in this chapter is on the development option, where flexibility is of particular importance.[30] The development strategy has a significant impact on the profitability of an oil project. It requires large investment costs, and is made early in the project's lifetime where information concerning future oil prices is uncertain. Hence, the selection of the development strategy is a challenging task for the decision-maker.

Valuing real options

The most familiar model for the pricing of options is the Black-Scholes model, developed in the early 1970s. Under the Black-Scholes formula, there are five variables that need to be estimated in order to calculate the option value.[31]

These are:

- The current price of the underlying stock, S_T.
- The exercise price, E.
- Annual volatility of stock price, σ (a measure of the amount by which the stock price could change during the time to maturity of the option).
- Risk free interest rate, i
- Time to expiration, T.

In addition to these factors, Merton (1973) generalised the Black-Scholes model to allow the incorporation of a sixth parameter, dividend yield, d, which is the dividend per share divided by the market price at time of purchase.[32]

The development of an oil field is analogous to a financial option. To acquire an offshore oil field, the company must first bid for an exploration license for exclusive rights to explore a particular offshore block. In general, the exploration license lasts five years during which the oil company has to make a decision on whether to proceed with the development or to return the block to the host government. Table 7.3 summarizes the analogies between financial options, real options and extends the comparison to a petroleum development project.

Using the financial options analogy, the current estimate of the expected value of the undeveloped reserve on which the oil company has an option to invest in (current asset value) can be viewed as the current stock price. The exercise price for the undeveloped reserve would refer to development cost (investment) incurred should the project be carried out. The annual volatility of the option refers to the measure of the amount by which the current asset estimate can change during the length of the option. Since the current value of the undeveloped reserve is assumed to be only a function of the oil price, the annual volatility is that of oil price. The risk free rate of interest used to calculate financial options is the same for real options. The time to expiration is related to the maximum time that the investment decision can be postponed. The length of the exploration license or the relinquishment date[33] can be viewed as the time to maturity of the option. At expiration, if the option was not exercised before, the firm either presents the development investment plan (commits to start the investment immediately) or returns the concession to the government. Finally, the dividend of the oil project is the net production revenue less the rate of depletion, also called the cash flow rate (net cash flow as a percentage of the project value) or the net convenience yield.

Let V_{et} be the present value of the expected cash flows from the project, in other words, V_{et} is the present value of the operating revenues less operating costs and tax.

$$V_{et} = R_{et} - OE_{et} - T_{et} \tag{7.16}$$

Where:

- R_{et} is the present values of the expected revenue cash flow in period t;
- OE_{et} is the present values of the expected cost cash flow in period t;
- T_{et} is the present values of the expected tax cash flow in period t.

Let I'_{et} be the present value of the investment expenditure net of fiscal benefits.

$$I'_{et} = I_{et} - FB_{et} \tag{7.17}$$

Table 7.3 Analogy between financial and real options[34]

Option terminology	*Financial options*	*Real options*	*Petroleum project*
Value of underlying asset	Stock price	Gross project value (present value of expected cash flow)	Net present value of the developed reserve
Exercise price	Exercise price	Present value of investment expenditure	Present value of capital costs
Maturity time	Time to expiration	Time span during which the investment can be undertaken	Negotiated development period (relinquishment requirement)
Volatility	Volatility of stock price	Volatility of gross project value	Volatility of oil price
Risk free interest rate	Risk free interest rate	Risk free interest rate	Risk free interest rate
Dividend	Dividend	Net convenience yield	Net convenience yield

Where:

- I_{et} is the present value of capital expenditures in period t;
- FB_{et} is the present value of investment fiscal benefits in period t.

The project cash flows can be obtained when the company decides to develop the field. In this case, the company exercises its option by paying the exercise price, I_{et}, net of fiscal benefits.[35] Therefore, the immediate exercise of the option generates a net pay-off, or the net value of the project, which is the NPV_{et}, where:

$$NPV_{et} = V_{et} - I'_{et} \tag{7.18}$$

Let F_r be the value of the real option, in this case the undeveloped oil field. This value is determined from the partial differential equation based on the Black-Scholes model, as follows[36]:

$$\tfrac{1}{2}\sigma_v^2 V_{et}^2 F''(V) + (i - \delta) V_{et} V F'(V) - iF = 0 \tag{7.19}$$

This equation is solved subject to the following boundary conditions[37]:

$$F(0,t) = 0$$

$$F(V,t) = \max(V_t - I, 0)$$

$$F(V^*,t) = V^* - I$$
$$F'(V^*,t) = 1 \qquad (7.20)$$

Where:

- δ is the dividend yield
- F' is the first derivative of F
- F'' is the second derivative of F
- V^* is the threshold, which is the critical value of V where the real option is *deep-in-the-money* and the value of waiting is zero.

The decision to exercise the option and develop of the field is taken in the light of the option value, as explained below and further illustrated in Figure 7.2.

- If $V_{et} > I'_{et}$, $NPV_{et} > 0$ and the option is *in-the-money*. However, the company should consider exercising its option when it is deep in the money, where $V > V^*$, the option premium is zero and the option value, F_r, is equal to its intrinsic value, NPV_{et}.
- If $V_{et} = I'_{et}$, $NPV_{et} = 0$ and the option is *at-the-money*. In this case, $F_r = 0$.
- If $V_{et} < I'_{et}$, $NPV_{et} < 0$ and the option is *out-of-the-money*. Also, in this case, $F_r = 0$, because the option value cannot be negative.[38]

Subsequently, because the option value cannot be negative, it can be said that the pay-off from a real option is equal to:

$$V_{et} - I'_{et}, \text{ if } V_{et} > I'_{et}$$
$$0, \text{ if } V_{et} < I'_{et}$$

Through its double effect on the net pay-off, firstly on the project value and secondly on the investment expenditure, taxation is likely to affect the decision to exercise the option or the timing of the investment.

ROT and MAP model

ROT is based on the same concepts as MAP, namely DAPT and contingent claims analysis. To value an asset, the cash flows occurring at each period are split into different components, then valued separately depending on the risk inherent to each component.

As oil price is assumed to be the only source of uncertainty, revenues are adjusted for risk while the other components, mainly costs, are discounted at the risk free rate. Once the individual components of the cash flow are valued, the project value is determined by adding up the individual components' values. Because ROT is based on the same concepts applied in MAP, it also benefits from the major advantages of the MAP approach, namely the separ-

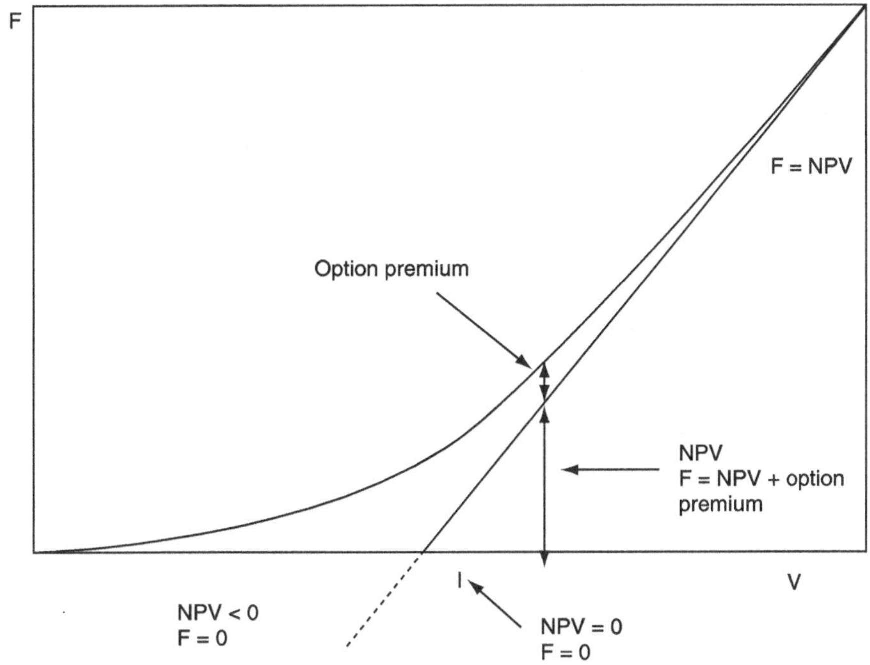

Figure 7.2 Investment decisions and real options.[39]

ate discounting of the cash flow components and the incorporation of a rigorous oil price model.

However, while MAP assumes a forward contract to model oil price uncertainty, ROT considers financial options. Both forward contracts and financial options are the most common financial derivatives used, but they differ in the following way. While a forward contract *obliges* the holder of the contract to exercise its right at a specified price and day, the option gives its owner the *right* (not the obligation) to buy or sell some asset at a specified price. As such, the option gives more flexibility than the forward contract.

Consequently, the application of ROT to value real projects, which are analogous to financial options, allows the incorporation of management flexibility in decision making. Furthermore, when MAP is extended to incorporate flexibility, the model is referred to as real options technique.

7.3.4 DCF and ROT comparison: practical examples

This section presents the empirical analysis used to evaluate the effect of taxation on investment timing through its effect on project value as well as the post-tax cost of investment.

Methodology

The purpose of the analysis below is firstly to compare the DCF and ROT and secondly to identify the impact of different tax structures on the value of waiting and as such on the timing of development of a particular field. The analysis can allow identifying any related investment distortions, hence addressing the neutrality of the regime.

To compute the real option value, as well as the value of waiting, timing software developed by Dias (2002) is used. This software comprises Excel spreadsheets that use a simple model analogy of real options with the American call option.

For the purpose of this chapter, the software is used to calculate the real option value. The software requires inputs, namely the discounted values of the expected cash flow, V_{et}, and of the investment expenditures, I'_{et}, the time to expiration, the dividend yield and the nominal risk free interest rate.

In order to isolate the fiscal effects on investment expenditures, the following steps are adopted:

Firstly, the total field's profitability, NPV_{et}, is calculated as follows:

$$NPV_{et} = R_{et} - OE_{et} - CE_{et} - T_{et} \tag{7.21}$$

Secondly, the field's profitability, V_{et}, is calculated in the same way as NPV but this time assuming capital expenditures, CE_{et}, equal to zero.

Finally, the difference between NPV_{et} and V_{et} gives the value of investment expenditures net of fiscal benefits, I'_{et}.

Once calculated, the values are inserted into the timing software in order to determine the option value.

Assumptions

The analysis in the section below uses the same economic assumptions and tax scenarios as presented in both Chapters 5 and 6. But in terms of tax scenarios, and for reasons of simplicity, only three scenarios are used for comparison, namely; UK_{75}, UK_{83} and UK_{93a} in addition to the pre-tax scenario. The following assumptions are also added:

- The time to expiration, T, is assumed to be five years. In the UK, the production licence covers the most important stages of exploration and development as well as actual production. Under the first four licencing rounds the rights under a production licence last for an initial period of six years, under the fifth licencing round licences are granted for a period of four years. Also, Emhjellen (1999), Dias (2001) and Siew (2001) assume an expiration period of five years, as a typical time for relinquishment.
- The dividend yield, δ, is assumed to be two per cent in annual terms, similarly to the real risk-free rate. According to Pickles and Smith (1993)

and Dias (2001) the risk free interest rate is a good practical value for the dividend yield.

- λ, the speed of reversion of oil prices, is assumed to tend to zero, hence, oil prices are assumed to follow a GBM, rather than an MRP as used in Section 7.2. This assumption is adopted for the following reasons.

Firstly, early models of Black and Scholes (1973), and Paddock, Siegel and Smith (1988) assume a GBM, which is much simpler to use than the mean reversion model. The same assumption is also implemented in several studies, such as those of Zhang (1997) and Lund (2001). As put by Laughton (1998), 'there may be problems with the use of this particular class of models of price reversion in the consideration of projects with timing flexibility' (p.93). Pindyck (2001) also argues that the GBM assumption is unlikely to lead to large errors in the optimal investment rule, as the speed of reversion is relatively very slow.

Secondly, the timing software uses the same assumption and as such the chapter adopts the GBM assumption for reasons of consistency.

Since uncertainty is modelled differently in GBM and in the mean reversion model,[40] the two models have different implications for the term structure of the risk discount factor. Under the mean reversion assumption, the risk discount rate declines from a short-term rate toward zero in the long term, whereas the risk discount rate is constant under GBM. Consequently, higher values are likely to result under the mean reversion assumption. According to Bradley (1998), although there are quantitative differences in the two oil price models, the qualitative features of the two models are the same.

Under GBM, the risk discount factor used to adjust oil revenues for risk is assumed as follows:

$$\mathrm{RDF}_t = \exp(-\phi\sigma t) \qquad (7.22)$$

With ϕ, the price of risk.[41]

The discounted values are obtained by applying the time discount factor, TDF, where:

$$TDF_t = \exp(-it) \qquad (7.23)$$

The evaluation is carried out firstly in nominal terms then the results are deflated, and given in £M.

Findings

Table 7.4 displays the profitability of the 25 selected oil fields evaluated using DCF and ROT under the pre-tax scenario – where no tax applies. The main finding is that the two discounting methods produce different projects NPV.

Pre-tax comparison

The ROT values are always lower than DCF (except for one field – Leadon), most probably as a result of the discrete discounting of the cash flow components under ROT. The difference is particularly significant for the fields with positive NPV under DCF, but with a negative NPV as calculated with ROT. This is the case of Birch, Beatrice, Heather, and Captain. The difference between the two methods is sometimes more pronounced relatively to the difference between MAP and DCF, as discussed in Section 7.2. Such a variance relates mainly to the underlying models.

Firstly, with MAP the use of mean reversion model for oil price reduces the long-term discounting for revenues. With ROT, however, revenues' discounting grows over time, due to the GBM assumption. Secondly, while revenues are adjusted for risk, costs are discounted at the risk free rate under ROT, similarly to MAP. With DCF, however, both revenues and costs are discounted at the risk-adjusted rate. Consequently, the difference between DCF and ROT is more significant for low revenue and high cost fields, like Beatrice, Heather and Captain.

For instance, in the case of Captain, the discounted costs' value is higher than the discounted revenue value, because CAPEX alone, constitutes about 50 per cent of revenues on an undiscounted basis. However, for fields, like Leadon and Schiehallion, with high revenues and low costs, the difference between the two techniques is small. For Schiehallion, for example, the total costs constitute only 25 per cent of the total revenues, on an undiscounted basis.

Furthermore, under DCF, all fields have a positive NPV, except Tiffani field. Following the concept of 'now or never', the development of all of the 24 oil fields can be carried out. With ROT, however, 11 fields have a value of waiting, significant in the case of six fields. As such, under the ROT concept of 'wait and see', the development of such fields can be delayed instead of being carried out today. This can explain why authors, like Ekern (1988), argued that the option analysis may yield results partly conflicting with the recommendations of the traditional DCF method.

In fact, if a field has a negative NPV under DCF, it is probably that its development would never be undertaken. But ROT leads to a more flexible outcome, where the development would be delayed and undertaken under more favourable conditions. For instance, the development of Tiffani field can be delayed instead of abandoned. However, because the value of waiting for this field is substantial, it is unlikely that the development of the field will be undertaken. When the value of waiting is small or zero, both ROT and DCF lead to the same conclusion with regard to the development decision. This applies to 14 fields from the selected sample, as shown in Table 7.4.

Table 7.4 Oil field profitability under DCF and ROT- pre-tax scenario

Pre-tax Scenario	*DCF* £M	*ROT* £M	*Difference* (%)	*Option Value* £M	*Value of Waiting* £M
Very small					
Argyll	258.93	202.4	21.8%	202.4	0.0
Arkwright	68.19	49.2	27.8%	49.2	0.0
Birch	45.49	−7.1	115.6%	14.0	21.1
Blake	239.28	212.8	11.1%	212.8	0.0
Kappa	149.2	79.5	46.7%	79.5	0.0
Highlander	306.59	268.2	12.5%	268.2	0.0
Janice	139.91	108.7	22.3%	125.9	17.2
Tiffani	−249.45	−412.1	65.2%	3.5	415.6
Thelma	194.22	193.5	0.4%	193.5	0.0
Toni	157.28	147.1	6.5%	147.1	0.0
Small					
Arbroath	436.38	289.2	33.7%	289.2	0.0
Auk	866.71	177.3	79.5%	177.3	0.0
Balmoral	108.45	38.2	64.8%	95.6	57.4
Beatrice	108.27	−200.8	285.5%	19.6	220.4
Heather	129.83	−97.2	174.9%	19.3	116.5
Leadon	486.5	531.4	−9.2%	531.4	0.0
Montrose	217.47	79.2	63.6%	84.0	4.8
Osprey	233.6	164.1	29.8%	167.7	3.6
Scapa	347.77	288.0	17.2%	288.0	0.0
Medium					
Captain	440.46	−28.8	106.5%	102.5	131.3
Clair	364.31	326.3	10.4%	326.3	0.0
Maureen	403.74	271.5	32.8%	303.4	31.9
Tern	621.64	414.7	33.3%	414.7	0.0
Large					
Alba	885.92	594.6	32.9%	600.1	5.5
Schiehallion	1302.05	1202.8	7.6%	1202.8	0.0

Effect of tax on the value of waiting

As discussed previously, taxation can affect the option value through its effect on V, the present value of the expected cash flows and I, the present value of capital expenditures. While an increase in taxation is likely to reduce the value of V, higher tax reliefs have the opposite effect on I. The total effect depends on the amount of the tax and its capital expenditure relief. Consequently, tax instruments, like Royalty, are expected to increase the value of waiting, since they are imposed on revenues and may offer limited reliefs for development costs. However, profits-related tax instruments, like PRT and CT, are expected to encourage early development, as they offer several capital expenditure reliefs, particularly PRT.

Table 7.5 displays the value of waiting in the case of the 25 oil fields under the three tax scenarios selected for this analysis, in addition to the pre-tax scenario.

Under Scenario UK_{75}, there is a significant reduction in the profitability of all fields, regardless of their size (e.g. Janice, Leadon, Tern and Schiehallion). Four fields, two very small (Kappa and Janice), and two small (Balmoral and Beatrice) even have a negative profitability compared with the Base Scenario. Under Scenario UK_{83}, there is a reduction in profitability but it is less pronounced compared with Scenario UK_{75}. In fact, compared with the pre tax scenario, the profitability of only one very small field, Janice, becomes negative. But the two scenarios generate a value of waiting for certain fields, although those fields have a zero value of waiting under the pre-tax Scenario.

Under Scenario UK_{75}, the ROT results indicate that 14 oil fields have a value of waiting, significant in the case of 10 fields. Such a result is not surprising. Since Royalty is imposed on revenues, and when combined with costs discounted at the risk free rate under ROT, the result is a significantly lower NPV value, and as such consequently a higher value of waiting. Under Scenario UK_{83}, 11 fields have a value of waiting, significant for eight fields. This indicates that in the UK, both the pre-1983 and post-1983/pre-1993 packages impact the development timing and can lead to postponing development activity, but the effect of pre-1983 structure is more substantial. Nevertheless, for certain fields, like Captain, there is a reduction in the value of waiting under Scenario UK_{83}. This is possibly due to investment expenditure's fiscal benefits, which are significant for fields with large capital expenditures, like Captain.

On the one hand, taxes can reduce the value of expected cash flows, and consequently they can increase the value of waiting and the possibility of delaying investment. But on the other hand, fiscal benefits can reduce the investment expenditure value, leading to an opposite effect on the value of waiting. Tax instruments, such as Royalty with limited capital expenditure reliefs, can lead to a significant increase in the value of waiting thereby encouraging investment delay and leading to delay and probably loss of fiscal revenue, unlike PRT and CT.

Effect of the value of waiting on tax receipts

As a consequence of the flexibility option, the oil fields with a significant value of waiting are not going to be developed today, but instead their development is postponed. This in turn can affect the timing of fiscal receipts.

Using the ROT concept, where the development of fields with a significant value of waiting can be postponed, the effect of various tax scenarios on government revenues can vary as compared with DCF analysis. Under DCF analysis, fields do not have a value for waiting, hence as long as the NPV is positive (and substantial) the fields will be developed and revenues will accrue to the government. However, under ROT, the suspension of

Table 7.5 Value of waiting under different tax structures

Scenario	*UK_{75} 12.5% Royalty, 70% PRT, 52% CT*				*UK_{83} 75% PRT, 33% CT*				*UK_{93a} 30% CT*			
	DCF £M	*ROT* £M	*Option value* £M	*Value of waiting* £M	*DCF* £M	*ROT* £M	*Option value* £M	*Value of waiting* £M	*DCF* £M	*ROT* £M	*Option value* £M	*Value of waiting* £M
Very small												
Argyll	97	60.2	60.2	0.0	148	117.1	117.1	0.0	180	137.2	137.2	0.0
Arkwright	22	11.0	12.3	1.3	39	30.1	30.1	0.0	11	31.8	31.8	0.0
Birch	6	−19.1	2.1	21.2	25	−9.1	6.9	16.0	21	−8.9	8.6	17.5
Blake	71	60.5	60.5	0.0	124	116.2	116.2	0.0	163	143.6	143.6	0.0
Kappa	−12	−92.4	0.0	92.3	62	−17.9	7.1	25.0	66	−9.1	11.4	20.5
Highlander	85	61.3	61.3	0.0	151	129.1	129.1	0.0	200	180.8	180.8	0.0
Janice	21	−268.8	0.1	268.9	79	63.8	65.6	1.8	84	67.9	96.8	28.9
Tiffani	−262	−429.1	0.0	412.0	−251	−412.1	0.0	412.1	−251	−412.1	0.7	412.8
Thelma	58	66.8	66.8	0.0	105	120.6	120.6	0.0	130	132.5	132.5	0.0
Toni	40	43.0	43.0	0.0	71	91.6	91.6	0.0	101	97.8	97.8	0.0
Small												
Arbroath	436	29.8	31.6	1.8	159	147.7	147.7	0.0	306	193.4	193.4	0.0
Auk	867	−24.6	5.9	30.5	370	33.3	39.4	6.1	298	98.8	98.8	0.0
Balmoral	108	−70.5	1.4	71.9	32	−28.8	15.0	43.8	604	−22.7	40.8	63.5
Beatrice	108	−255.7	0.0	255.7	30	−200.8	0.8	201.6	39	−200.8	7.0	207.8
Heather	130	−140.5	0.0	140.5	54	−105.8	2.0	107.8	39	−105.0	6.7	111.7
Leadon	487	167.3	167.3	0.0	176	274.4	274.4	0.0	50	360.4	360.4	0.0
Montrose	217	−19.4	7.6	27.0	110	31.8	36.6	4.8	313	36.1	45.3	9.2
Osprey	234	38.9	44.4	5.5	117	101.8	101.8	0.0	153	107.5	111.8	0.0
Scapa	348	93.2	93.2	0.0	176	155.6	155.6	0.0	206	192.7	192.7	0.0
Medium												
Captain	64	−140.1	1.0	141.1	170	−80.0	11.9	91.9	2581	−69.2	25.5	94.7
Clair	68	200.5	200.5	0.0	140	200.5	200.5	0.0	278	279.9	279.9	0.0
Maureen	31	−23.9	40.8	64.7	105	−23.9	53.4	77.3	238	−23.9	120.3	144.2
Tern	58	89.1	89.1	0.0	157	197.1	197.1	0.0	174	269.1	272.9	3.8
Large												
Alba	83	126.0	126.0	0.0	177	271.1	271.1	0.0	574	387.8	397.1	0.0
Schiehallion	79	322.4	322.4	0.0	328	495.0	495.0	0.0	868	809.9	815.0	0.0

development of certain fields results in a reduction in government revenue, as shown in Table 7.6.

Scenario UK_{75}, illustrating the pre-1983 fiscal package, has the most significant impact. If this scenario is imposed on the 25 oil fields selected, it can generate a reduction in total government revenue of 42 per cent. This results from the fact that the development of 10 oil fields, particularly small fields, is not profitable today and as such it is suspended. The other scenarios generate less critical effects, as both PRT and CT provide significant fiscal reliefs encouraged by this early development. This result also confirms the conclusion in Chapter 6 that had the 1975 fiscal package still applied, many fields would not have been developed.

None of the tax structures evaluated in this section can be described as entirely neutral. In particular, the pre-1983 fiscal package results in the suspension of the development of 10 oil fields, leading almost to halving the total fiscal take, as noted above – the most significant reduction as compared with other scenarios. Imposing IT solely (Scenario UK_{93a}) generates a significant reduction in government's revenues as a result of suspending the development of some small and medium size fields. This is mainly due to the fact that PRT offers various reliefs that can reduce the value of waiting and thereby encourage early development.

In mature provinces, such as the UKCS, developing discovered fields is likely to be the most important concern, in order to sustain production as well as maintain the interest of oil companies in the province. Any delay in the development of certain fields is not an outcome preferred by the government, which generally aims to receive receipts as early as possible. As such, it can be concluded that in the UK the major changes to the fiscal regime, particularly that of 1983, have maintained investment and government revenue in response to the changing nature of the North Sea province. However, the abolition of PRT in 1993 had a less significant impact in terms of investment timing, due to the fact that small fields were protected against the payment of this tax.

Table 7.6 Change in government revenue under ROT concept

Reduction in Revenue	*Scenario UK 75*	*Scenario UK 83*	*Scenario UK 93a*
Very small fields: (£M)	2271.1	1854.1	1356.0
(%)	18%	0%	0%
Small fields: (£M)	3941.7	5789.6	2904.7
(%)	166%	47%	62%
Medium fields: (£M)	5628.5	5073.1	2190.0
(%)	41%	34%	62%
Large fields: (£M)	8832.5	7917.0	3344.0
(%)	0%	0%	0%
Total (£M)	20673.8	20633.8	9794.7
(%)	42%	17%	29%

7.4 SUMMARY AND CONCLUSION

This chapter has opened some alternative possibilities for assessing the economics of an oil project. The difficult issue for company executives and decision-makers, which we have tried to narrow and clarify, is whether the gains of different and undoubtedly more complicated calculations of benefit outweigh the extra burdens of grappling with the unfamiliar. It is not an easy choice to make in advance, especially in an industry such as oil where uncertainties abound at every point.

The chapter has considered two alternatives to conventional DCF methods – the MAP model and ROT. Comparing results from deploying these two techniques against results from DCF procedures allows us to discern whether the newer techniques truly make a significant and beneficial difference and therefore whether they should be recommended as a replacement for traditional techniques.

MAP allows a more accurate evaluation and incorporation of the risk components of the cash flow. ROT integrates an additional important feature in investment decision-making, which provides a marked increase in flexibility. This can be a real gain. Flexibility in decision-making permits companies to postpone the development of an oil field, until economic conditions become more favourable or uncertainty is reduced. The petroleum industry has a significant managerial flexibility due to the long life nature of oil projects. Previous studies have argued that such flexibility can add value to projects. Neglecting it in oil ventures can lead to an under-valuation of assets and a consequential misallocation of resources in the economy.

A growing body of empirical work suggests that because the DCF technique, in its simplistic form, is based on the static concept of 'now or never', it fails to account for the existence of flexibility in investment decisions and as such it can undervalue a project. ROT could prove a more useful technique than DCF precisely because it allows the incorporation of flexibility in the valuation of projects. Although ROT was originally developed for the appraisal of financial derivatives, the analogy between petroleum projects and financial options allows the application of ROT to value oil projects.

Not surprisingly, the results in this chapter show that differences in outcomes do indeed occur in the economics of a particular project when different techniques are applied.

Accuracy can be valuable and inaccuracy can be costly. That is the case for more complex procedures, despite the obvious extra burden which falls on a company's financial brainpower and the natural dislike for new methods for which the gains are not always clear and immediate. This is what MAP and ROT promise; a more difficult road than conventional methods. But by overcoming some of the limitation of DCF they also hold out the promise of greater accuracy and precision, which in the end could be immensely valuable.

But inside big corporations there is a wide range of managers, board members and many others from various disciplines who need to be familiar with project economics, not just leaving it all to economists. For this reason, the financial evaluation technique needs to be simple and applicable among all companies. The DCF method meets these two requirements. The more sophisticated MAP and ROT are unlikely to capture many sponsors.

For company executives, as well as for tax planners it is a hard choice to call. The sums and exercises in this chapter may assist in the process and are intended to make it a little easier.

8 Sharing the oil wealth

The political and social contexts

An examination of the perceptions, popular beliefs and political pressures underlying petroleum policies.

8.1 NO ORDINARY INDUSTRY

Oil industry executives sometimes like to argue that they work in 'just another big industry' and that they should be treated just like other industries. But they are wrong. The oil industry is no ordinary industry, petroleum taxation is no ordinary tax and the surrounding political and economic circumstances are unlike those to be found in any other fiscal area. The imposition of petroleum taxes tends in almost every instance to be accompanied by intense political debate, discussion and tension. Oil is, in short, different, and its extraction and production generates different attitudes and different resulting policies and approaches from those governing other tax measures and policies.

A variety of reasons are at work in shaping the background mood and context in which petroleum tax policy is formed. First, there is invariably the deeply embedded popular notion that all natural resources, and oil in particular, belong to the nation, the state (in the UK case, the Crown) and that proceeds from their extraction should go mainly to the owners. Second, there is the popular assumption, also deep-rooted but not always valid, that security of energy supplies and 'ownership' of oil and gas resources in the ground are connected. There is also the related assumption that oil and gas resources will somehow insulate the country or region in which they have been found from the vagaries of world oil markets and oil politics. Third, a popular mood can also develop that with oil being dubbed 'black gold' a flow of prosperity and benefits is somehow going to reach every citizen. Fourth, the discovery of large hydrocarbon deposits in a particular region can, and does, often give rise to internal arguments within the overall national jurisdiction as to whether the benefits should be localised rather than shared nationally. In the UK North Sea case this arose in acute form in the debate about Scottish separatism and nationalism. In a completely different context, the Darfur tragedy has as one of its underlying causes the debate as to how different regions and tribes should share the expanding proceeds from oil being developed and produced, while Iraq's unity has long been jeopardised by Kurdish and other regional claims to oil proceeds.

These ideas have played their part, to different degrees, in the formulation of petroleum tax regimes round the world, and have been duly reflected in ripples on the political surface as policy is shaped. We will look at them in turn.

8.2 'IT IS OUR OIL'

The concept that all natural and mineral resources under any territory 'belong' to the state or sovereign authority in which they have been discovered is well established, but it has not always prevailed and does not prevail to this day in the USA.

On the contrary, United States law governing the ownership of mineral resources in the ground remains rooted in the ancient common law provision that 'to whomever the soil belongs, he owns also to the sky and the depths'. US law and practice has been built up from this viewpoint which was no doubt carried to America by the early settlers and reflected the free and pioneering spirit, and the robust hostility to the dominance of the British crown, which were their hallmarks. US landowners therefore have enjoyed from the start, and continue to enjoy, title to the oil under their feet and much of US case law has been concerned all along not with this almost unchallenged right but with the tricky legal problems of ownership where oil has 'migrated' through underground structures from territory of one owner to another.

This doctrine and system has come to be called 'the concessionary system' (although it should not be confused with the granting of concessions by the state to oil companies, also labelled the concessionary system or pattern in contrast to the contractual system, as discussed in Chapter 3). It stands in clear contrast to the so-called domanial system of law and practice in every other oil-producing country in the world, where the resource in the ground has now come to be regarded unambiguously state property, whether it has been 'discovered' and exploited or not.

This now almost universal assumption (except in the USA) is by far the most important influence working on the minds of policy-makers when it comes to sharing the proceeds of oil once it is extracted. Carried one stage further it can be, and is, used to support the contention that if the nation owns the oil in the first place then the proceeds from the extraction and sale of what it owns should therefore also predominantly belong to the state, or in democratic parlance, 'the people', although with appropriate allowances for the costs of their extraction.

This is a debate which continues and is reflected in the choices which government authorities make, already explained in earlier chapters, between concessionary and contractual relations with oil companies themselves. At the wellhead governments may or may not agree to permit private oil companies to own and sell the oil. The pattern has varied both as between different oil producers and over time in the twentieth century. As recounted in Chapter 4, the UK initially sought full contractual control of North Sea oil but eventually settled for a compromise, with concessions to private oil companies but also with contractual participation in oil production in all fields (eventually lapsing). But elsewhere today the clear trend is towards full government control.

Either way, and whatever the full nature of the government/industry relationship, what might be called the subterranean issue has been resolved in the state's favour and is now the general rule. Reinforcement for this view comes from the United Nations itself, where General Assembly Resolution Number 636 (VII) asserts the 'right of peoples to use and exploit the mineral resources *inherent in their sovereignty*'. This leaves little room for further argument. In the ground the oil belongs to the state. Oil tax regimes start from this central and fundamental point. Offshore, the issue is still more clear cut, even in the USA. No private landholders own the sea. What lies beneath it is the undisputed property of the state and belongs to the state. The full costs of what is extracted must be realistically covered out of the proceeds, but it is the state, so it is assumed, which should and must be the prime and main beneficiary.

A far higher 'take' is felt to be justified from the revenues and the profits oil companies generate than is the case with other forms of production or income-creating activities. The 'sharing' calculation becomes one of deciding what to leave, rather than what to take. Thus, tax rates of eighty or ninety percent are seen as 'fair', or indeed whatever rates are consistent with the continued willingness of operators to invest in the extraction sequence, to cover extraction and production costs and to secure a reasonable rate of return. The petroleum tax policy 'debate' therefore turns almost entirely on what these costs are, or are likely to be, in widely differing sets of circumstances, and what should be left to operating enterprises to meet them.

The British experience as the UK emerged as a major oil producing country with the development of the North Sea in the 1960s and 1970s provides an interesting case study. From the start the state was seen not only as the rightful owner of North Sea oil but also as a key participant in its production. This 'ownership' was to be expressed both through the share of revenues and profits to be taken by the state in tax and by direct participation by the state in ownership of the oil as it came out of the ground (or seabed). The Labour Government which came to power in 1974, just as North Sea production was taking off, at first had an even more extreme stance. This was, in the words of its election manifesto 'to ensure not only that the North Sea and Celtic Sea oil and gas resources are in full public ownership, but that the operation of getting and distributing them is under full Government control with majority public participation'. Needless to say this highly socialistic approach greatly alarmed the oil companies who had already invested large sums in North Sea exploration and development, incentivised by the relatively light tax regime under the outgoing Conservative Government – so light that it had been possible to offset profits against losses incurred in operations elsewhere and in debts to foreign governments. As a Parliamentary Committee pointed out in the early seventies, this generous tax pattern, if continued, could well result in no revenues at all reaching the British Government and people. The oil companies were therefore resigned to the prospect of a tougher and tighter tax regime but remained deeply worried as to the full implications of participation and what it might mean.

On the government side, it soon dawned on the new Labour administration (1974) that, despite the yearnings for 'full control' in practice it would be necessary to attract and depend upon vigorous private sector activity to extract the oil in novel and challenging conditions. So while the concept of government participation in oil production and sale was retained on a limited basis, the earlier dreams of an all-powerful and all-controlling state oil company were toned down sharply. The key question became therefore one of deciding what should be left to the operators and oil companies in the way of proceeds so as firstly to continue to attract oil companies world-wide to invest in the speedy development of the North Sea and secondly to cover fully the costs of discovery and identification of fields, development and production in a profitable manner and with an attractive rate of return. This meant first, devising a tax regime which the oil companies would accept generally as fair, and second, defining the degree of participation by the State and the machinery for exercising it.

Needless to say, views differed sharply on what the costs and the desirable rate of return ought to be. There was the added difficulty that since the North Sea was a new province, involving completely novel forms of development and production, no one knew what the costs of production might be or how they might vary as between the larger and more accessible fields and the smaller, deeper or more difficult ones. In deciding its tax 'take' or share the British government was therefore having in a sense to 'fly blind' and found itself in bitter arguments with investors and the oil industry.

At the outset the sheer complexity, riskiness and prolonged nature of the overall oil delivery sequence was simply not grasped by the policy-makers, let alone by the general public. The full set of phases, from exploration to development to production (and possibly to eventual decommissioning and abandonment) was outside the understanding of government officials, and the huge sums involved – up to $2 or $3 billion to bring a larger field to production – beyond official comprehension. Only after prolonged discussions, and as the full large scale of the infrastructure required for recovery of oil from deep under the North Sea floor became apparent, was a sensible balance found between the interests of the state and of the operators. Even then, the records show that different oil companies took very different views about the levels of tax proposed and the reliefs offered for the more difficult and smaller fields.

This is not the place to describe the full history and origins of the British petroleum tax regime as it first emerged in the early 1970s, although the details of the final (1974) package have been examined in an earlier chapter. But suffice it to say that very rough guesses had to be made about the levels of taxation the oil industry would tolerate and which would maintain incentives and momentum in the North Sea, and would stand the test of time.

The British experience shows that full public ownership and control was not the best path for the novel conditions and the fast development of the North Sea. But elsewhere, stronger impulses towards total state ownership and control have prevailed. This is because both political and geological priorities vary widely between different oil producing jurisdictions. History and experience also play their part. Thus in the Gulf region in the 1960s the mood was moving strongly in favour of total state control of all oil (and gas) resources and their extraction and production, both in reaction to a previous era in which it was believed that foreign interests (the IOCs) had been far too dominant and because there was no matching of the urgency evident in the North Sea (at least on the UK side). On the contrary, the emphasis was, and remains, far more on controlled depletion (keeping the resource in the ground) than on rapid development and production. Through the last quarter of the twentieth century the idea of surrendering any element of 'ownership' to outside interests therefore became less and less acceptable. This was the thinking behind the Saudi-Arabian ejection of American oil interests from the Aramco consortium. In Venezuela the same shift of direction is visible although the motives are different. There, the populist impulses of President Chavez have led to a rapid dismissal of foreign oil interests and the nationalisation of most oil assets in the name of the people. The language may be blunter and more ideological but the outcome is the same – national and indigenous ownership is asserted.

8.3 'WE WILL BE SAFE'

The second major influence governing the approach to petroleum taxation relates to the unique nature of the commodity. Second only to water, oil is the lifeblood of a society – certainly of a more developed modern society. The security of its supply is rightly deemed essential to national survival. The ownership of oil and other hydrocarbon resources by a country has therefore come to be seen as some sort of guarantor of energy security within that state.

This was certainly the case in the 1970s in the UK as North Sea oil production began to grow. With the country battered by coal strikes and with OPEC threatening not merely to raise crude prices by shutting up production, but also to impose actual embargoes on oil sales unless Western consumer countries took a firmer line against Israel, it was assumed that the possession of North Sea oil would insulate the British economy against shortages and oil price volatility. These assumptions were widely shared and deeply embedded in the public mind, and therefore influential in shaping oil policy, although they were in the British experience flawed and based on a fundamental misunderstanding of the nature of the world oil industry. Dependence on imported oil, and in particular oil from the hostile and unreliable Middle East and Arab world, could be minimised, so it was believed, so long as the oil companies were not allowed to 'steal' the oil and sell it elsewhere.

The story is told of how Edward Heath, the British Prime Minister in 1973 at the time of the first major oil crisis induced by OPEC action, summoned the leaders of major oil companies to his official country residence, Chequers, to seek assurances that whatever happened in the outside world, the UK would be 'alright' so far as oil supplies were concerned and that British oil consumers would have priority. He was said to have been dumbfounded to learn from the oil companies that this was not the case and that they, as North Sea producers, had the legal right to sell their oil wherever they chose in world markets. They had an obligation to land their oil on UK soil, but that was all. They could and would sell it where they wished. They had invested in the North Sea on the basis that it was an international oil province and that is what it remained. Mr. Heath was even more astonished to hear the chairman of BP, Sir Eric Drake, a company then 68 per cent owned by the British Government, take the same line. There could be no mistake. The British Government could take its 'share' of oil proceeds through taxation, but it had no legal control over the direction of oil sales.

The assumption that a country's oil resources give it added energy security is both natural and influential in the public attitude to oil companies, and therefore inevitably in the minds of politicians and policy makers. It gives rise to the idea that the public, or the state on the people's behalf, is entitled not merely to a share in the oil wealth but has some sort of right to the oil and its proceeds. Hence again the instinct to impose tax at the highest possible rate on oil-producing, oil-processing and oil-marketing entities.

8.4 BENEFITS FOR ALL?

A third major influence on the approach to petroleum fiscal policy has been the popular belief that oil wealth will bring easy benefits to all. Thus at the time of the expansion of North Sea production in the UK in the 1970s there was much talk of a North Sea 'bonanza'. The discussion was considerably amplified by prevailing conditions and public attitudes in the UK at the time. These were that the nation was in dire economic straits, that it was burdened with a large balance of payments deficit, a weak currency and an archaic economic structure in urgent need of reform. North Sea oil was depicted in the media as a special and fortuitous blessing and rescue prospect, 'manna from heaven' so to speak. Opinion formers confidently predicted that it would resuscitate the flagging British economy and almost literally 'lubricate' the necessary structural reforms required to enable the UK to compete internationally. It followed that as large a proportion as possible of the proceeds of North Sea oil should be appropriated by the government on behalf of the public purse and the people's welfare. Those responsible for designing and establishing the new fiscal regime for the North Sea therefore had to operate under these intense political pressures as they sought to balance a 'fair share' for the country against the need to maintain incentives and encourage the fastest possible development of North Sea resources.

The 'bonanza' attitude has not certainly been confined to the British experience. In many oil producing countries expanding oil production and revenues have raised high expectations, often magnified by extravagant promises from political figures. Countries like Venezuela provide a good example of what can, and does, happen. In extreme populist mode President Hugo Chavez has not only insisted that the oil companies sell out to the state on highly disadvantageous terms but promised that the wealth will be spread out as never before in the form of distributions of welfare and subsidies to the people. This is taking the concept of 'sharing' to its limits. It remains to be seen how long it will be before all investment in new fields, especially the Orinoco belt heavy mineral oil, slows to a total halt, and also what effect the new flows of 'easy' money will have on the rest of the Venezuelan economy.

In the main Middle-East oil producing states the 'sharing' concept is also deeply entrenched in a variety of forms, ranging from light or even zero tax levels on the general populace, to generous subsidies, notably on fuel itself and on oil and gas related power sources. Since oil revenues in, for example, the Gulf states, raised either by petroleum taxation or by direct appropriation where all oil is state-owned, support the entire budget, the need to 'visit' the public to raise taxes is minimised, as is also, therefore, the need for accountability on the part of the authorities for their expenditures and general use of funds. The commonest sharing device, and the one usually regarded as a virtual 'right' by the public, is heavily subsidised gasoline. For example, in Teheran the price was held for several years at eighteen cents a litre. The results have been highly predictable. Inflated demand, combined with severe under-investment in refining facilities, has led Iran, one of the world's largest oil producers, into heavy importing and rationing of refined oil products.

Behind all these dispositions, in which various governments find ways of both tapping their oil wealth and of at least appearing to share it widely, lies the so-called curse of oil syndrome. The chief features of this syndrome are, first, the widespread assumption that the money will always flow and therefore that the need for, and incentive to, promote diversification and new economic enterprises is minimal. Second, there is the tendency for these money flows to be held in government and official hands, or in the hands of those well-connected with power and authority. Third, there are the consequent sharp disparities in wealth between the fortunate beneficiaries of oil wealth flows and the general public. Fourth, the resultant tensions caused by very visible inequalities and by lack of balanced economic growth outside the oil and gas sectors provide fertile soil for political instability and discontent.

For these symptoms any attempts to divert a larger share of oil revenues away from the operators provide no remedies, since taking more from the oil producing sector can only mean more wealth in limited private hands. Pressure can be, and is, eased from time to time by distributive measures, through subsidies and 'free' energy, as described above, or through outright hand-outs to the public; but the basic and inherent imbalances of oil and gas dominated economies remain, unless and until corrected by falling oil output and consequently falling revenues.

Dubai and Bahrain both provide examples of a break from this paralysing pattern. Both countries have sought, with varying degrees of success, to diversify and create 'new' non-oil economies. Qatar has acted without waiting for the 'rainy day' of falling revenues. Still with hydrocarbon earnings at their height it has sought to 'share the wealth' from its gas operations between the inevitable very large concentrations in ruling family hands and the development of ambitious projects in the high-tech and educational fields intended to bring tangible benefits to its small population. Nevertheless, over all these arrangements a single question continues to hang, namely to what extent is 'the oil wealth' actually being shared with the public and the citizenry and how much is being diverted for private use or lost in general government budgetary deficits or expended on 'white elephant' public projects?

In the British case it was more a matter of using the new revenue flows to avert otherwise inevitable penalties, and to assist the public budget in financing and cushioning disruptive and painful structural changes, rather than producing some visible 'bonanza' – to the great disappointment of the taxpaying public who had been led to expect something juicier and more immediate. Angry demands arose to know 'where the oil wealth had gone'. In the case of less open societies the answers have been offered by pointing to heavy fuel subsidies, lavish infrastructural works, superbly equipped new hospitals, schools and universities. Whether this accounts for the full 'take' of revenues from indigenous oil activities remains obscure, and indeed elaborate measures are kept in place to keep it obscure. Whether the government authority's share is being secured through petroleum tax regimes, in the case of private sector companies, or through straight budgetary appropriation of surpluses, in the case of state-owned concerns, little is revealed which can provide a clear means of assessing whether the public are getting their share and how much is being either wasted or disappearing into the private bank accounts of high officials and rulers.

What can however be concluded is that in every oil province there is a public waiting to receive some benefits, and to raise the political temperature if they feel those benefits are not adequate. The grass roots pressure on policy-makers when it comes to formulating fiscal regimes for the oil companies is therefore invariably one way – take more. As the crude oil price rises this pressure rises also. The fact that the overall costs of the extraction process – research, discovery, development, production – may also be rising, interests the political and governing classes hardly at all.

8.5 REGIONAL RIVALRIES

A fourth key influence on petroleum fiscal policy and arrangements must be examined. This is where a dispute arises not only as to which parts of 'the State' should share the proceeds but also which different regions and societies within a nation state reckon that they are entitled to keep the largest share.

The argument always sounds a powerful one. Oil revenues, so it goes, secured by the State, through taxation or otherwise, should be used for the benefit of the peoples and regions from which the oil comes. In the UK North Sea case this debate surfaced in virulent form over Scotland's 'share'. Separatists and nationalists were anyway looking for arguments to support Scotland's retirement from the Union and its return to its ancient independent state. They therefore clamoured loudly for near-punitive tax rates on North Sea production and for a much larger share of total proceeds to be directed towards Scotland's needs. The bulk of the oil, they argued, lay in Scottish and not British waters. The debate continues, if anything with rising intensity as nationalist political fortunes in Scotland have flourished and oil companies have reported giant profit increases.

But Scotland is not the only place where bitter regional feuds are driven by oil prospects. At least in part the horrific tribal conflicts in the Darfur region of Western Sudan are driven by oil revenue greed and arguments as to the destination of oil revenues. Wars in Somalia have oil motives, as they have had in Angola. Russian federal politics are heavily influenced by arguments over oil proceeds, with oil-producing areas, such as for instance Tartarstan, furiously contesting the demands of the central Moscow authorities for revenues. Elsewhere in the fractious Caucasus conflicts tend to be about oil and gas transmission, rather than production, but the principle is the same – local claims for benefits versus central desires for revenues. Most vividly of all, the oil resources of Iraq are a source of intense regional rivalries and divisive influences which add further to the threats of national disintegration. In the north the Kurds lay claim to the rich Kirkuk fields while in the south Shia dominated areas assert their claim to what they see as their oil. Those in the middle areas, and around Baghdad, fear that in any break up, or loose federal arrangement, they might be left with little or nothing – a fear which plays a central part in the struggle of the Iraqi authorities to set up a balanced new oil industry structure and petroleum taxation regime.

8.6 CONCLUSION

We have analysed four major influences on the formation of petroleum industry taxation – the deep-rooted belief that oil belongs to the state and the people, the conviction that indigenously produced oil provides energy security, the hopes that oil revenues will provide easy living and the potential for regional disputes over the proceeds.

We may conclude from this analysis that petroleum tax regimes are born out of circumstances and that these circumstances are invariably highly political. The popular notion is that oil belongs to the people and that the oil recovery and extracting industries should therefore be pushed to the edge in yielding up the proceeds of their activities. The 'fair' share for the sovereign power should be very large and the amount left to the operating entities, whether private companies or state-owned bodies, should be cut to the bare minimum.

This unavoidable political pressure creates for those designing and implementing petroleum tax systems intensely difficult dilemmas. No set of government ministers, whether autocratic, democratic or something in between, can afford to be seen as 'soft' on oil companies or to be backward in claiming their country's full share of oil revenues. Further pressures to be 'tough' come from the mounting political influence of green lobbies and those concerned with climate change and the effects of ever-growing fossil fuel burning. The oil companies and their profits make one more easy target in the search for environmental 'villains' – an image which the companies themselves have struggled to shake off by investing increasingly in 'green' and renewable energy technologies

Hence, while the policy-maker knows that a balance is essential between, on the one hand tax take, and on the other hand incentives for companies to operate in what is a high risk business requiring the prospect of high returns, the nature of politics creates a constant and growing bias towards tipping the balance in the state's favour, and therefore the constant danger of 'killing the goose which lays the golden eggs', or to put it less picturesquely, of simply driving away the oil companies. Few politicians, and even fewer members of the general public, are interested in such matters as marginal fields, rising costs and real life challenges facing oil companies, and very few appreciate the enormous investment risks involved in the search for and production of crude oil, especially in testing environments such as deep sea regions or very hot or very cold climates.

It is the unenviable task of policy-makers to stand between vociferous public opinion and the iron laws of investment. Too weak an outcome and the policy-makers can find themselves dismissed, or worse. Too tough a pressure and the oil companies slide away to easier provinces elsewhere. Somewhere in between is the ideal balance, regarded as 'fair and reasonable' by both sides, but as difficult to find is the optimum or ideal petroleum tax structure itself, as explained in Chapter 2.

Yet it is a search that no government authority in any country which seeks a healthy and expanding oil and gas sector, and clear benefits for its peoples, can afford for one moment to abandon.

9 Sharing the wealth

The way forward

9.1 SOME GUIDING AXIOMS

The chief aim of preceding chapters has been to show that petroleum taxation is a subject of great complexity and variety, and subject to continued evolution. It is surrounded and shaped by multi-facetted geological, technical, and market factors together with unstable and unpredictable political influences. Many substantial and probably insurmountable obstacles lie in the way of an ideal petroleum fiscal system. It has yet to be invented and probably never will be.

As long as oil remains a major and increasingly scarce source of energy, the issue of the tax 'take' and of the balance between government desire for revenue and the industry's appetite for investment coupled with attractive returns, will remain central to the public debate.

Government and oil companies are the principal players in the upstream sector of the petroleum industry, but their individual focus is one of competing rather than complementary objectives, though the balance varies from basin to basin. Governments normally seek to generate high levels of take from oil related activity while oil companies want to ensure an appropriate, predictable and sufficient level of profitability in their operations. Since taxation removes a considerable slice of the producers' profits, oil companies prefer fiscal systems that result in a low overall tax level thereby allowing high post-tax returns. The challenge is to design a fiscal regime that meets those two competing objectives. Further, several complications are associated with petroleum taxation.

The principal source of complication is related to the determination of economic rent. Measuring economic rent requires knowledge of the differing costs of the individual factors of production as well as their opportunity costs. The difficulty in measuring each of these components is what makes the determination of economic rent and its capture difficult and controversial. Further, because the size of a given discovery and its related exploitation costs can vary substantially, economic rent will vary from field to field. Although this problem can be partly overcome by a progressive tax system, it is difficult to make conventional fiscal systems sufficiently flexible and focused on resource rent across a wide range of unpredictable parameters.

An ideal tax exists just in theory, but is a useful paradigm against which to test actual or proposed fiscal systems. Controversy will always prevail since there is no objective yardstick that determines sharing the oil wealth between the government and the industry. But fiscal terms could be tailored in such a way as to be attractive for both large as well as small discoveries while safeguarding the economic long-term interests of the oil companies.

To illustrate and delineate these issues, as well as to establish valid and worthwhile conclusions and guideposts for future policy, we have both examined the theory and underlying mechanics of petroleum taxation and visited a range of existing petroleum tax regimes around the world, both established and in the process of development. We have also been able to look in detail at the history and particular circumstances lying behind them. This has enabled us to tabulate the varying experiences of the tax policy-makers and their political overlords, identifying both the flaws encountered in their evolution and the useful lessons to be learned for policy-makers in the future, as they design new regimes (as, for instance, in Iraq) or seek to improve existing ones.

A further section of the overall picture has been provided by drawing comparisons between various petroleum tax systems and assessing their effectiveness in both raising revenue and satisfying the needs and best interests of both national governments and the operatives and enterprises engaged in oil extraction. Working on a hypothetical basis, tax scenarios have been applied to a variety of conditions in selected countries so as to examine 'what if' outcomes (Chapter 6). Alternative evaluation and computation methods have also been tested over the same ground (Chapter 7). In earlier chapters, the conventional distinctions in relations between the official state and the oil companies are examined and analysed, and it is shown how in practice these become easily blurred, with conditions in particular as between oil companies on contract from the state to produce oil, and oil companies awarding concessions to exploit given territory (under licence), often overlapping.

A particular emphasis has been placed on the sequential and also very risky nature of the oil industry everywhere. The successive phases of identification of possible deposits, exploration, development – where that exploration yields positive results – and finally production and transmission to refiners and markets, are each in themselves significant processes demanding the highest degree of specialist skills and, in a sense, constituting separate, although clearly connected, industrial processes. In each phase the risks are different, the technology is different and the operating conditions are different. And so, too, are the investment conditions and investor attitudes which drive the whole industry forward.

Applying a regime focussed entirely on end revenues to such a diffuse set of processes, spread out usually over a prolonged timescale, and where the costings are often no more than guesswork, although always tempting for governments and tax authorities, invites considerable dangers and prospects of unintended consequences. The text (Chapter 4) draws particular attention to the British experience on this front where, as the North Sea opened up, the authorities attempted to apply a tax regime which would balance fairly the claims of the state with the returns required by the industry and its investors.

Certain guiding axioms emerge clearly from our overall appraisal which it is useful to summarise.

There is a paramount need for fiscal stability

If anything, the general trend in the twenty-first century has been towards more fiscal instability driven by sharp swings in oil prices. Again and again governments succumb to the temptation to change tax levels and structures simply in response to oil price changes, the assumption being that higher crude prices must mean higher returns to the oil companies. As has been shown, that is not necessarily the case. Parallel cost increases can cancel out revenue increases, and often do.

Stability is an intangible yet crucial attribute of a fiscal regime. It directly affects the confidence of investors in government policy, particularly in the case of petroleum extraction activity, where long-term projects are the norm. New oil field developments take two to seven years to bring into production and will be producing for 10–25 years. Consequently, such investment decisions are not driven by short-term oil and gas price movements, but instead by the longer term perspective on prices. The project will have to be sufficiently robust to endure many commodity price cycles during its life cycle. Fiscal policy, which focuses on 'creaming off' rent at the peak of the each cycle whilst ignoring the pain of the troughs, is unlikely to attract and sustain a basin's full investment potential.

Regime modifications should not be undertaken on a frequent basis nor be of a major or structural nature nor undertaken without advanced warning, as they can negatively affect investors' confidence. Oil prices are volatile and it is almost impossible to track every change. If a government introduces fiscal changes based on high oil prices, then it could be argued that they should consider the corollary – namely that it should reduce tax rates if oil prices fall. However, our examination suggests that a wiser policy would be to accept that short-term fluctuations in oil prices should not be the basis for the application of fiscal changes. Uncertainty regarding future global oil resources and economics is so significant that the EIA (2005) considered a wide range of potential world oil price paths, which in 2030 range from \$34 to \$96 per barrel. Short-term oil prices change generally in response to 'news'. As such they rarely take account of the supply/demand balance, which in any case is unknown at the time. Consequently, using the oil price as the basis for taxation is simply inappropriate.

If governments are unable to deliver fiscal stability for political and constitutional reasons then the additional fiscal risk created will be required to be remunerated via a higher return to investors. Therefore unstable fiscal regimes will in the long run be required to offer to investors a lower level of government take than if more stability was on offer.

In evaluating a fiscal regime, looking only at the level of tax rates can be very misleading

One cannot make judgements about the effectiveness or strengths of a fiscal regime, simply by looking at the tax rate. Several factors, such as fiscal reliefs and the process of calculating the tax base, can lead to significant differences among fiscal packages, while different structures and regimes can produce the same results in terms of revenue and tax 'take'.

What works in one country does not necessarily work in another

A high level of government take is not prudent in cases of high-risk exploration and high-cost development, or for those provinces with remaining modest petroleum potential, as is the case in the UKCS. The cost of producing oil can overwhelm any price incentive. Large price incentives are needed to increase production while the costs of production are rising. As Chapter 4 demonstrates, in the case of the UKCS there are still substantial volumes to come. But this situation requires very large investment, given the rising costs and the shrinking of fields' size.

The appropriate regime would improve the profitability of marginal fields in order to persuade oil companies to develop these discoveries. In countries where oil production has started to decline, fiscal regimes can be tuned to compensate for the decline in production by encouraging existing and new companies to sustain production and develop the remaining less profitable fields

Oil ownership tends to be a legal and political rather than an economic issue

As discussed in Chapter 8 the ownership of oil resources in the ground or under the seabed is more or less a closed and settled issue (except in the USA). However, differences of view persist about the desirable degree of state 'ownership' in oil at the wellhead, and in the various stages of oil production and on the role private enterprise should play. Moreover opinion about the amount of private involvement can vary over time, as popular impulses to 'own' the entire oil industry process in a producing country clash with the realisation that private sector skills are needed to get the oil out.

As has been shown, similar economic outcomes can be achieved under different tax regimes and different patterns of relations between governments and oil operatives, depending on how the regime is structured and how the fiscal terms are set.

Petroleum taxation – its structure, levels and general stability of application – is a key factor in affecting oil and gas activity at all stages

There are, evidently, many other factors which shape the activity and development of an oil province, the geology being the fundamental one but such things as the crude oil price, current and expected, and the availability of new technology also being significant. But the crucial point is that tax is the only factor which is under direct government control. It is the 'sharp instrument' which decides. Public ownership, nationalisation, part ownership (as with the UK's participation model in the 1970s) can all change perceptions, and give the illusion of State control. But when it comes to the key economics of oil field investment, development and production, it is through the tax system that real control can be exercised, regardless of who owns what in legal terms.

9.2 FINAL NOTE

Throughout this work we have returned again and again to the underlying states of mind, or philosophies, which govern the entire industry and provide the raison d'etre for the main features and characteristics of petroleum taxation – notably that the oil 'belongs' to the state (and the people), that the industries, enterprises and other entities concerned with its extraction and marketing are 'different' from all other industries and that the total 'take' by the state, whether via straightforward taxation or other means, should therefore be much higher than is the norm with company and industry taxation. These are the embedded assumptions underlying the overall concept of 'fair shares', and 'sharing the oil wealth', and they are, certainly, open to a number of different interpretations – interpretations which may vary according to the wider political and social mood in a society at any one time, and may also vary through time as perceptions – and hard facts such as the crude oil price – change.

It has to be kept at the forefront of the reader's mind that the global processes which constitute the oil industry are undergoing very rapid change, driven by technology, by geology, by geo-politics and to some extent by ideology. As the Preface to this volume observes, the old multi-national oil companies are having to adjust their role as the younger national oil companies exert their muscle and spread their ambitions outside their home territories. The so-called 'easy' oil of the vast Middle East deposits may well be running down (although more slowly than some pessimists predict) but the 'new' oil is getting both more costly to extract (despite cost-reducing technologies) from remoter areas, more risky in geo-political terms and more jealously guarded by its nation state proprietors.

Attitudes can naturally change over time, swinging to and fro, and have done so in the twentieth century. In the twentieth century era of the legendary Seven Sister major international oil companies the mood swung from, first, acquiescence and even welcome in oil producing countries for the outsiders with their vast capital resources and access to technology, and then sharply against them in the 1960s–1990s as nationalist instincts mounted and leaders in the traditional oil-producing countries became convinced that they could 'do it all themselves'. While this remains the dominant doctrine the policy pendulum has now swung marginally back in some producer governments towards recognition of the need for an enhanced role once again for the IOCs, although a different one from the past, combined also with recognition that national oil companies need to spread their wings and become global players.

Finally, full account has also to be taken of fast-changing attitudes to fossil fuel consumption generally and rising concerns both about shorter term global pollution and longer term climate change dangers. While it is easy to make too much of these, and to dramatise changing attitudes as leading to 'the end of oil', the arrival of an age of zero carbon emissions and the like, it is certainly the case that the planet's energy mix is changing and that the familiar pattern of the last century or so of petroleum dominance across the whole energy spectrum may be giving way to a radical rebalancing of both world energy supplies and world energy consumption. But the view amongst some governments that in order to promote renewable forms of energy, taxes from oil and gas activity should be increased and hypothecated to fund the deployment of the greener energy sources. This adds further complexity to the role and purpose of oil and gas taxation.

All these factors, and many more, make the art of establishing and applying an appropriate petroleum tax framework ever more demanding and requiring an even more sensitive and flexible appreciation of the industry and its ways. Controversy about taxation will always prevail and will be the constant plaything of shifting government priorities and political pressures. It will always be in the nature of subjects such as taxation of oil companies that short term objectives, being pursued by transient politicians, will clash with longer term aims, with governments torn between the hunger for immediate revenues and the inclination to keep the precious oil resource in the ground through careful depletion policies – always the much preferred option in the countries with the largest reserves such as Saudi-Arabia.

If this volume can contribute to an understanding of these deeply complex issues, which embed a volatile and increasingly unpredictable blend of conflicting objectives, political desires and practical ambitions, then it will have done its modest job.

Notes

1 Petroleum taxation: art and science

1 As referred to in Crossman (2004), p.12.

2 The taxation of oil: theoretical background

1 HM Treasury and Customs, 2006.
2 Taxation is one of the mechanisms by which the government attempts to capture economic rent from petroleum activity. Other mechanisms, such as competitive bidding, also known as auction licencing, can be used. 'Competitive bidding in the absence of collusion should lead to the state's receiving a large part of any economic rent accruing from oil and gas production' (Robinson and Morgan, 1978, p.193). But competitive bidding can deal with foreseeable rent and not with unexpected rent.
3 The introduction of a new energy producing sector can affect other sectors in the economy. The discovery of natural gas in the Netherlands in the 1960s had adverse effects on the Dutch manufacturing sector, mainly through the appreciation of the real exchange rate. By the end of the 1970s, when the high gas income from the gas resources fell, the (uncompetitive) traditional industries could not compensate for the loss of revenues from the energy sector and as a consequence unemployment rose. For this reason, the negative consequence for traditional industries of a natural resource discovery has commonly been referred to as the Dutch disease in the economic literature.
4 The theory of optimal taxation concentrates primarily on personal income taxes and focuses on the effects of taxation on households rather than producers. A detailed discussion of optimal taxation theory can be found in Ramsey (1927), Diamond and Mirrlees (1971a, b), Dasgupta and Stiglitz (1971), Samuelson (1986), and Heady (1993). Altay (2000) presents a detailed summary of the different studies on optimal tax theory.
5 Garnaut and Clunies, A.R. 1983, p. 26.
6 The concept of risk is discussed in more detail in Chapter 6.
7 Andrews-Speed, 1998, p.14.
8 Watkins, 2001, p.17.
9 Detailed study is done by Raja (1999), also refer to Smith (1999) and Bond *et al* (1987).
10 Dickson, 1999, p.1.
11 Banfi et al., 2003, p.2.
12 Kooten and Bulte, 2001, p.65.
13 Raja, 1999, p.2.

14 For a more detailed analysis of international tax systems, namely Concessionary and Contractual systems, see Chapter 3.
15 Stiegeler, 1985, p.376.
16 After its proposer Brown (1948).
17 See Chapter 3, China Sliding Scale Royalty.
18 Explained in detail in Chapter 5.

3 Comparing fiscal regimes

1 Nicholas Kaldor's tax reform proposals were addressed primarily to improving the equity of direct taxation. But his proposals often took a näive view of the potential for improved tax administration and failed to come to terms with political realities.
2 Johnston, 2001.
3 Blinn et al (1986).
4 Johnston (2001).
5 For a detailed analysis see Chapter 4.
6 Robinson and Morgan (1978), Robinson and Rowland (1978), Brent (1991), Quinlan (1998).
7 Norwegian Petroleum Directorate, 2007.
8 EU Commission, 2006.
9 EIA, 2007.
10 Barrows, 2000, p.105.
11 Johnston, 2001.

4 The UK petroleum fiscal regime

1 A detailed numeric computation of the tax instruments is carried out in Chapter 5.
2 The department became 'Department for Business, Enterprise and Regulatory Reform' in 2007.
3 Entitled 'United Kingdom Offshore Oil and Gas Policy'.
4 Before 1975, there were two elements of the UK North Sea fiscal regime: Royalty charged at 12.5 per cent and Corporation Tax charged at 50 per cent. The Oil Taxation Act (1975) established the Petroleum Revenue Tax and the main regulations governing the administration of the tax.
5 Royalty is not charged on a field but on the licence. In general, there is no difference between the field and the licence but there are several cases where a licence covers more than one field or where a field extends into the area covered by more than one licence. For reasons of simplicity, it will be assumed that there is no difference between the field and the licence.
6 This difference is explained in more detail in Chapters 5 and 6, where Australia PRT is compared with the UK PRT.
7 OGJ, 1993c.
8 In 2003, the UK Government abolished PRT on tariffs receipts. In fact, a field, which is liable to PRT and provides services in relation to another field, had to pay PRT on the tariffs received from the new field. However, with the 2003 changes, such payments were abolished on new business.
9 HM Treasury and Customs, 2006.
10 Nelsen, 1991, p.143.
11 As referred to in Miller (2000).
12 See Chapter 3.
13 UK Oil and Gas, as of 2006.
14 Rowland, 1983, p.235.

15 Robinson and Morgan, 1978, p.201.
16 UKOG, 1984, p.1.
17 As referred to in Rowland (1983), p.1.
18 Watkins, 2000.
19 Recoverable reserves are 'that proportion of the oil and gas in the reservoir that can be removed using currently available techniques' (DTI, Oil and Gas Glossary, 2003).
20 Reuters, 2004, p.1.

5 The economics of petroleum projects

1 We should distinguish between commercial success rate and technical success rate. Global exploration commercial success rate over the period 1994–2003 was 17 per cent, compared with 32 per cent global technical success rate (including non-commercial discoveries) for the same period. Onshore, the difference is narrow, but offshore the difference tends to be more significant, as many discovered fields are not big enough to develop.
2 In some countries, like the UK, the exploration, appraisal and development stages are incorporated into one single stage, the exploration stage, which covers broadly the period from the obtaining of the licence to the time when a decision is made to develop, or not, a field.
3 Oil Industry Accounting Committee, 2003.
4 Appendix B illustrates the computation of each tax and NCF of an oil field under the UK petroleum fiscal regime.
5 Devereux and Morris (1983) assume that the conveying and treating costs represent 37.6 per cent of capital expenditure depreciated over 8 years (i.e. 4.7 per cent of CAPEX per year) and 4.5 per cent of operating costs. As such, the authors represent the Royalty take in a given period t as in the following:

$$ROY_t = (R_t - (0.047^* \Sigma\ CE_t) - (0.045^* OE_t))^* 0.125$$

6 However, the introduction of the Cross Field Allowance (CFA) in 1987, enabling 10 per cent of the development costs on a new field to be offset against PRT liabilities on another field operated by the same company, was one of the exceptions to the general principle that PRT is a field-based tax.
7 Unrelieved costs are carried forward for relief in subsequent years.
8 The rate was initially 75 per cent but it was reduced to 35 per cent in 1979.
9 The government refunds prior period tax payments.
10 Before 1979, 500,000 tonnes of oil were allowed for each period with a maximum cumulative allowance of 10 million tonnes.
11 Losses are cumulative negative cash flows.
12 'This was aimed at preventing companies manipulating their levels of borrowing between ring fence and non-ring fence activities to minimize the impact of the supplementary charge' (Inland Revenue, 2003).
13 The computation of the other structures is the same. The two differences are: 1. No Royalty applies, 2. ST is calculated on the same basis as CT, with the exception that financing costs are not allowed for deduction.
14 For a detailed example see Appendix C.
15 For a detailed example see Appendix D.
16 Based on 1990 PSC model.
17 For an applied example see Appendix C.
18 See Chapter 3.
19 Based on 1996 PSA.
20 For an applied example see Appendix C.

21 See Chapter 3, Table 3.2.
22 See Table 3.3, Chapter 3.
23 Based on the year 2000 Buyback model.
24 For an applied example see Appendix C.
25 Among others, Robinson and Morgan (1978), Rowland (1983), Rowland and Hann (1987), Kemp and Rose (1982), Kemp and Stephens (1997), and Martin (1997).
26 Chapter 7 explores other financial evaluation techniques.
27 Other methods include the Internal Rate of Return (IRR) and Discounted Payback method.
28 A dollar that is paid or received today is not the same as a dollar that is paid or received in a years time. This difference is recognised and accounted for by the time value of money concept.
29 Kemp et al (1997), express the EMV by the following:

$$EMV = p_s NPV - (1 - p_s)EC$$

Where:

- p_s is the probability of success.
- EC the exploration costs.

30 See survey undertaken in 1998 by Mohiuddin and Ash-Kuri on 30 companies. 83 per cent of these maintained that prospectivity was the most important factor in their investment decisions, while fiscal terms came close second at 80 per cent and political stability third. In practice of course the investor has to have a firm hold on all these factors, and many others besides.

6 Regimes and outcomes

1 Except Argyll field, which was decommissioned in 1992, but it is included in the fields' sample as a model field that can represent the production life cycle of many very small newly developed fields.
2 Fields' cost and production database, including past and prospective information, are provided by the Global Economic Model (GEM), which is an Excel spreadsheet economic evaluation tool developed by WoodMackenzie, a well-established consultancy company in the E&P sector of the petroleum industry.
3 See Chapter 4.
4 For instance, in the UK, to compute CT taxable profit, a company's profit in a particular field is equal to its interest in that field multiplied by the profit generated (after deduction of PRT, if it applies). A company's assessable profit for CT is the sum of different profits from each of the fields it holds an interest.
5 BP Statistical Review, 2005.
6 See Kemp and Rose (1983), Rowland (1983), Kemp and Stephens (1997), Martin (1997) and Bradley (1998).
7 Johnston, 2002, p.25.

7 Other financial evaluation techniques

1 The DCF technique can be more sophisticated, but in this book a more simplistic version of the technique is followed, as adopted in majority of previous studies.
2 Among others, Robinson and Morgan (1978), Rowland (1983), Rowland and Hann (1987), Kemp and Rose (1982), Kemp and Stephens (1997), and Martin (1997).

3 The term 'project' in this book refers to an oilfield.
4 See Chapter 6.
5 Ibid.
6 The concept of flexibility is discussed in detail in Section 6.3.
7 The risk is also called non-diversifiable, systemic, market or macro-eoconomic risks because it is correlated with the overall economy and cannot be completely removed by diversification strategy.
8 The risk is also called diversifiable, non-systemic, local, private or project-specific risks, because it is not correlated with the overall economy and can be removed almost completely by diversification strategy, of course if the company has sufficient size to pursue diversification.
9 See section on oil price model.
10 See Section below.
11 For further detail see Appendix F.
12 Dixit and Pindyck, 1994, p.75.
13 Under the assumption of Mean Reversion Model for oil prices, the variance is given by:

$$v\,(P_t - P') = \frac{\sigma^2}{2\lambda}(1 - e^{-2\lambda t}) \qquad (7.13)$$

14 For a detailed explanation see Appendix F.
15 See Paddock et al (1988), Pindyck (1988), Dixit and Pindyck (1994) and Lund (2001).
16 A half-life of five yeas for the mean reversion of oil prices was assumed by Laughton and Jacoby (1992) and Emhjellen and Alaouze (2001) and is the value estimated by Pindyck (1997, p.7).
17 As assumed by Jacoby and Laughton (1992), Laughton (1997) and Emhjellen (1999).
18 See Section 6.2.1.
19 Emhjellen, 1999, p.59.
20 Among others, Dixit and Pindyck (1994), Laughton (1998), Laughton et al (2000), Zettl (2002), and Dias (2001).
21 This analogy is developed in Section 7.3.2.
22 Emhjellen, 1999, p. 59.
23 See Chapter 2.
24 Dixit and Pindyck, 1995, p.113.
25 See Chapter 6.
26 Pike and Neale, 1996, p.319.
27 This example is adapted from Bodie and Merton (2000).
28 Dixit and Pindyck, 1995, p.113.
29 For a field life cycle, See Chapter 5.
30 When development plans are made, exploration and appraisal costs are considered as sunk costs and are normally disregarded. At the production stage, operators may choose to wait (i.e. temporarily stop production) if, for instance, oil prices decline. In this case, although there are no direct costs associated with the decision to wait, the operator is still faced with the fixed operating costs, hence making postponing production less attractive. Furthermore, as Lund (1987) argued, the economic significance of flexibility at the abandonment stage is small. However, one should also consider that companies may have contractual arrangements that limit their choice; another problem can also occur when reservoir ownership is divided and agreement is required among the parties.
31 See Appendix F for a review of the Black-Scholes model.

32 As referred to by Bodie and Merton (2000), p.400.
33 When the lease must be given back to the government because the development of the project has not been undertaken (Emhjellen, 1999, p.69).
34 Adapted from Dias (2001).
35 I'_{et} is equivalent to the exercise price, E, in the case of a financial option, as assumed on p. 208.
36 For a derivation of this equation see Appendix D.
37 For an explanation, see Appendix D.
38 See Section 7.3.2.
39 Adapted from Dias (2001).
40 See Section 7.2.
41 As defined in Section 7.2.

Appendix E Oil price model

1 Adapted from Baker et al. (1998) and Emhjellen (1999).

Appendix F The black-scholes model

1 Adapted from Bodie and Merton (2000).
2 Adapted from Dias (2001) and Emhjellen (1999).

Glossary

Abandon: To cease work on a well, which is non-productive. Also used in the context of field abandonment.

Abandonment Allowance: An allowance for expenditure incurred in respect of abandoning a field.

Appraisal Expenditure: Costs incurred in survey, exploitation and appraisal of licence areas not yet under development or in production.

Appraisal Well: A well drilled as part of an appraisal drilling programme which is carried out to determine the physical extent, reserves and likely production rate of a field.

Barrel: A unit of volume measurement used for petroleum and its products 7.5 barrels = 1 ton.

Barrel of Oil Equivalent (boe): A term used to express the gas volume in terms of its energy equivalent in barrels of oil; 6 thousand cubic feet of gas equals 1 bbl of crude oil.

bbl: Abbreviation of one barrel of oil.

b/d: Abbreviation of barrel per day.

bn: Abbreviation of billion.

bnbbl: Abbreviation of billion of barrels.

bnbbloe: Abbreviation of billion barrels of oil equivalent.

bnt: Abbreviation of billion tonnes.

Commercial Discovery: The term applies to any discovery that would be economically feasible to develop under a given fiscal system. A field that satisfied these conditions would then be granted commercial status, and the contractor would then have the right to develop the field.

Commercial field: Field judged to be capable of producing sufficient net income to be worth developing.

Concession: An agreement between a government and a company that grants the company the right to explore for, develop, produce, transport, and market hydrocarbons or minerals within a fixed area for a specific amount of time. The concession and production and sale of hydrocarbons from the concession is then subject to rentals, royalties, bonuses, and taxes.

Under a concessionary agreement the company would hold title to the resources that are produced.

Contractor: An oil company operating in a country under a production sharing contract or a service contract on behalf of the host government for which it receives either a share of production or a fee.

Contractor take: The total contractor after-tax share of profits.

Cost of Capital: The minimum rate of return on capital required to compensate debt holders and equity investors for bearing risk. Cost of capital is computed by weighting the after-tax cost of debt and equity according to their relative proportions in the corporate capital structure.

Cost Oil: A term most commonly applied to production sharing contracts which refers to the oil (or revenues) used to reimburse the contractor for exploration costs, development capital costs, and operating costs.

Cross Field Allowance (CFA): An element of immediate relief qualifying field development costs where a participator on a new taxable development has, or expects to have, profits in another taxable field.

Decommissioning: Term used for the re-use, recycling and disposal of redundant oil and gas facilities.

Development expenditure: All costs including financing costs, E&A expenditures incurred in bringing a field to commercial production and is defined as tangible assets.

Development Phase: The phase in which a proven oil or gas field is brought into production by drilling production (development) wells.

Discovery: An Exploration well which has encountered hydrocarbons.

Enhanced Oil Recovery: A process whereby oil is recovered other than by natural pressure in a reservoir.

Entitlements: The shares of production to which the operating company and the government or government agencies are authorized to lift. Generally, legal entitlement equals profit oil plus cost oil in a PSC.

Exploration drilling: Drilling carried out to determine whether hydrocarbons are present in a particular area or structure.

Exploration expenditure: All costs, including premium payments, associated with acquisition of new acreage, drilling of exploratory wells and other costs incurred in evaluating commercial viability of geological entities.

Exploration phase: The phase of operations which covers the search for oil or gas by carrying out detailed geological and geophysical surveys followed up where appropriate by exploratory drilling.

Exploration well: A well in an unproven area or prospect, may also be known as a 'wildcat well'.

Field: A geographical area under which an oil or gas reservoir lies.

Fiscal System: Technically, the legislated taxation structure for a country including royalty payments. The term includes all aspects of contractual and fiscal elements that make up a given government-foreign oil company relationship.

Gold Plating: When a company or contractor makes unreasonably large expenditures due to lack of cost-cutting incentives. This kind of behaviour could be encouraged where a contractor's compensation is based in part on the level of capital and operating expenditure.

Government Take: The total government share of profit oil or revenues not associated with cost recovery. Same as government after-tax equity split and government marginal take.

Incentives: Fiscal or contractual elements emplaced by host governments that make petroleum exploration or development more economically attractive. Includes such things as tax credits, lower government take, uplift, and investment credit.

Investment Credit: A fiscal incentive where the government allows a company to recover an additional percentage of tangible capital expenditure.

M: Abbreviation of million.

mmbbl: Abbreviation of million barrels.

mmbbl/d: Abbreviation of million barrels per day.

mmboe: Abbreviation of million barrels oil equivalent.

Mt: Abbreviation of million tonnes.

Marginal Field: A field that may not produce enough net income to make it worth developing at a given time; should technical or economic conditions change, such a field may become commercial.

Oil Allowance: A gross production relief that reduces effective PRT rate, but cannot be used to create a loss.

Oil Equivalent: Used when adding together volumes of oil, gas and NGL. It is defined as the energy obtained from burning the various types of petroleum. One tonne of oil equivalent = one tonne of oil = 100 cubic meters of natural gas.

Oil Taxation Act (OTA): Came into force in 1975, introducing PRT.

Operator: The company that has legal authority to drill wells and undertake production of hydrocarbons are found.

Operating Profit (or Loss): The difference between business revenues and the associated costs and expenses exclusive of interest or other financing expenses, and extraordinary items, or ancillary activities. Synonymous with net operating profit (or loss), operating income (or loss), and net operating income (or loss).

Petroleum: A generic name for hydrocarbons, including crude oil, natural gas liquids, natural gas and their products.

Possible Reserves: Those reserves which at present cannot be regarded as 'probable' but are estimated to have a significant but less than 50 per cent chance of being technically and economically producible.

Probable Reserves: Those reserves which are not yet proven but which are estimated to have a better than 50 per cent chance of being technically and economically producible.

Progressive Taxation: Where tax rates increase as the basis to which the tax increases. Or where tax rates decrease as the basis decreases. The opposite of regressive taxation.

Proven Field: An oil and/or gas field whose physical extent and estimated reserves have been determined.

Proven Reserves: Those reserves that on the available evidence are virtually certain to be technically and economically producible (i.e. having a better than 90 per cent chance of being produced).

Recoverable Reserves: That proportion of the oil and/gas in a reservoir that can be removed using currently available techniques.

Ring-fencing: A cost centre based fiscal device that forces contractors or concessionaries to restrict all cost recovery and or deductions associated with a given license (or sometimes a given field) to that particular cost centre. The cost centres may be individual licenses or on a field-by-field basis. For example, exploration expenses in one non-producing block could not be deducted against income for tax calculations in another block. Under PSC, ring-fencing acts in the same way; cost incurred in one ring fenced block cannot be recovered from another block outside the ring fence.

Royalty payments: As part of some early UKCS licence round conditions there was an obligation to pay a royalty on 'value of the petroleum' which is deductible in computing PRT and CT.

Significant Discovery: A DTI definition of a well which flow tested, or would have flowed, at a rate of 1000 barrels of oil a day or 15 million cubic feet of gas a day.

Sliding Scales: A mechanism in a fiscal system that increases effective taxes and/or royalties based upon profitability or some proxy for profitability, such as increased levels of oil or gas production.

UKOOA: Abbreviation of United Kingdom Oil Offshore Association.

Uplift: Common terminology for a fiscal incentive whereby the government allows the contractor to recover some additional percentage of tangible capital expenditure.

List of acronyms

APRT	Advance Petroleum Revenue Tax
BT	Brown Tax
CAPEX	Capital Expenditures
CFA	Cross Field Allowance
CIT	Corporate Income Tax
CT	Corporation Tax
DAPT	Derivative Asset Pricing Theory
DCF	Discounted Cash Flow
DMO	Domestic Market Obligation
E and A	Exploration and Appraisal
E and P	Exploration and Production
EIA	Energy Information Administration
FTP	First Tranche Petroleum
FYA	First Year Allowance
GBM	Geometric Brownian Motion with Drift
GR	Gross Royalty
HRIT	Higher Rates of Proportional Income Tax
IOCs	International Oil Companies
IT	Income Tax
MAP	Modern Asset Pricing
MRPs	Mean Reverting Processes
NCF	Net Cash Flow
NPV	Net Present Value
OPEX	Operating Expenditures
PRRT	Petroleum Resource Rent Tax
PRT	Petroleum Revenue Tax
PSA	Production-Sharing Agreement
PSC	Production-Sharing Contract
PSCs	Production-Sharing Contracts
RDF	Risk Discount Factor
ROT	Real Options Theory
ROY	Royalty
RRT	Resource Rent Tax

RSA	Risk Service Agreement
SPD	Supplementary Petroleum Duty
SPT	Special Petroleum Tax
ST	Supplementary Tax
T&R	Tax and Royalty regimes
TDF	Time Discount Factor
UKCS	United Kingdom Continental Shelf
VAT	Value Added Tax
WDA	Writing Down Allowance

Appendices

Appendix A

Example of post tax NCF of an oil field under a concessionary regime

Year	*Production* *000b/d* *(A)*	*Oil Price* *£/bbl* *(B)*	*Revenues* *£M* *(C)*	*Total OPEX* *£M* *(D)*	*Total CAPEX* *£M* *(E)*	*Pre-tax NCF* *£M* *(F)*	*Total Gov Take* *£M* *(G)*	*Post-Tax NCF* *£M* *(H)*	*Real NCF* *£M* *(I)*
2002	0.0	13.0	0.0	0.0	110.0	−110.0	0.0	−110.0	−110.0
2003	0.0	13.3	0.0	0.0	235.0	−235.0	0.0	−235.0	−229.2
2004	0.0	13.7	0.0	0.0	220.0	−220.0	0.0	−220.0	−209.3
2005	44.0	14.0	224.8	54.0	50.0	120.8	2.5	118.3	109.7
2006	69.5	14.4	364.0	58.7	25.0	280.3	25.7	254.6	230.4
2007	70.0	14.7	375.8	58.8	58.0	259.0	49.6	209.4	184.8
2008	92.0	15.1	506.3	66.8	73.0	366.5	231.9	134.5	115.8
2009	81.0	15.5	456.9	68.4	121.0	267.4	202.1	65.4	54.9
2010	73.4	15.9	424.3	69.3	37.0	318.0	217.0	100.9	82.6
2011	77.6	16.3	460.1	65.7	11.0	383.4	314.2	69.3	55.3
2012	78.2	16.7	474.7	63.9	70.0	340.8	277.3	63.5	49.5
2013	74.0	17.1	460.7	64.1	50.9	345.7	281.1	64.6	49.0
2014	86.0	17.5	548.8	72.4	10.4	466.0	385.0	81.0	60.0
2015	74.0	18.0	484.0	68.8	5.4	409.8	335.4	74.4	53.8
2016	60.0	18.4	402.3	63.1	0.0	339.2	273.1	66.1	46.6
2017	48.0	18.9	329.9	57.4	0.0	272.5	214.4	58.1	39.9
2018	42.0	19.4	295.8	49.4	0.0	246.5	203.3	43.2	29.0
2019	34.0	19.9	245.5	48.5	0.0	197.0	172.2	24.8	16.2
2020	29.0	20.4	214.6	46.8	0.0	167.8	146.7	21.1	13.5
2021	25.0	20.9	189.6	47.3	0.0	142.4	124.5	17.9	11.1

2022	23.5	21.4	182.7	41.9	0.0	140.8	123.2	17.7	10.7
2023	22.0	22.0	175.3	34.9	0.0	140.5	122.8	17.6	10.4
2024	0.0	22.5	0.0	0.0	110.0	−110.0	−94.2	−15.8	−7.9
2025	0.0	23.1	0.0	0.0	0.0	0.0	0.0	0.0	0.0
Totals:	1103.2		6816.2	1100.1	1186.7	4529.4	3607.8	921.6	666.9

(A) Daily oil production in 000bbl
(B) Base Brent oil price of \$19.5/bbl, constant exchange rate of US \$1.5 = £1STG and constant inflation rate of 2.5%
(C) Annual oil revenue in £M, where: (C) = (A) × (B) ×365/1000
(D) Operating expenditures in £M
(E) Capital expenditures in £M
(F) Pre-tax NCF = (C) – (D) – (E)
(G) Total Government take = Royalty + Special tax + Income tax
(H) Post-tax NCF = (F)–(G)
(I) Real post-tax NCF = (H)/Inflation factor

Appendix B

Example of tax take computation in the UKCS

(Based on the 1975 structure)

Table B1 Pre-tax & post-tax net cash flow

Year	*Production 000bl/d (A)*	*Oil Price £/bbl (B)*	*Revenues £M (C)*	*Total OPEX £M (D)*	*Total CAPEX £M (E)*	*Pre-tax NCF £M (F)*	*Total Gov Take £M (G)*	*Post-Tax NCF £M (H)*	*Real NCF £M (I)*
2002	0.0	13.0	0.0	0.0	110.0	–110.0	0.0	–110.0	–110.0
2003	0.0	13.3	0.0	0.0	235.0	–235.0	0.0	–235.0	–229.2
2004	0.0	13.7	0.0	0.0	220.0	–220.0	0.0	–220.0	–209.3
2005	44.0	14.0	224.8	54.0	50.0	120.8	2.5	118.3	109.7
2006	69.5	14.4	364.0	58.7	25.0	280.3	25.7	254.6	230.4
2007	70.0	14.7	375.8	58.8	58.0	259.0	49.6	209.4	184.8
2008	92.0	15.1	506.3	66.8	73.0	366.5	231.9	134.5	115.8
2009	81.0	15.5	456.9	68.4	121.0	267.4	202.1	65.4	54.9
2010	73.4	15.9	424.3	69.3	37.0	318.0	217.0	100.9	82.6
2011	77.6	16.3	460.1	65.7	11.0	383.4	314.2	69.3	55.3
2012	78.2	16.7	474.7	63.9	70.0	340.8	277.3	63.5	49.5
2013	74.0	17.1	460.7	64.1	50.9	345.7	281.1	64.6	49.0
2014	86.0	17.5	548.8	72.4	10.4	466.0	385.0	81.0	60.0
2015	74.0	18.0	484.0	68.8	5.4	409.8	335.4	74.4	53.8
2016	60.0	18.4	402.3	63.1	0.0	339.2	273.1	66.1	46.6
2017	48.0	18.9	329.9	57.4	0.0	272.5	214.4	58.1	39.9
2018	42.0	19.4	295.8	49.4	0.0	246.5	203.3	43.2	29.0
2019	34.0	19.9	245.5	48.5	0.0	197.0	172.2	24.8	16.2

2020	29.0	20.4	214.6	46.8	0.0	167.8	146.7	21.1	13.5
2021	25.0	20.9	189.6	47.3	0.0	142.4	124.5	17.9	11.1
2022	23.5	21.4	182.7	41.9	0.0	140.8	123.2	17.7	10.7
2023	22.0	22.0	175.3	34.9	0.0	140.5	122.8	17.6	10.4
2024	0.0	22.5	0.0	0.0	110.0	–110.0	–94.2	–15.8	–7.9
2025	0.0	23.1	0.0	0.0	0.0	0.0	0.0	0.0	0.0
Totals:	1103.2		6816.2	1100.1	1186.7	4529.4	3607.8	921.6	666.9

(A) Daily oil production in 000bbl
(B) Base Brent oil price of $19.5/bbl, constant exchange rate of US $1.5 = £1STG and constant inflation rate of 2.5%.
(C) Annual oil revenue in £M, where: (C) = (A) × (B) × 365/1000
(D) Operating expenditures in £M
(E) Capital expenditures in £M
(F) Pre-tax NCF = (C) – (D) – (E)
(G) Total Government take = Royalty + PRT + CT (See tables 2–6)
(H) Post-tax NCF = (F)–(G)
(I) Real post-tax NCF = (H)/Inflation factor

Table B2 PRT calculation (part 1)

Year	*Period*	*Revenues* *£M* *(J)*	*Royalty* *£M* *(K)*	*Total OPEX* *£M* *(L)*	*Total CAPEX* *£M* *(M)*	*Uplift 35%* *£M* *(N)*	*Net Profit 1* *£M* *(O)*	*Cumulative Losses* *£M* *(P)*	*Loss c/f Set-Off* *£M* *(Q)*	*Net Profit 2* *£M* *(R)*
2002	1	0.0	0.0	0.0	25.0	8.8	–33.8	–33.8	0.0	0.0
2002	2	0.0	0.0	0.0	85.0	29.8	–114.8	–148.5	0.0	0.0
2003	1	0.0	0.0	0.0	125.0	43.8	–168.8	–317.3	0.0	0.0
2003	2	0.0	0.0	0.0	110.0	38.5	–148.5	–465.8	0.0	0.0
2004	1	0.0	0.0	0.0	115.0	40.3	–155.3	–621.0	0.0	0.0
2004	2	0.0	0.0	0.0	105.0	36.8	–141.8	–762.8	0.0	0.0
2005	1	71.6	0.0	25.6	35.0	12.3	–1.2	–764.0	0.0	0.0
2005	2	153.4	2.5	28.5	15.0	5.3	102.2	–661.7	102.2	0.0
2006	1	178.3	12.4	29.2	15.0	5.3	116.4	–545.3	116.4	0.0
2006	2	186.2	13.3	29.5	10.0	3.5	129.9	–415.5	129.9	0.0
2007	1	190.9	15.3	29.5	27.5	9.6	109.0	–306.5	109.0	0.0
2007	2	185.5	15.5	29.3	30.5	10.7	99.6	–206.9	99.6	0.0
2008	1	259.1	22.5	33.6	33.0	11.6	158.4	–48.5	158.4	0.0
2008	2	248.1	20.5	33.2	40.0	14.0	140.4	0.0	48.5	91.9
2009	1	248.7	15.9	34.2	72.5	0.0	126.1	0.0	0.0	126.1
2009	2	209.1	9.0	34.2	48.5	0.0	117.5	0.0	0.0	117.5
2010	1	212.9	11.1	34.7	21.0	0.0	146.1	0.0	0.0	146.1
2010	2	212.4	17.1	34.7	16.0	0.0	144.6	0.0	0.0	144.6
2011	1	247.0	23.4	32.8	6.0	0.0	184.8	0.0	0.0	184.8
2011	2	214.3	20.8	32.8	5.0	0.0	155.7	0.0	0.0	155.7
2012	1	232.4	22.3	31.9	32.5	0.0	145.8	0.0	0.0	145.8
2012	2	243.7	23.0	31.9	37.5	0.0	151.3	0.0	0.0	151.3
2013	1	231.1	23.4	31.9	27.8	0.0	148.0	0.0	0.0	148.0
2013	2	231.1	23.4	32.3	23.1	0.0	152.4	0.0	0.0	152.4
2014	1	275.4	28.4	36.0	5.2	0.0	205.8	0.0	0.0	205.8
2014	2	275.4	28.4	36.4	5.3	0.0	205.4	0.0	0.0	205.4
2015	1	243.0	24.9	34.2	2.7	0.0	181.2	0.0	0.0	181.2

2015	2	243.0	25.0	34.6	2.7	0.0	180.7	0.0	0.0	180.7
2016	1	202.0	20.4	31.3	0.0	0.0	150.2	0.0	0.0	150.2
2016	2	202.0	20.5	31.7	0.0	0.0	149.8	0.0	0.0	149.8
2017	1	165.7	16.8	28.5	0.0	0.0	120.3	0.0	0.0	120.3
2017	2	165.7	17.1	28.9	0.0	0.0	119.7	0.0	0.0	119.7
2018	1	148.7	15.5	24.5	0.0	0.0	108.6	0.0	0.0	108.6
2018	2	148.7	15.5	24.8	0.0	0.0	108.3	0.0	0.0	108.3
2019	1	127.0	12.9	24.1	0.0	0.0	90.0	0.0	0.0	90.0
2019	2	119.8	12.0	24.4	0.0	0.0	83.4	0.0	0.0	83.4
2020	1	111.6	11.2	23.3	0.0	0.0	77.2	0.0	0.0	77.2
2020	2	104.2	10.3	23.6	0.0	0.0	70.4	0.0	0.0	70.4
2021	1	99.2	9.7	23.5	0.0	0.0	66.0	0.0	0.0	66.0
2021	2	91.6	8.7	23.8	0.0	0.0	59.0	0.0	0.0	59.0
2022	1	93.9	9.4	20.8	0.0	0.0	63.7	0.0	0.0	63.7
2022	2	90.0	8.8	21.1	0.0	0.0	60.1	0.0	0.0	60.1
2023	1	88.2	9.1	17.3	0.0	0.0	61.9	0.0	0.0	61.9
2023	2	88.2	9.0	17.5	0.0	0.0	61.7	0.0	0.0	61.7
2024	1	0.0	0.0	0.0	110.0	0.0	–110.0	0.0	0.0	0.0
2024	2	0.0	0.0	0.0	0.0	0.0	0.0	0.0	0.0	0.0
Totals		6839.2	605.0	1100.1	1186.7	269.9	3677.5		764.0	3787.5

(J) Oil revenues per 6-month period
(K) Royalty = 12.5 per cent × (J) – C&T costs.
The Conveying & Treating (C&T) Costs are approximately 70% of the CAPEX of the platform depreciated over eight years or the life of the field, whichever is the shorter, 60% of total platform operating costs and 100% of the costs of transportation.
(L) Operating expenditures per 6-month period
(M) Capital expenditures per 6-month period
(N) Uplift = 35% × (M).
It applies until the field reaches payback (i.e. when Net Profit 2 (R) turns positive).
(O) Net Profit 1 = (J) – (K) – (L) – (M) – (N)
(P) Cumulative losses = Losses in period t + losses from period t–1
(Q) Losses carried-forward: when Net Profit 1 (O) turns positive, Cumulative losses (P) start to be written off. Any loss, which is not written off, is carried forward to the following period, until all losses are written off (in this case, in year 2008).
(R) Net Profit 2 = Net-Profit 1 after all losses are written off.

Table B3 PRT calculations

Net Profit 2 *£M* *(R)*	*Oil Allowance* *£M* *(S)*	*Taxable Profit* *£M* *(T)*	*PRT Rate* *%* *(U)*	*Mainstream PRT* *£M* *(V)*	*Safeguard Limit* *£M* *(W)*	*Base PRT* *£M* *(X)*	*PRT Loss Repayment* *£M* *(Y)*	*PRT Paid* *£M* *(Z)*
0.0	0.0	0.0	70	0.0	0.0	0.0	0	0.0
0.0	0.0	0.0	70	0.0	0.0	0.0	0	0.0
0.0	0.0	0.0	70	0.0	0.0	0.0	0	0.0
0.0	0.0	0.0	70	0.0	0.0	0.0	0	0.0
0.0	0.0	0.0	70	0.0	0.0	0.0	0	0.0
0.0	0.0	0.0	70	0.0	0.0	0.0	0	0.0
0.0	0.0	0.0	70	0.0	0.0	0.0	0	0.0
0.0	0.0	0.0	70	0.0	0.0	0.0	0	0.0
0.0	0.0	0.0	70	0.0	0.0	0.0	0	0.0
0.0	0.0	0.0	70	0.0	0.0	0.0	0	0.0
0.0	0.0	0.0	70	0.0	0.0	0.0	0	0.0
0.0	0.0	0.0	70	0.0	0.0	0.0	0	0.0
0.0	0.0	0.0	70	0.0	0.0	0.0	0	0.0
91.9	28.3	63.6	70	44.5	63.0	44.5	0	44.5
126.1	29.0	97.0	70	67.9	66.3	66.3	0	66.3
117.5	29.0	88.4	70	61.9	40.3	40.3	0	40.3
146.1	29.8	116.4	70	81.5	41.2	41.2	0	41.2
144.6	29.8	114.9	70	80.4	36.0	36.0	0	36.0
184.8	30.5	154.3	70	108.0	0.0	108.0	0	108.0
155.7	30.5	125.2	70	87.6	0.0	87.6	0	87.6
145.8	31.3	114.5	70	80.1	0.0	80.1	0	80.1
151.3	31.3	120.0	70	84.0	0.0	84.0	0	84.0
148.0	32.1	115.9	70	81.2	0.0	81.2	0	81.2
152.4	32.1	120.3	70	84.2	0.0	84.2	0	84.2
205.8	32.9	172.9	70	121.1	0.0	121.1	0	121.1
205.4	32.9	172.5	70	120.7	0.0	120.7	0	120.7
181.2	33.7	147.5	70	103.3	0.0	103.3	0	103.3

180.7	33.7	146.9	70	102.8	0.0	102.8	0	102.8
150.2	34.6	115.6	70	80.9	0.0	80.9	0	80.9
149.8	34.6	115.2	70	80.6	0.0	80.6	0	80.6
120.3	35.5	84.9	70	59.4	0.0	59.4	0	59.4
119.7	35.5	84.3	70	59.0	0.0	59.0	0	59.0
108.6	36.4	72.2	70	50.6	0.0	50.6	0	50.6
108.3	0.0	108.3	70	75.8	0.0	75.8	0	75.8
90.0	0.0	90.0	70	63.0	0.0	63.0	0	63.0
83.4	0.0	83.4	70	58.4	0.0	58.4	0	58.4
77.2	0.0	77.2	70	54.0	0.0	54.0	0	54.0
70.4	0.0	70.4	70	49.3	0.0	49.3	0	49.3
66.0	0.0	66.0	70	46.2	0.0	46.2	0	46.2
59.0	0.0	59.0	70	41.3	0.0	41.3	0	41.3
63.7	0.0	63.7	70	44.6	0.0	44.6	0	44.6
60.1	0.0	60.1	70	42.0	0.0	42.0	0	42.0
61.9	0.0	61.9	70	43.3	0.0	43.3	0	43.3
61.7	0.0	61.7	70	43.2	0.0	43.2	0	43.2
0.0	0.0	0.0	70	0.0	0.0	0.0	77	–77.0
0.0	0.0	0.0	70	0.0	0.0	0.0	0	0.0
3787.5	643.5	3144.0		2200.8	246.7	2092.9	77	2015.9

(R) Net Profit 2 = Net-Profit 1 after all losses are written off (as calculated in Table 2).
(S) The Oil Allowance starts to apply when Net Profit 2 becomes positive.
For detailed computation of the allowance, see Table 4.
(T) Taxable Profit = (R) – (S)
(U) PRT rate that applies to the taxable profit (T)
(V) Mainstream PRT = (U) × (V)/100

At this stage the Safeguard applies. This is a form of tapering relief.

(W) Safeguard Limit. For detailed computations of the Safeguard, see Table 5
(X) Base PRT: During the period where the Safeguard applies (the period until the field has reached payback plus half of that number of periods), the mainstream PRT (V) is compared with the Safeguard limit (W). The field pays whichever is less.
(Y) PRT loss repayment represents the repayment of Abandonment costs.
(Z) PRT paid = (X) – (Y)

Table B4 Oil allowance calculation

Year	*Period*	*Oil Product. Mmbbl (AA)*	*Oil Rev. £M (J)*	*Allow. 1 period (BB)*	*Allow. Available Bbl (CC)*	*Total Available £ (DD)*	*Allow. Utilized £ (EE)*	*Allow. Utilized bbl (FF)*	*Cumulative Allow. Utilized bbl (GG)*
2002	1	0.0	0.0	1.9	0.0	0.0	0.0	0.0	0.0
2002	2	0.0	0.0	1.9	0.0	0.0	0.0	0.0	0.0
2003	1	0.0	0.0	1.9	0.0	0.0	0.0	0.0	0.0
2003	2	0.0	0.0	1.9	0.0	0.0	0.0	0.0	0.0
2004	1	0.0	0.0	1.9	0.0	0.0	0.0	0.0	0.0
2004	2	0.0	0.0	1.9	0.0	0.0	0.0	0.0	0.0
2005	1	5.1	71.6	1.9	0.0	0.0	0.0	0.0	0.0
2005	2	11.0	153.4	1.9	0.0	0.0	0.0	0.0	0.0
2006	1	12.4	178.3	1.9	0.0	0.0	0.0	0.0	0.0
2006	2	13.0	186.2	1.9	0.0	0.0	0.0	0.0	0.0
2007	1	13.0	190.9	1.9	0.0	0.0	0.0	0.0	0.0
2007	2	12.6	185.5	1.9	0.0	0.0	0.0	0.0	0.0
2008	1	17.2	259.1	1.9	1.9	0.0	0.0	0.0	0.0
2008	2	16.4	248.1	1.9	1.9	28.3	28.3	1.9	1.9
2009	1	16.1	248.7	1.9	1.9	29.0	29.0	1.9	3.8
2009	2	13.5	209.1	1.9	1.9	29.0	29.0	1.9	5.6
2010	1	13.4	212.9	1.9	1.9	29.8	29.8	1.9	7.5
2010	2	13.4	212.4	1.9	1.9	29.8	29.8	1.9	9.4
2011	1	15.2	247.0	1.9	1.9	30.5	30.5	1.9	11.3
2011	2	13.2	214.3	1.9	1.9	30.5	30.5	1.9	13.1
2012	1	13.9	232.4	1.9	1.9	31.3	31.3	1.9	15.0
2012	2	14.6	243.7	1.9	1.9	31.3	31.3	1.9	16.9
2013	1	13.5	231.1	1.9	1.9	32.1	32.1	1.9	18.8
2013	2	13.5	231.1	1.9	1.9	32.1	32.1	1.9	20.6
2014	1	15.7	275.4	1.9	1.9	32.9	32.9	1.9	22.5
2014	2	15.7	275.4	1.9	1.9	32.9	32.9	1.9	24.4
2015	1	13.5	243.0	1.9	1.9	33.7	33.7	1.9	26.3

2015	2	13.5	243.0	1.9	1.9	33.7	33.7	1.9	28.1
2016	1	11.0	202.0	1.9	1.9	34.6	34.6	1.9	30.0
2016	2	11.0	202.0	1.9	1.9	34.6	34.6	1.9	31.9
2017	1	8.8	165.7	1.9	1.9	35.5	35.5	1.9	33.8
2017	2	8.8	165.7	1.9	1.9	35.5	35.5	1.9	35.6
2018	1	7.7	148.7	1.9	1.9	36.4	36.4	1.9	37.5
2018	2	7.7	148.7	0.0	0.0	0.0	0.0	0.0	0.0
2019	1	6.4	127.0	0.0	0.0	0.0	0.0	0.0	0.0
2019	2	6.0	119.8	0.0	0.0	0.0	0.0	0.0	0.0
2020	1	5.5	111.6	0.0	0.0	0.0	0.0	0.0	0.0
2020	2	5.1	104.2	0.0	0.0	0.0	0.0	0.0	0.0
2021	1	4.7	99.2	0.0	0.0	0.0	0.0	0.0	0.0
2021	2	4.4	91.6	0.0	0.0	0.0	0.0	0.0	0.0
2022	1	4.4	93.9	0.0	0.0	0.0	0.0	0.0	0.0
2022	2	4.2	90.0	0.0	0.0	0.0	0.0	0.0	0.0
2023	1	4.0	88.2	0.0	0.0	0.0	0.0	0.0	0.0
2023	2	4.0	88.2	0.0	0.0	0.0	0.0	0.0	0.0
2024	1	0.0	0.0	0.0	0.0	0.0	0.0	0.0	0.0
2024	2	0.0	0.0	0.0	0.0	0.0	0.0	0.0	0.0
Totals		402.7	6839.2			643.5	643.5	37.5	

(AA) Oil production in Million Barrels per six-month period. It is equal to daily production (A) × (365/2)/1000

(J) Similar to revenues as determined in Table 2

(BB) Oil Allowance per period is limited to a maximum of 250,000 tonne.
As 1tonne = 7.5 bbl, the Oil Allowance per period is 250×7.5/1000 = 1.9.

(CC) The available Oil Allowance per period depends on the oil production per period (AA):
- If (BB) > (AA), the Oil Allowance available is equal to (AA)
- If (BB) < (AA), the Oil Allowance available is equal to (BB)

(DD) Oil Allowance per period expressed in £.

(EE) Oil Allowance utilised in £. The Oil Allowance per period (DD) is compared with Net Profit 2 (R):
- If (DD) < (R), then the Oil Allowance utilised in £ is equal to (DD)
- If (DD) > (R), then the Oil Allowance utilised in £ is equal to (R).

(FF) The Oil Allowance utilised is expressed in Barrels.

(GG) The cumulative Oil Allowance utilised. When it reaches 37.5 (=7.5bbl×5Mt, where 5 Mt is the maximum cumulative Oil Allowance available for an oil field), the Oil Allowance relief stops applying

Table B5 safeguard calculation

Year	*Period*	*Adjusted Profit £M (HH)*	*Payback £M (II)*	*Safeguard Base £M (JJ)*	*Safeguard Period (KK)*	*Safeguard Limit £M (W)*
2002	1	0.0	−33.8	25.0	0.0	0.0
2002	2	0.0	−148.5	110.0	0.0	0.0
2003	1	0.0	−317.3	235.0	0.0	0.0
2003	2	0.0	−465.8	345.0	0.0	0.0
2004	1	0.0	−621.0	460.0	0.0	0.0
2004	2	0.0	−762.8	565.0	0.0	0.0
2005	1	46.0	−764.0	600.0	0.0	0.0
2005	2	122.5	−661.7	615.0	0.0	0.0
2006	1	136.7	−545.3	630.0	0.0	0.0
2006	2	143.4	−415.5	640.0	0.0	0.0
2007	1	146.1	−306.5	667.5	0.0	0.0
2007	2	140.7	−206.9	698.0	0.0	0.0
2008	1	203.0	−48.5	731.0	0.0	0.0
2008	2	194.4	91.9	771.0	0.0	63.0
2009	1	198.6	218.0	771.0	1.0	66.3
2009	2	166.0	335.4	771.0	2.0	40.3
2010	1	167.1	481.6	771.0	3.0	41.2
2010	2	160.6	626.2	771.0	4.0	36.0
2011	1	190.8	811.0	771.0	0.0	0.0
2011	2	160.7	966.8	771.0	0.0	0.0

(HH) The Adjusted Profit = Revenues (J) – Royalty (K) – OPEX (L)

(II) The payback period, *K*, can be found as the minimum value of *K* for which the following relationship is satisfied:

$$\sum_{t=1}^{K} (R_t - ROY_t - OE_t) > \sum_{t=1}^{K} CE_t(1 + up_t)$$

As such, 2008 is the year during which the field reaches payback. From the start of production, payback is reached after eight periods (four years) therefore the Safeguard will apply for four additional periods (two years), until 2010.

(JJ) Safeguard base is the cumulative Capital Expenditures (M)

(KK) Safeguard period is the period during which the Safeguard applies. It is equal to the Payback period (from the startg of production) plus half of that period.

(W) Safeguard limit = 80%× [(HH)–15%× (JJ)] (see Table 3). The Safeguard limit is then compared to the mainstream PRT as calculate in Table 2 (V):

- If (HH) < 15 per cent of (JJ), no PRT is paid.
- If (HH) > 15 per cent of (JJ), mainstream PRT is compared to the Safeguard limit (W) and the company pays whichever is the smaller amount.

Table B6 Corporation tax calculation

Rev *£M* *(J)*	*Roy.* *£M* *(K)*	*Total OPEX* *£M* *(L)*	*Capital Allow.* *£M* *(LL)*	*PRT Paid* *£M* *(Z)*	*Pre-Tax Income* *£M* *(MM)*	*Cum. Losses* *£M* *(NN)*	*Loss c/f Set-Off* *£M* *(OO)*	*Taxable Income* *£M* *(PP)*	*CT Rate* *%* *(QQ)*	*CT* *£M* *(RR)*	*CT Loss Repay* *£M* *(SS)*	*CT Paid* *£M* *(TT)*
0.0	0.0	0.0	25.0	0.0	−25.0	−25.0	0.0	0.0	52	0.0	0.0	0.0
0.0	0.0	0.0	85.0	0.0	−85.0	−110.0	0.0	0.0	52	0.0	0.0	0.0
0.0	0.0	0.0	125.0	0.0	−125.0	−235.0	0.0	0.0	52	0.0	0.0	0.0
0.0	0.0	0.0	110.0	0.0	−110.0	−345.0	0.0	0.0	52	0.0	0.0	0.0
0.0	0.0	0.0	115.0	0.0	−115.0	−460.0	0.0	0.0	52	0.0	0.0	0.0
0.0	0.0	0.0	105.0	0.0	−105.0	−565.0	0.0	0.0	52	0.0	0.0	0.0
71.6	0.0	25.6	35.0	0.0	11.0	−554.0	11.0	0.0	52	0.0	0.0	0.0
153.4	2.5	28.5	15.0	0.0	107.5	−446.5	107.5	0.0	52	0.0	0.0	0.0
178.3	12.4	29.2	15.0	0.0	121.7	−324.8	121.7	0.0	52	0.0	0.0	0.0
186.2	13.3	29.5	10.0	0.0	133.4	−191.5	133.4	0.0	52	0.0	0.0	0.0
190.9	15.3	29.5	27.5	0.0	118.6	−72.8	118.6	0.0	52	0.0	0.0	0.0
185.5	15.5	29.3	30.5	0.0	110.2	0.0	72.8	37.4	52	19.4	0.0	19.4
259.1	22.5	33.6	33.0	0.0	170.0	0.0	0.0	170.0	52	88.4	0.0	88.4
248.1	20.5	33.2	40.0	44.5	109.9	0.0	0.0	109.9	52	57.1	0.0	57.1
248.7	15.9	34.2	72.5	66.3	59.7	0.0	0.0	59.7	52	31.1	0.0	31.1
209.1	9.0	34.2	48.5	40.3	77.2	0.0	0.0	77.2	52	40.2	0.0	40.2
212.9	11.1	34.7	21.0	41.2	104.9	0.0	0.0	104.9	52	54.6	0.0	54.6
212.4	17.1	34.7	16.0	36.0	108.6	0.0	0.0	108.6	52	56.5	0.0	56.5
247.0	23.4	32.8	6.0	108.0	76.8	0.0	0.0	76.8	52	39.9	0.0	39.9
214.3	20.8	32.8	5.0	87.6	68.1	0.0	0.0	68.1	52	35.4	0.0	35.4
232.4	22.3	31.9	32.5	80.1	65.6	0.0	0.0	65.6	52	34.1	0.0	34.1
243.7	23.0	31.9	37.5	84.0	67.3	0.0	0.0	67.3	52	35.0	0.0	35.0
231.1	23.4	31.9	27.8	81.2	66.9	0.0	0.0	66.9	52	34.8	0.0	34.8
231.1	23.4	32.3	23.1	84.2	68.2	0.0	0.0	68.2	52	35.5	0.0	35.5
275.4	28.4	36.0	5.2	121.1	84.8	0.0	0.0	84.8	52	44.1	0.0	44.1
275.4	28.4	36.4	5.3	120.7	84.6	0.0	0.0	84.6	52	44.0	0.0	44.0

243.0	24.9	34.2	2.7	103.3	78.0	0.0	0.0	78.0	52	40.6	0.0	40.6
243.0	25.0	34.6	2.7	102.8	77.8	0.0	0.0	77.8	52	40.5	0.0	40.5
202.0	20.4	31.3	0.0	80.9	69.3	0.0	0.0	69.3	52	36.0	0.0	36.0
202.0	20.5	31.7	0.0	80.6	69.1	0.0	0.0	69.1	52	36.0	0.0	36.0
165.7	16.8	28.5	0.0	59.4	60.9	0.0	0.0	60.9	52	31.7	0.0	31.7
165.7	17.1	28.9	0.0	59.0	60.8	0.0	0.0	60.8	52	31.6	0.0	31.6
148.7	15.5	24.5	0.0	50.6	58.0	0.0	0.0	58.0	52	30.2	0.0	30.2
148.7	15.5	24.8	0.0	75.8	32.5	0.0	0.0	32.5	52	16.9	0.0	16.9
127.0	12.9	24.1	0.0	63.0	27.0	0.0	0.0	27.0	52	14.0	0.0	14.0
119.8	12.0	24.4	0.0	58.4	25.0	0.0	0.0	25.0	52	13.0	0.0	13.0
111.6	11.2	23.3	0.0	54.0	23.2	0.0	0.0	23.2	52	12.0	0.0	12.0
104.2	10.3	23.6	0.0	49.3	21.1	0.0	0.0	21.1	52	11.0	0.0	11.0
99.2	9.7	23.5	0.0	46.2	19.8	0.0	0.0	19.8	52	10.3	0.0	10.3
91.6	8.7	23.8	0.0	41.3	17.7	0.0	0.0	17.7	52	9.2	0.0	9.2
93.9	9.4	20.8	0.0	44.6	19.1	0.0	0.0	19.1	52	9.9	0.0	9.9
90.0	8.8	21.1	0.0	42.0	18.0	0.0	0.0	18.0	52	9.4	0.0	9.4
88.2	9.1	17.3	0.0	43.3	18.6	0.0	0.0	18.6	52	9.6	0.0	9.6
88.2	9.0	17.5	0.0	43.2	18.5	0.0	0.0	18.5	52	9.6	0.0	9.6
0.0	0.0	0.0	110.0	–77.0	–33.0	0.0	0.0	–33.0	52	0.0	17.2	–17.2
0.0	0.0	0.0	0.0	0.0	0.0	0.0	0.0	0.0	52	0.0	0.0	0.0
6839.2	605.0	1100.1	1186.7	2015.9	1931.5		565.0	1931.5		1021.5	17.2	1004.4

(LL) Capital Allowances providing 100% deduction of CAPEX (M)
(MM) Pre-tax Income = J – K– L– AL– Z
(NN) Cumulative Losses = Losses in period t + losses from period t–1
(OO) Losses carried-forward: when the pre-tax income (MM) becomes positive, Cumulative losses (NN) start to be written off. Any loss, which is not written off, is carried forward to the following period, until all losses are written off (in this case, in year 2007).
(PP) Taxable Income = pre-tax income (MM) after all losses are written off.
(QQ) CT rate
(RR) CT income = (QQ) × (PP)
(SS) Loss repayment represents the relief for Abandonment costs
(TT) CT paid = (RR) – (SS)

Appendix C

International comparison

Table C1 Oil field pre-tax NCF

Year	*Period*	*Total Production 000b/d (A)*	*Revenue £M (B)*	*Total Opex £M (C)*	*Total Capex £M (D)*	*Pre-tax NCF £M (E)*	*Real NCF £M (F)*	*Discounted Pretax CF £M (G)*
2002	0	0.0	0.0	0.0	0.0	0.0	0.0	0.0
2003	1	0.0	0.0	0.0	55.0	–55.0	–53.6	–48.5
2004	2	0.0	0.0	0.0	70.0	–70.0	–66.6	–54.5
2005	3	25.0	127.9	39.1	60.0	28.8	26.7	19.8
2006	4	34.0	178.3	43.7	15.0	119.6	108.2	72.5
2007	5	35.5	190.9	40.2	0.0	150.7	133.0	80.6
2008	6	33.5	184.7	39.2	0.0	145.5	125.2	68.7
2009	7	32.0	180.9	38.5	0.0	142.4	119.5	59.4
2010	8	35.5	205.7	40.2	5.0	160.5	131.4	59.1
2011	9	31.5	187.2	38.2	10.0	138.9	110.9	45.1
2012	10	24.0	146.2	34.5	0.0	111.7	87.0	32.0
2013	11	24.5	153.0	49.3	0.0	103.8	78.8	26.2
2014	12	26.7	171.1	27.7	0.0	143.4	106.2	32.0
2015	13	21.3	139.9	30.2	5.0	104.7	75.7	20.6
2016	14	17.4	117.3	53.1	5.0	59.2	41.7	10.3
2017	15	20.0	138.1	43.1	7.0	88.0	60.5	13.5
2018	16	20.0	141.6	21.7	10.0	109.9	73.6	14.9
2019	17	19.0	137.9	20.4	1.0	116.5	76.2	13.9
2020	18	17.0	126.5	21.2	1.0	104.4	66.5	11.0

2021	19	14.0	106.8	21.9	1.0	83.9	52.2	7.8
2022	20	11.0	86.1	20.1	1.0	65.0	39.4	5.3
2023	21	9.0	72.2	18.7	1.0	52.5	31.1	3.8
2024	22	8.0	65.8	17.9	1.0	46.9	27.0	3.0
2025	23	7.0	59.0	17.2	1.0	40.8	23.0	2.3
2026	24	6.0	51.9	16.4	0.0	35.5	19.5	1.8
2027	25	6.0	53.2	16.7	0.0	36.5	19.5	1.6
2028	26	5.0	45.4	16.4	0.0	29.0	15.2	1.1
2029	27	5.0	46.6	16.8	0.0	29.8	15.2	1.0
2030	28	0.0	0.0	0.0	40.0	–40.0	–19.9	–1.2
2031	29	0.0	0.0	0.0	0.0	0.0	0.0	0.0
Totals:		487.9	3114.2	742.4	289.0	2082.7	1523.1	503.1

Table C2 Oil field under Australian regime

Year	PRRT calculations						CIT Calculations				
	Gross Revenues £M (H)	*Comp. CAPEX £M (I)*	*Loss CF £M (J)*	*Taxable Income (K)*	*PRRT at 40% (L)*	*Dep. £M (M)*	*Taxable Income £M (N)*	*CT at 30% £M (O)*	*Gov. Take £M (P)*	*Real NCF Post-tax £M (Q)*	*Disc.NCF Post-tax £M (R)*
2002	0.0	0.0	0.0	0.0	0.0	0.0	0.0	0.0	0.0	0.0	0.0
2003	0.0	55.0	55.0	0.0	0.0	0.0	0.0	0.0	0.0	–53.6	–48.5
2004	0.0	133.3	133.3	0.0	0.0	0.0	0.0	0.0	0.0	–66.6	–54.5
2005	88.8	213.2	124.5	0.0	0.0	7.4	81.4	24.4	24.4	4.0	3.0
2006	134.6	158.2	23.6	0.0	0.0	8.0	126.6	38.0	38.0	73.9	49.5
2007	150.7	27.1	0.0	123.6	49.4	8.0	93.2	28.0	77.4	64.7	39.2
2008	145.5	0.0	0.0	145.5	58.2	8.0	79.2	23.8	82.0	54.7	30.0
2009	142.4	0.0	0.0	142.4	57.0	8.0	77.4	23.2	80.2	52.2	25.9
2010	165.5	5.0	0.0	160.5	64.2	8.3	93.0	27.9	92.1	56.0	25.2
2011	148.9	10.0	0.0	138.9	55.6	8.8	84.6	25.4	80.9	46.3	18.8
2012	111.7	0.0	0.0	111.7	44.7	8.8	58.2	17.5	62.2	38.6	14.2
2013	103.8	0.0	0.0	103.8	41.5	8.8	53.5	16.0	57.6	35.1	11.7
2014	143.4	0.0	0.0	143.4	57.4	8.8	77.2	23.2	80.5	46.6	14.0
2015	109.7	5.0	0.0	104.7	41.9	9.1	58.7	17.6	59.5	32.7	8.9
2016	64.2	5.0	0.0	59.2	23.7	9.5	31.0	9.3	33.0	18.5	4.6
2017	95.0	7.0	0.0	88.0	35.2	10.0	49.8	14.9	50.1	26.0	5.8
2018	119.9	10.0	0.0	109.9	43.9	10.9	65.1	19.5	63.5	31.1	6.3
2019	117.5	1.0	0.0	116.5	46.6	11.0	60.0	18.0	64.6	33.9	6.2
2020	105.4	1.0	0.0	104.4	41.7	11.1	52.6	15.8	57.5	29.9	4.9
2021	84.9	1.0	0.0	83.9	33.6	11.2	40.2	12.0	45.6	23.8	3.6
2022	66.0	1.0	0.0	65.0	26.0	11.3	28.7	8.6	34.6	18.4	2.5
2023	53.5	1.0	0.0	52.5	21.0	11.4	21.1	6.3	27.3	14.9	1.8
2024	47.9	1.0	0.0	46.9	18.7	11.6	17.5	5.3	24.0	13.2	1.5
2025	41.8	1.0	0.0	40.8	16.3	11.8	13.7	4.1	20.5	11.5	1.2
2026	35.5	0.0	0.0	35.5	14.2	11.8	9.5	2.8	17.0	10.1	0.9

2027	36.5	0.0	0.0	36.5	14.6	11.8	10.1	3.0	17.6	10.1	0.8
2028	29.0	0.0	0.0	29.0	11.6	11.8	5.6	1.7	13.3	8.2	0.6
2029	29.8	0.0	0.0	29.8	11.9	11.8	6.1	1.8	13.7	8.2	0.5
2030	0.0	0.0	0.0	0.0	0.0	0.0	0.0	0.0	0.0	–19.9	–1.2
2031	0.0	0.0	0.0	0.0	0.0	0.0	0.0	0.0	0.0	0.0	0.0
Totals:	2371.7	635.7	336.3	2072.3	828.9	249.0	1293.8	388.1	1217.1	622.4	177.4

PRRT Calculation

(H) Gross Revenue = Revenue (B) – OPEX (C)
(I) Compounded $CAPEX_t = CAPEX_t$ (D) + $LossCF_{t-1}$ (J) × 1.15
(J) Any losses not written off are carried for the following period.
(K) Taxable Income = Gross Revenue (H) – Compounded Capex (I)
(L) PRRT = 40 per cent × Taxable Profit (K)

CT Calculation

(M) Depreciation = CAPEX are depreciated on a straight-line basis over field life.
(N) Taxable Income = Revenue (B) – OPEX (C) – Depreciation (M) – PRRT (L)
(O) CT = 30 per cent × Taxable Income (N)

Pre-tax NCF Calculation

(P) Total Government Take = PRRT (L) + CT (O)
(Q) Real NCF Post-tax = [Pre-tax NCF (E) – Government Take (P)]/Inflation Factor
(R) Discounted NCF Post-tax = Real NCF (Q) × Discount factor.

Table C3 Oil field under Norwegian regime

Year	*ST Calculations*						*CT calculations*			
	Dep. £M (S)	*Uplift* £M (T)	*ST Base* £M (U)	*Loss CF* £M (V)	*Taxable Income* £M (W)	*ST Payable 50%* £M (X)	*CT Base* £M (Y)	*Loss CF* £M (Z)	*Taxable Income* £M (AA)	*CT Payable 28%* £M (BB)
2002	0.0	0.0	0.0	0.0	0.0	0.0	0.0	0.0	0.0	0.0
2003	9.2	2.8	–11.9	–11.9	0.0	0.0	–9.2	–9.2	0.0	0.0
2004	20.8	6.3	–27.1	–39.0	0.0	0.0	–20.8	–30.0	0.0	0.0
2005	30.8	9.3	48.7	0.0	9.7	4.8	57.9	0.0	27.9	7.8
2006	33.3	10.0	91.3	0.0	91.3	45.6	101.3	0.0	101.3	28.4
2007	33.3	10.0	107.3	0.0	107.3	53.7	117.3	0.0	117.3	32.8
2008	33.3	10.0	102.1	0.0	102.1	51.1	112.1	0.0	112.1	31.4
2009	24.2	7.3	111.0	0.0	111.0	55.5	118.2	0.0	118.2	33.1
2010	13.3	3.8	148.4	0.0	148.4	74.2	152.2	0.0	152.2	42.6
2011	5.0	0.8	143.2	0.0	143.2	71.6	143.9	0.0	143.9	40.3
2012	2.5	0.0	109.2	0.0	109.2	54.6	109.2	0.0	109.2	30.6
2013	2.5	0.0	101.3	0.0	101.3	50.6	101.3	0.0	101.3	28.4
2014	2.5	0.0	140.9	0.0	140.9	70.4	140.9	0.0	140.9	39.4
2015	3.3	0.0	106.4	0.0	106.4	53.2	106.4	0.0	106.4	29.8
2016	3.3	0.0	60.9	0.0	60.9	30.4	60.9	0.0	60.9	17.0
2017	2.8	0.0	92.2	0.0	92.2	46.1	92.2	0.0	92.2	25.8
2018	4.5	0.0	115.4	0.0	115.4	57.7	115.4	0.0	115.4	32.3
2019	4.7	0.0	112.9	0.0	112.9	56.4	112.9	0.0	112.9	31.6
2020	4.8	0.0	100.5	0.0	100.5	50.3	100.5	0.0	100.5	28.1
2021	4.2	0.0	80.7	0.0	80.7	40.4	80.7	0.0	80.7	22.6
2022	3.5	0.0	62.5	0.0	62.5	31.2	62.5	0.0	62.5	17.5
2023	2.5	0.0	51.0	0.0	51.0	25.5	51.0	0.0	51.0	14.3
2024	1.0	0.0	46.9	0.0	46.9	23.4	46.9	0.0	46.9	13.1
2025	0.8	0.0	41.0	0.0	41.0	20.5	41.0	0.0	41.0	11.5
2026	0.7	0.0	34.8	0.0	34.8	17.4	34.8	0.0	34.8	9.7
2027	0.5	0.0	36.0	0.0	36.0	18.0	36.0	0.0	36.0	10.1
2028	0.3	0.0	28.7	0.0	28.7	14.4	28.7	0.0	28.7	8.0
2029	0.2	0.0	29.6	0.0	29.6	14.8	29.6	0.0	29.6	8.3
2030	0.0	0.0	0.0	0.0	0.0	0.0	0.0	0.0	0.0	0.0
2031	0.0	0.0	0.0	0.0	0.0	0.0	0.0	0.0	0.0	0.0
Totals:	248.0	60.0	2063.7	–50.9	2063.7	1031.9	2123.7	–39.2	2123.7	594.6

Table C4 Oil field under Norwegian regime

Year	*Pre-tax NCF* *£M* *(CC)*	*Total tax Take* *£M* *(DD)*	*Abandonment cost* *(EE)*	*Abandonment grant* *£M* *(FF)*	*Post-tax NCF* *£M* *(GG)*	*Real NCF Post-tax* *£M* *(HH)*	*Dis. NCF Post-tax* *£M* *(II)*
2002	0.0	0.0	0.0	0.0	0.0	0.0	0.0
2003	–55.0	0.0	0.0	0.0	–55.0	–53.6	–48.5
2004	–70.0	0.0	0.0	0.0	–70.0	–66.6	–54.5
2005	28.8	12.7	0.0	0.0	16.1	14.9	11.1
2006	119.6	74.0	0.0	0.0	45.6	41.3	27.7
2007	150.7	86.5	0.0	0.0	64.1	56.6	34.3
2008	145.5	82.5	0.0	0.0	63.0	54.2	29.8
2009	142.4	88.6	0.0	0.0	53.8	45.2	22.4
2010	160.5	116.8	0.0	0.0	43.7	35.8	16.1
2011	138.9	111.9	0.0	0.0	27.0	21.6	8.8
2012	111.7	85.2	0.0	0.0	26.5	20.7	7.6
2013	103.8	79.0	0.0	0.0	24.8	18.8	6.3
2014	143.4	109.9	0.0	0.0	33.5	24.8	7.5
2015	104.7	83.0	0.0	0.0	21.7	15.7	4.3
2016	59.2	47.5	0.0	0.0	11.7	8.3	2.0
2017	88.0	71.9	0.0	0.0	16.1	11.1	2.5
2018	109.9	90.0	0.0	0.0	19.9	13.3	2.7
2019	116.5	88.0	0.0	0.0	28.5	18.6	3.4
2020	104.4	78.4	0.0	0.0	25.9	16.5	2.7
2021	83.9	63.0	0.0	0.0	20.9	13.0	1.9
2022	65.0	48.7	0.0	0.0	16.2	9.8	1.3
2023	52.5	39.8	0.0	0.0	12.7	7.5	0.9
2024	46.9	36.5	0.0	0.0	10.3	5.9	0.7
2025	40.8	32.0	0.0	0.0	8.9	5.0	0.5
2026	35.5	27.1	0.0	0.0	8.3	4.6	0.4
2027	36.5	28.1	0.0	0.0	8.4	4.5	0.4
2028	29.0	22.4	0.0	0.0	6.6	3.5	0.3
2029	29.8	23.1	0.0	0.0	6.7	3.4	0.2
2030	0.0	0.0	40.0	30.6	–9.4	–4.6	–0.3
2031	0.0	0.0	0.0	0.0	0.0	0.0	0.0
Totals:	2122.7	1626.5	40.0	30.6	486.9	349.8	92.4

(Continued overleaf)

Table C4 (Continued)

ST Calculation:

(S) Depreciation for CAPEX (D) is allowed on Six year straight-line basis
(T) Uplift applies on CAPEX (D) at a rate of 5% over Six years
(U) ST Base = Revenue (B) – OPEX (C) – Depreciation (S) – Uplift (T)
(V) Any loss not written off in a particular period is carried forward to a following period.
(W) Taxable Income is equal to the ST base (U) when all losses have been written off.
(X) ST Payable = 50% × Taxable Income (W)

CT Calculation:

(Y) CT Base = Revenue (B) – OPEX (C) – Depreciation (S)
(Z) Any loss not written off in a particular period is carried forward to a following period.
(AA) Taxable Income is equal to the CT base (Y) when all losses have been written off.
(BB) CT Payable = 28% × Taxable Income (AA)

Post-Tax NCF Calculation:

(CC) Pre-tax NCF excluding Abandonment Cost (EE)
(DD) Total Government Take = ST (X) + CT (BB)
(EE) Abandonment Cost
(FF) Abandonment Cost Grant = 76.6% × Abandonment Cost (EE), where 76.6% is the effective tax rate.
(GG) Post Tax NCF = Pre-tax NCF (CC) – Government Take (DD) – Abandonment Cost Grant (FF)
(HH) Real NCF Post-tax = Post-tax NCF (GG)/Inflation Factor
(II) Discounted NCF Post-tax = Real NCF (HH) × Discount factor.

Table C5 Oil field under Indonesian regime

Year	*FTP calculation*				
	Total FTP 20% £M (JJ)	*Gov. Share 64%* *£M* *(KK)*	*Contractor Share 36%* *£M* *(LL)*	*Net Revenue* £M (MM)	*DMO* £M (NN)
2002	0.0	0.0	0.0	0.0	–
2003	0.0	0.0	0.0	0.0	–
2004	0.0	0.0	0.0	0.0	–
2005	25.6	16.4	9.2	102.3	–
2006	35.7	22.8	12.8	142.6	–
2007	38.2	24.4	13.7	152.7	–
2008	36.9	23.6	13.3	147.7	–
2009	36.2	23.2	13.0	144.7	–
2010	41.1	26.3	14.8	164.6	13.9
2011	37.4	24.0	13.5	149.7	12.6
2012	29.2	18.7	10.5	117.0	9.9
2013	30.6	19.6	11.0	122.4	10.3
2014	34.2	21.9	12.3	136.9	11.5
2015	28.0	17.9	10.1	112.0	9.4
2016	23.5	15.0	8.4	93.8	7.9
2017	27.6	17.7	9.9	110.5	9.3
2018	28.3	18.1	10.2	113.3	9.6
2019	27.6	17.7	9.9	110.3	9.3
2020	25.3	16.2	9.1	101.2	8.5
2021	21.4	13.7	7.7	85.5	7.2
2022	17.2	11.0	6.2	68.8	5.8
2023	14.4	9.2	5.2	57.8	4.9
2024	13.2	8.4	4.7	52.6	4.4
2025	11.8	7.6	4.2	47.2	4.0
2026	10.4	6.6	3.7	41.5	3.5
2027	10.6	6.8	3.8	42.6	3.6
2028	9.1	5.8	3.3	36.4	3.1
2029	9.3	6.0	3.4	37.3	3.1
2030	0.0	0.0	0.0	0.0	0.0
2031	0.0	0.0	0.0	0.0	0.0
Totals:	622.8	398.6	224.2	2491.3	152.0

Table C6 Oil field under Indonesian regime

Year	*Cost Recovery Calculation*							
	Intangible CAPEX £M (OO)	*Tangible CAPEX £M (PP)*	*Dep. £M (QQ)*	*Inv. Credits £M (RR)*	*Total Cost Recovery £M (SS)*	*Cost Recovery Limit £M (TT)*	*Cost CF £M (UU)*	*Cost recovery allowed £M (VV)*
2002	0.0	0.0	0.0	0.0	0.0	0.0	0.0	0.0
2003	16.3	38.8	0.0	0.0	16.3	0.0	0.0	0.0
2004	25.0	45.0	0.0	0.0	25.0	0.0	16.3	0.0
2005	27.5	32.5	29.1	21.7	117.4	102.3	41.3	102.3
2006	11.3	3.8	22.7	0.0	77.7	142.6	56.3	134.0
2007	0.0	0.0	17.1	0.0	57.3	152.7	0.0	57.3
2008	0.0	0.0	12.8	0.0	52.0	147.7	0.0	52.0
2009	0.0	0.0	37.2	0.0	75.7	144.7	0.0	75.7
2010	3.8	1.3	1.5	0.0	45.5	164.6	0.0	45.5
2011	7.5	2.5	0.9	0.0	46.6	149.7	0.0	46.6
2012	0.0	0.0	0.6	0.0	35.2	117.0	0.0	35.2
2013	0.0	0.0	0.5	0.0	49.8	122.4	0.0	49.8
2014	0.0	0.0	0.7	0.0	28.3	136.9	0.0	28.3
2015	1.3	3.8	1.7	0.0	33.2	112.0	0.0	33.2
2016	3.8	1.3	1.0	0.0	57.9	93.8	0.0	57.9
2017	5.2	1.7	1.2	0.0	49.5	110.5	0.0	49.5
2018	7.5	2.5	1.5	0.0	30.7	113.3	0.0	30.7
2019	0.3	0.8	2.2	0.0	22.9	110.3	0.0	22.9
2020	0.3	0.8	1.3	0.0	22.7	101.2	0.0	22.7
2021	0.3	0.8	1.3	0.0	23.4	85.5	0.0	23.4
2022	0.3	0.8	1.3	0.0	21.7	68.8	0.0	21.7
2023	0.3	0.8	0.8	0.0	19.7	57.8	0.0	19.7
2024	0.3	0.8	0.8	0.0	18.9	52.6	0.0	18.9
2025	0.3	0.8	0.8	0.0	18.2	47.2	0.0	18.2
2026	0.0	0.0	0.6	0.0	17.0	41.5	0.0	17.0
2027	0.0	0.0	0.4	0.0	17.1	42.6	0.0	17.1
2028	0.0	0.0	0.3	0.0	16.7	36.4	0.0	16.7
2029	0.0	0.0	0.2	0.0	17.1	37.3	0.0	17.1
2030	0.0	0.0	0.0	0.0	0.0	0.0	0.0	0.0
2031	0.0	0.0	0.0	0.0	0.0	0.0	0.0	0.0
Totals:	110.7	138.2	138.2	21.7	1013.1	2491.3	113.8	1013.1

Table C7 Oil field under Indonesian regime

Profit oil			*Income Tax*				*Gov. take & Contractor NCF*			
Total Profit Oil	*Gov. Share 64%*	*Contractor Share 36%*	*Bonus*	*Contractor Total Profit*	*Taxable Income*	*Income tax 44%*	*Gov. Take*	*NCF*	*Real NCF*	*Contractor Dis. NCF*
£M (WW)	*£M (XX)*	*£M (YY)*	*£M (ZZ)*	*£M (AAA)*	*£M (BBB)*	*£M (CCC)*	*£M (DDD)*	*£M (EEE)*	*£M (FFF)*	*£M (GGG)*
0.0	0.0	0.0	0.0	0.0	0.0	0.0	0.0	0.0	0.0	0.0
0.0	0.0	0.0	0.0	0.0	0.0	0.0	0.0	–55.0	–53.6	–48.5
0.0	0.0	0.0	0.0	0.0	0.0	0.0	0.0	–70.0	–66.6	–54.5
0.0	0.0	0.0	0.0	9.2	30.9	13.6	30.0	–1.2	–1.1	–0.8
8.6	5.5	3.1	0.0	15.9	15.9	7.0	35.4	84.2	76.2	51.1
95.4	61.1	34.4	0.0	48.1	48.1	21.2	106.7	44.0	38.8	23.5
95.7	61.3	34.5	0.0	47.8	47.8	21.0	105.9	39.5	34.0	18.7
69.0	44.2	24.9	0.0	37.9	37.9	16.7	84.0	58.4	49.0	24.3
119.1	76.2	42.9	0.0	57.7	43.8	19.3	135.7	24.8	20.3	9.1
103.1	66.0	37.1	0.0	50.6	38.0	16.7	119.3	19.6	15.7	6.4
81.8	52.4	29.5	0.0	40.0	30.1	13.3	94.2	17.5	13.6	5.0
72.7	46.5	26.2	0.0	37.2	26.9	11.8	88.3	15.5	11.8	3.9
108.5	69.5	39.1	0.0	51.4	39.8	17.5	120.4	23.0	17.0	5.1
78.8	50.4	28.4	0.0	38.4	29.0	12.8	90.5	14.2	10.3	2.8
36.0	23.0	13.0	0.0	21.4	13.5	5.9	51.9	7.3	5.2	1.3
61.0	39.0	21.9	0.0	31.9	22.6	9.9	75.9	12.1	8.3	1.9
82.5	52.8	29.7	0.0	39.9	30.3	13.4	93.8	16.0	10.7	2.2
87.5	56.0	31.5	0.0	41.4	32.1	14.1	97.1	19.5	12.7	2.3
78.5	50.3	28.3	0.0	37.4	28.8	12.7	87.7	16.7	10.6	1.8
62.0	39.7	22.3	0.0	30.0	22.8	10.0	70.6	13.3	8.3	1.2
47.2	30.2	17.0	0.0	23.2	17.4	7.6	54.7	10.3	6.2	0.8
38.1	24.4	13.7	0.0	18.9	14.0	6.2	44.7	7.9	4.6	0.6

33.7	21.6	12.1	0.0	16.9	12.4	5.5	39.9	7.0	4.0	0.4
29.0	18.6	10.5	0.0	14.7	10.7	4.7	34.8	6.0	3.4	0.3
24.5	15.7	8.8	0.0	12.6	9.1	4.0	29.8	5.6	3.1	0.3
25.5	16.3	9.2	0.0	13.0	9.4	4.1	30.8	5.7	3.0	0.2
19.6	12.6	7.1	0.0	10.3	7.3	3.2	24.6	4.4	2.3	0.2
20.2	12.9	7.3	0.0	10.6	7.5	3.3	25.3	4.4	2.3	0.2
0.0	0.0	0.0	0.0	0.0	0.0	0.0	0.0	–40.0	–19.9	–1.2
0.0	0.0	0.0	0.0	0.0	0.0	0.0	0.0	0.0	0.0	0.0
1478.2	946.1	532.2	0.0	756.4	626.1	275.5	1772.1	310.6	230.3	58.6

Tables C5–C7: Oil Field under Indonesian Regime

FTP & DMO Calculation:

(JJ) First Tranche Petroleum (FTP) = 20% × Revenue (B)
(KK) Government Share of FTP = 64% × Total FTP (JJ)
(LL) Contractor Share of FTP = 36% × Total FTP (JJ)
(MM) Net Revenue = Revenue (B) – FTP (JJ)
(NN) Domestic Market Obligation = Revenue (B) × 75% × 25% × 36%
After 60 months of production (i.e. 5 years), the contractor sells 25% of its share of oil (36%) to national oil company at 25% of the market price (Price differential of 75%)

Cost Recovery Calculation:

(OO) Intangible CAPEX = 75% × Development and Drilling expenditures + 25% × Facilities (Equipment and Transportation), which are provided separately in GEM.
(PP) Tangible CAPEX = Total CAPEX (D) – Intangible CAPEX (OO)
(QQ) Depreciation on tangible CAPEX at 25% per year, using the Declining Balance method with the undepreciated amount written off in year five
(RR) Investment credits = 15.5% × Facilities and Equipment.
(SS) Total Cost Recovery = OPEX (C) + Intangible CAPEX (OO) + Depreciation (QQ) + Investment Credits (RR)
(TT) Cost Recovery Limit = 80% × Total Revenue (B) (or 100% of Net Revenue (MM)
(UU) Any cost recovery, which exceeds the limit is carried forward to the following period.
(VV) Cost Recovery Allowed = Minimum of Cost Recovery Limit (TT) and Total Cost Recovery (SS), taking into account Cost Carried Forward (UU).

(Continued overleaf)

Table C7 (Continued)

Profit Oil Calculation:

(WW) Total Profit Oil = Total Revenue (B) – Total FTP (JJ) – Cost Recovery Allowed (VV)
(XX) Government Share of Profit Oil = 64% × Total Profit Oil (WW)
(YY) Contractor Share of Profit Oil = 36% × Total Profit Oil (WW)

Income Tax Calculation:

(ZZ) Bonus = 0, because in this example, the daily production of the field does not reach 50,000 bbl.
(AAA) Contractor Total Profit = Contractor Profit Oil (YY) + Contractor Share of FTP (LL)
(BBB) Taxable Income = Contractor Total Profit (AAA) + Investment Credits (RR) – DMO (NN) – Bonus (ZZ)

Government Take Contractor NCF:

(CCC) Total Government take = Government share of FTP (KK) + DMO (NN) + Bonus (ZZ) + Income Tax (BBB)
(DDD) Contractor NCF = Total Revenue (B) – OPEX (C) – CAPEX (D) – Gov. FTP (KK) – DMO (NN) – Gov. Profit Oil (XX) – Bonus (ZZ) – Income Tax (BBB)
(EEE) Real NCF = NCF (DDD)/Inflation Factor
(FFF) Discounted NCF = Real NCF (EEE) × Discount factor.

Table C8 Oil field under Chinese regime

Year	*Royalty* £M (EEE)	*VAT 5%* £M (FFF)	*Net Revenues* £M (GGG)	*Dep.* £M (HHH)	*Total Cost Recovery* £M (III)	*Cost Recovery Limit 62.5%* £M (JJJ)	*Cost CF* £M (KKK)	*Cost Recovery Allowed* £M (LLL)
2002	0.0	0.0	0.0	0.0	0.0	0.0	0.0	0.0
2003	0.0	0.0	0.0	55.0	55.0	0.0	0.0	0.0
2004	0.0	0.0	0.0	75.0	75.0	0.0	0.0	0.0
2005	1.0	6.4	120.4	66.7	105.9	79.9	0.0	79.9
2006	3.4	8.9	166.0	15.0	58.7	111.4	25.9	84.6
2007	3.9	9.5	177.4	0.0	40.2	119.3	0.0	40.2
2008	3.4	9.2	172.1	0.0	39.2	115.4	0.0	39.2
2009	2.9	9.0	168.9	0.0	38.5	113.0	0.0	38.5
2010	4.2	10.3	191.2	5.0	45.2	128.6	0.0	45.2
2011	2.9	9.4	174.9	10.0	48.2	117.0	0.0	48.2
2012	1.0	7.3	137.9	0.0	34.5	91.4	0.0	34.5
2013	1.1	7.7	144.3	0.0	49.3	95.7	0.0	49.3
2014	1.7	8.6	160.8	0.0	27.7	106.9	0.0	27.7
2015	0.3	7.0	132.6	5.0	35.2	87.5	0.0	35.2
2016	0.0	5.9	111.4	5.0	58.1	73.3	0.0	58.1
2017	0.0	6.9	131.2	7.0	50.1	86.3	0.0	50.1
2018	0.0	7.1	134.5	10.0	31.7	88.5	0.0	31.7
2019	0.0	6.9	131.0	1.0	21.4	86.2	0.0	21.4
2020	0.0	6.3	120.2	1.0	22.2	79.1	0.0	22.2
2021	0.0	5.3	101.5	1.0	22.9	66.8	0.0	22.9
2022	0.0	4.3	81.8	1.0	21.1	53.8	0.0	21.1
2023	0.0	3.6	68.6	1.0	19.7	45.1	0.0	19.7
2024	0.0	3.3	62.5	1.0	18.9	41.1	0.0	18.9
2025	0.0	3.0	56.1	1.0	18.2	36.9	0.0	18.2
2026	0.0	2.6	49.3	0.0	16.4	32.4	0.0	16.4
2027	0.0	2.7	50.5	0.0	16.7	33.2	0.0	16.7
2028	0.0	2.3	43.2	0.0	16.4	28.4	0.0	16.4
2029	0.0	2.3	44.3	0.0	16.8	29.1	0.0	16.8
2030	0.0	0.0	0.0	0.0	0.0	0.0	0.0	0.0
2031	0.0	0.0	0.0	0.0	0.0	0.0	0.0	0.0
Totals:	25.9	155.7	2932.6	260.7	1003.1	1946.4	25.9	873.2

Table C9 Oil field under Chinese regime

Profit oil				*Income Tax*		*Gov. Take & Contractor NCF*			
Total Profit Oil £M (MMM)	*Gov. Share of Profit Oil* % (NNN)	*Gov. Share* £M (OOO)	*Contractor Share* £M (PPP)	*Taxable Income* £M (QQQ)	*Income tax 33%* £M (RRR)	*Gov. Take* £M (SSS)	*NCF* £M (TTT)	*Real NCF* £M (UUU)	*Discounted Pretax CF* £M (VVV)
0.0	0.0	0.0	0.0	0.0	0.0	0.0	0.0	0.0	0.0
0.0	0.0	0.0	0.0	–55.0	0.0	0.0	–55.0	–53.6	–48.5
0.0	0.0	0.0	0.0	–75.0	0.0	0.0	–70.0	–66.6	–54.5
40.5	7.8	3.2	37.4	11.4	3.8	14.3	14.4	13.4	9.9
81.4	9.7	7.9	73.5	99.4	32.8	53.0	66.6	60.3	40.4
137.2	9.9	13.6	123.6	123.6	40.8	67.9	82.8	73.1	44.3
132.9	9.6	12.8	120.1	120.1	39.6	65.0	80.4	69.2	38.0
130.4	9.4	12.2	118.2	118.2	39.0	63.2	79.2	66.5	33.0
146.0	9.9	14.5	131.5	131.5	43.4	72.4	88.1	72.1	32.4
126.7	9.3	11.8	114.9	114.9	37.9	62.0	77.0	61.5	25.0
103.4	7.5	7.8	95.7	95.7	31.6	47.6	64.1	49.9	18.4
95.0	7.7	7.3	87.7	87.7	29.0	45.0	58.8	44.6	14.9
133.1	8.3	11.0	122.1	122.1	40.3	61.6	81.8	60.6	18.3
97.4	6.6	6.4	91.0	91.0	30.0	43.8	61.0	44.1	12.0
53.3	5.7	3.0	50.3	50.3	16.6	25.5	33.7	23.7	5.9
81.1	6.0	4.9	76.2	76.2	25.2	36.9	51.1	35.1	7.8
102.8	6.0	6.2	96.6	96.6	31.9	45.1	64.7	43.4	8.8
109.6	5.9	6.5	103.2	103.2	34.0	47.4	69.1	45.2	8.3
98.0	5.6	5.5	92.5	92.5	30.5	42.4	62.0	39.5	6.5
78.5	5.1	4.0	74.5	74.5	24.6	34.0	49.9	31.0	4.6
60.7	4.4	2.6	58.0	58.0	19.1	26.1	38.9	23.6	3.2
48.9	4.0	2.0	46.9	46.9	15.5	21.1	31.5	18.6	2.3
43.6	4.0	1.7	41.8	41.8	13.8	18.8	28.0	16.2	1.8
37.9	4.0	1.5	36.4	36.4	12.0	16.5	24.4	13.7	1.4
32.9	4.0	1.3	31.6	31.6	10.4	14.3	21.1	11.6	1.1
26.8	4.0	1.1	25.7	25.7	8.5	11.8	17.2	9.0	0.7
33.9	4.0	1.4	32.5	32.5	10.7	14.7	21.8	11.7	1.0
27.4	4.0	1.1	26.3	26.3	8.7	12.1	17.7	9.0	0.6

0.0	0.0	0.0	0.0	0.0	0.0	0.0	0.0	0.0	0.0
0.0	0.0	0.0	0.0	0.0	0.0	0.0	0.0	0.0	0.0
2059.4		151.2	1908.2	1778.3	629.7	962.5	1160.2	826.3	237.3

Tables C8–C9: Oil Field under Chinese Regime

Cost Recovery Calculation:

(EEE) Royalty is calculated on a Sliding Scale Basis (See Chapter 3, Table 3.2). For example, the on the first tranche of production (<=20,000 bbl/d) Royalty rate is zero. On the second tranche of production (>20,000 bbl/d <=30,0000 bbl/d0 Royalty rate is 4% . . . Then, the total Royalty in one year is the sum of the Royalty payment on each tranche in that year. Finally, the annual Royalty value is determined by multiplying Total Royalty by the oil price.
(FFF) Value Added Tax = 5% × Total Revenue (B)
(GGG) Net Revenue = Total Revenue (B) – Royalty (EEE) – VAT (FFF)
(HHH) Depreciation is 100% of CAPEX as spent. Any unrecovered balance is carried forward to the following period and is compounded at a 9 per cent interest rate
(III) Cost Recovery = OPEX (C)– Depreciation (HHH)
(JJJ) Cost Recovery Limit = 62.5% × Total Revenue (B)
(KKK) Any cost recovery, which exceeds the limit, is carried forward to the following period.
(LLL) Cost Recovery Allowed = Minimum of Cost Recovery Limit (JJJ) and Total Cost Recovery (III), taking into account Cost Carried Forward (KKK).

Government Take & Contractor NCF:

(MMM) Total Profit Oil = Net Revenues (GGG) – Cost Recovery (LLL)
(NNN) Government Share of Profit Oil (%) is determined by the X Factor (See Table 3.3, Chapter 3), depending on annual Production.
(OOO) Government Share of Profit Oil = Government share in percentage (NNN) × Total Profit Oil (MMM)
(PPP) Contractor Share of Profit Oil = Total Profit Oil (MMM) – Government Share (OOO)
(QQQ) Taxable Income = Net Revenue (GGG) – OPEX (C) – Depreciation (HHH) – Government Share of Profit Oil (OOO)
(RRR) Income Tax = 33% × Taxable Income
(SSS) Total Government Take = Royalty (EEE) + VAT (FFF) + Gov. Share of Profit Oil (OOO) + Income Tax (RRR)
(TTT) Contractor NCF = Net Revenue (GGG) – OPEX (C) – Depreciation (HHH) – Income Tax (RRR) – Gov. Share of Profit Oil (OOO)
(UUU) Real NCF = NCF (DDD)/Inflation Factor
(VVV) Discounted NCF = Real NCF (EEE) × Discount factor.

Table C10 Oil field under Iraqi regime

Year	*Total cost* £M (WWW)	*Limit 50%* £M (XXX)	*Net Income* £M (YYY)	*Cumulative Net Income* £M (ZZZ)	*Cost Recovery allowed* £M (AAAA)	*Cost Unrecovered* £M (BBBB)	*Cumulative Unrecovered* £M (CCCC)	*Handover Date* (DDDD)
2002	0.0	0.0	0.0	0.0	0.0	0.0	0.0	–
2003	55.0	0.0	–55.0	–55.0	0.0	55.0	55.0	–
2004	70.0	0.0	–70.0	–125.0	0.0	70.0	125.0	–
2005	99.1	63.9	–35.2	–160.2	63.9	35.2	160.2	–
2006	58.7	89.1	30.5	–129.7	89.1	–30.5	129.7	–
2007	40.2	95.4	55.2	–74.5	95.4	–55.2	74.5	–
2008	39.2	92.3	53.1	–21.4	92.3	–53.1	21.4	–
2009	38.5	90.4	52.0	30.6	59.9	–21.4	**0.0**	Handover Date
2010	45.2	102.9	57.6	88.2	45.2	0.0	0.0	–
2011	48.2	93.6	45.4	133.6	48.2	0.0	0.0	–
2012	34.5	73.1	38.6	172.2	34.5	0.0	0.0	–
2013	49.3	76.5	27.3	199.4	49.3	0.0	0.0	–
2014	27.7	85.5	57.9	257.3	27.7	0.0	0.0	–
2015	35.2	70.0	34.8	292.0	35.2	0.0	0.0	–
2016	58.1	58.6	0.6	292.6	58.1	0.0	0.0	–
2017	50.1	69.0	19.0	311.6	50.1	0.0	0.0	–
2018	31.7	70.8	39.1	350.6	31.7	0.0	0.0	–
2019	21.4	69.0	47.6	398.2	21.4	0.0	0.0	–
2020	22.2	63.3	41.1	439.3	22.2	0.0	0.0	–
2021	22.9	53.4	30.5	469.8	22.9	0.0	0.0	–
2022	21.1	43.0	21.9	491.7	21.1	0.0	0.0	–
2023	19.7	36.1	16.4	508.1	19.7	0.0	0.0	–
2024	18.9	32.9	14.0	522.1	18.9	0.0	0.0	–
2025	18.2	29.5	11.3	533.4	18.2	0.0	0.0	–
2026	16.4	25.9	9.5	542.9	16.4	0.0	0.0	–
2027	16.7	26.6	9.9	552.9	16.7	0.0	0.0	–
2028	16.4	22.7	6.3	559.2	16.4	0.0	0.0	–
2029	16.8	23.3	6.5	565.7	16.8	0.0	0.0	–
2030	40.0	0.0	–40.0	525.7	0.0	40.0	40.0	–
2031	0.0	0.0	0.0	525.7	0.0	0.0	0.0	–
Totals:	1031.4	1557.1	525.7	8196.8	991.4			–

Table C1 Oil Field under Iraqi Regime

Cum. CAPEX Handover Date *£M* *(EEEE)*	*Remun. Index* *(FFFF)*	*Expected Cum. CAPEX* *£M* *(GGGG)*	*Overall Remun.* *£M* *(HHHH)*	*Contractor Remun.* *£M* *(IIII)*	*Cumulative Remun. to handover* *£M* *(JJJJ)*	*Balance to be recovered* *£M* *(KKKK)*	*8 Quarters* *£M* *(LLLL)*
0.0	1.5	200.0	300	0.0	0.0	300.0	0.0
55.0	1.5	200.0	300	0.0	0.0	300.0	0.0
125.0	1.5	200.0	300	0.0	0.0	300.0	0.0
185.0	1.5	200.0	300	12.8	12.8	287.2	0.0
200.0	1.5	200.0	300	17.8	30.6	269.4	0.0
200.0	1.5	200.0	300	19.1	49.7	250.3	0.0
200.0	1.5	200.0	300	18.5	68.2	231.8	0.0
200.0	**1.5**	**200.0**	**300**	**18.1**	**86.3**	**213.7**	0.0
200.0	1.5	200.0	300	0.0	0.0	0.0	106.9
200.0	1.5	200.0	300	0.0	0.0	0.0	106.9
200.0	1.5	200.0	300	0.0	0.0	0.0	0.0
200.0	1.5	200.0	300	0.0	0.0	0.0	0.0
200.0	1.5	200.0	300	0.0	0.0	0.0	0.0
200.0	1.5	200.0	300	0.0	0.0	0.0	0.0
200.0	1.5	200.0	300	0.0	0.0	0.0	0.0
200.0	1.5	200.0	300	0.0	0.0	0.0	0.0
200.0	1.5	200.0	300	0.0	0.0	0.0	0.0
200.0	1.5	200.0	300	0.0	0.0	0.0	0.0
200.0	1.5	200.0	300	0.0	0.0	0.0	0.0
200.0	1.5	200.0	300	0.0	0.0	0.0	0.0
200.0	1.5	200.0	300	0.0	0.0	0.0	0.0
200.0	1.5	200.0	300	0.0	0.0	0.0	0.0
200.0	1.5	200.0	300	0.0	0.0	0.0	0.0
200.0	1.5	200.0	300	0.0	0.0	0.0	0.0
200.0	1.5	200.0	300	0.0	0.0	0.0	0.0
200.0	1.5	200.0	300	0.0	0.0	0.0	0.0
200.0	1.5	200.0	300	0.0	0.0	0.0	0.0
200.0	1.5	200.0	300	0.0	0.0	0.0	0.0
200.0	1.5	200.0	300	0.0	0.0	0.0	0.0
200.0	1.5	200.0	300	0.0	0.0	0.0	0.0
5565.0				86.3	247.5	2152.5	213.7

Table C12 Oil field under Iraqi regime

Year	*Total Income £M (MMMM)*	*NCF £M (NNNN)*	*Real NCF £M* (OOOO)	*Discounted NCF £M (PPPP)*	*Gov. Take during contract £M (QQQQ)*
2002	0.0	0.0	0.0	0.0	0.0
2003	0.0	–55.0	–53.6	–48.5	0.0
2004	0.0	–70.0	–66.6	–54.5	0.0
2005	76.7	–22.4	–20.8	–15.4	51.1
2006	107.0	48.3	43.7	29.3	71.3
2007	114.5	74.3	65.6	39.8	76.4
2008	110.8	71.6	61.6	33.8	73.9
2009	78.0	39.5	33.1	16.5	102.9
2010	106.9	106.9	87.5	39.3	53.6
2011	106.9	106.9	85.3	34.7	32.1
2012	0.0	0.0	0.0	0.0	–
2013	0.0	0.0	0.0	0.0	–
2014	0.0	0.0	0.0	0.0	–
2015	0.0	0.0	0.0	0.0	–
2016	0.0	0.0	0.0	0.0	–
2017	0.0	0.0	0.0	0.0	–
2018	0.0	0.0	0.0	0.0	–
2019	0.0	0.0	0.0	0.0	–
2020	0.0	0.0	0.0	0.0	–
2021	0.0	0.0	0.0	0.0	–
2022	0.0	0.0	0.0	0.0	–
2023	0.0	0.0	0.0	0.0	–
2024	0.0	0.0	0.0	0.0	–
2025	0.0	0.0	0.0	0.0	–
2026	0.0	0.0	0.0	0.0	–
2027	0.0	0.0	0.0	0.0	–
2028	0.0	0.0	0.0	0.0	–
2029	0.0	0.0	0.0	0.0	–
2030	0.0	0.0	0.0	0.0	–
2031	0.0	0.0	0.0	0.0	–
Totals:	700.7	300.0	235.8	74.9	461.3

Tables C10–C12: Oil Field under Iraqi Regime

Cost Recovery Calculation:

(WWW) Total Costs = OPEX (C) + CAPEX (D)
(XXX) Cost Recovery Limit = 50% × Revenue (B)
(YYY) Net Income = Total Costs (WWW) – Cost Recovery Limit (XXX)
(ZZZ) Cumulative Net Income$_t$ = Net Income$_t$ (YYY) + Cumulative Income$_{t-1}$ (ZZZ)
(AAAA) Cost Recovery Allowed = Minimum between Total Costs (WWW) and Cost Recovery Limit (XXX)
(BBBB) Cost Unrecovered = Cost Recovery Allowed (AAAA) – Total Costs (WWW)
(CCCC) Cumulative Cost Unrecovered$_t$ = Cost Unrecovered$_t$ (BBB) + Cumulative Unrecovered$_{t-1}$ (CCCC)

(DDDD) When all costs are recovered (i.e. Cumulative Unrecovered = 0), the field reaches Handover date, which is in this example 2009.

Remuneration Calculation:

(EEEE) Cumulative CAPEX = Cumulative CAPEX (D) until field reaches Handover date.
(FFFF) Remuneration Index is assumed to be 1.5.
(GGGG) Expected Cumulative CAPEX = Maximum of Cumulative CAPEX (EEEE) to Handover date.
(HHHH) Overall Remuneration = Remuneration Index (FFFF) × Expected Cumulative CAPEX (GGGG)
(IIII) Contractor Remuneration = 10% × Revenue (B)
(JJJJ) Cumulative Remuneration of Contractor Remuneration (IIII)
(KKKK) Balance to be recovered = Overall Remuneration (HHHH) – Cumulative Remuneration (JJJJ)
(LLLL) Eight Quarters after Handover (i.e. Two years) means that the balance to be recovered at Handover will be recovered in 8 quarters, by equal instalments.

Contractor NCF Calculation:

(MMMM) Total Income = Contractor Remuneration (IIII) + 8 Quarters CAPEX (LLLL) + Cost Recovery Allowed (AAAA)
(NNNN) NCF = Total Income (MMMM) – Total Costs (WWW)
(OOOO) Real NCF = NCF (NNNN)/Inflation Factor
(PPPP) Discounted NCF = Real NCF (OOOO) × Discount factor.
(QQQQ) Government take during contract = Revenue (B) – Total Costs (WWW) – Contractor NCF (NNNN).

Appendix D

NPV £M under different tax scenarios using low oil price.

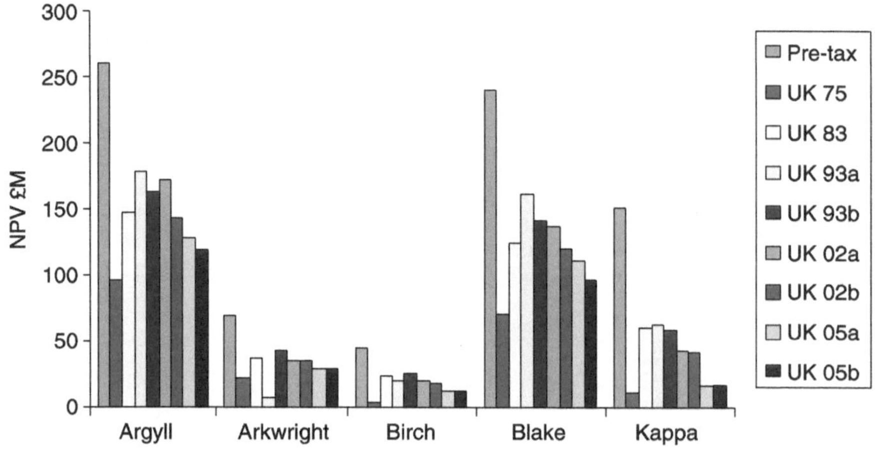

Figure D1 Very small fields.

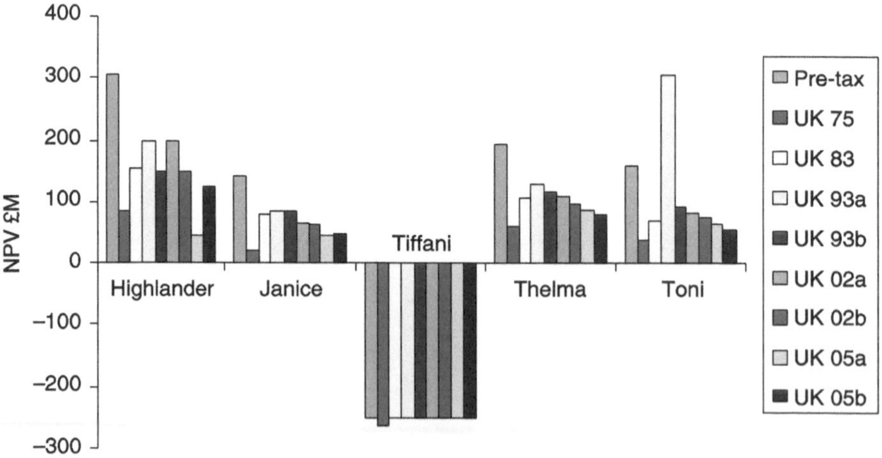

Figure D2 Very small fields (continued).

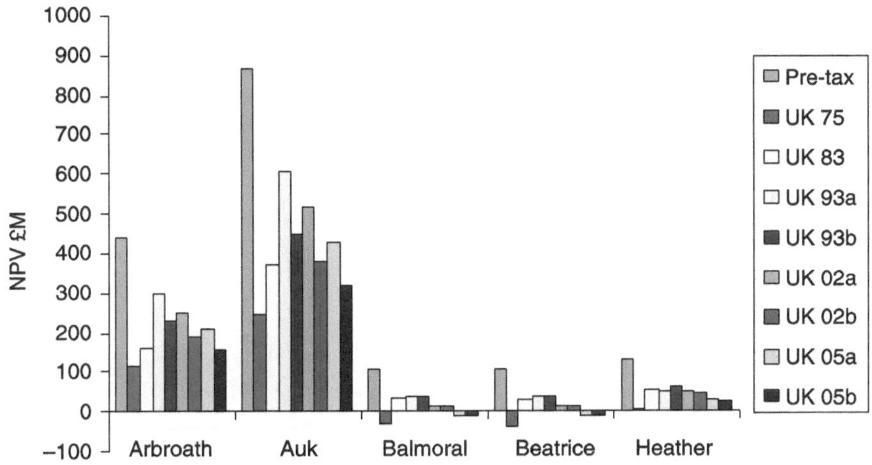

Figure D3 Small fields.

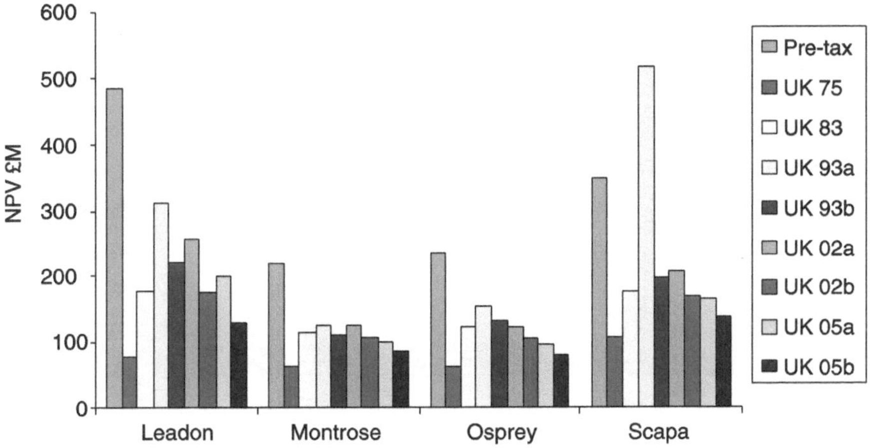

Figure D4 Small fields (continued).

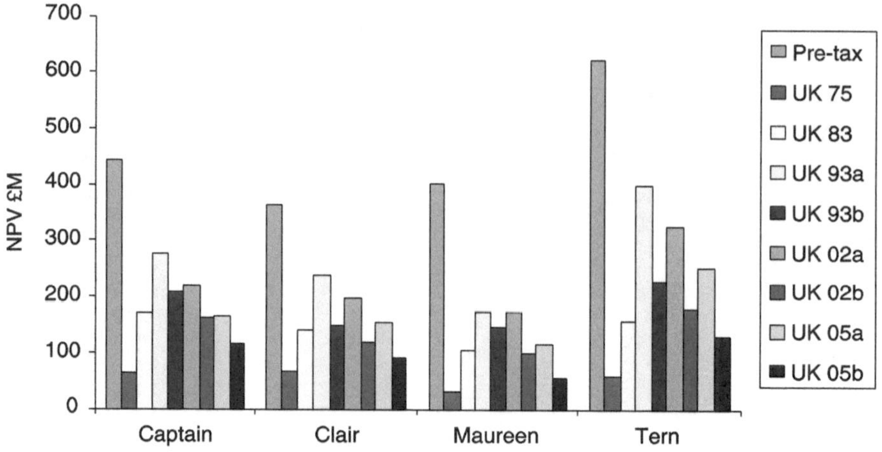

Figure D5 Medium fields.

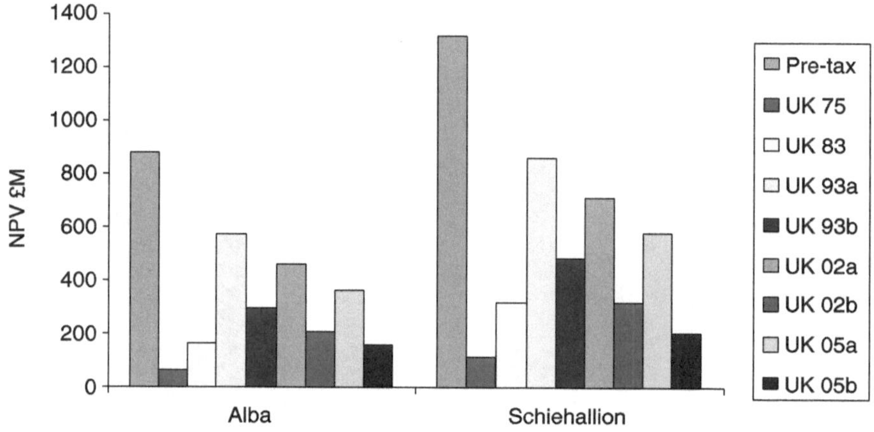

Figure D6 Large fields.

NPV £M under different tax scenarios using high oil price.

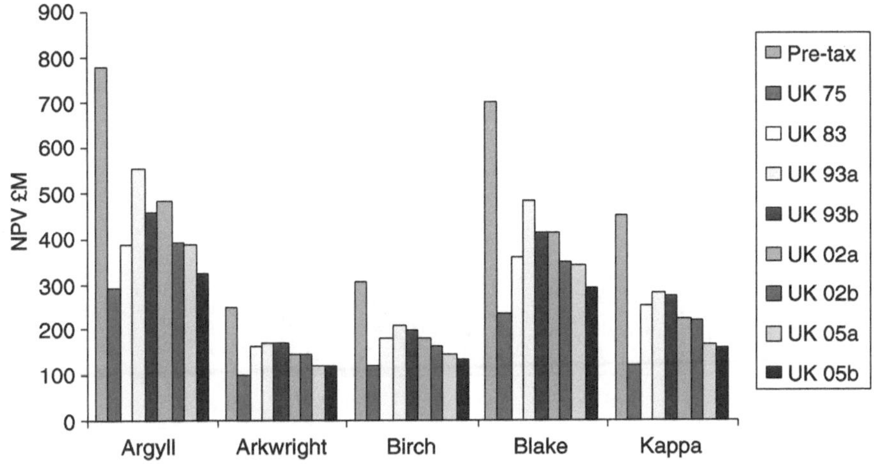

Figure D7 Very small fields.

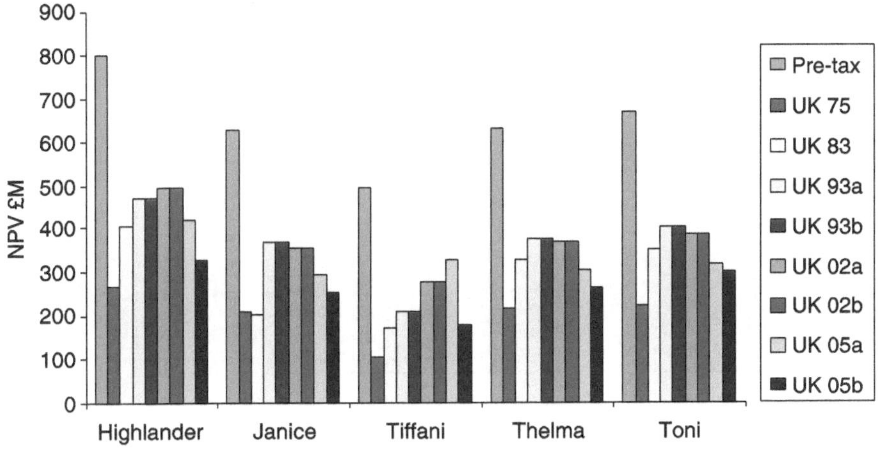

Figure D8 Very small fields (continued).

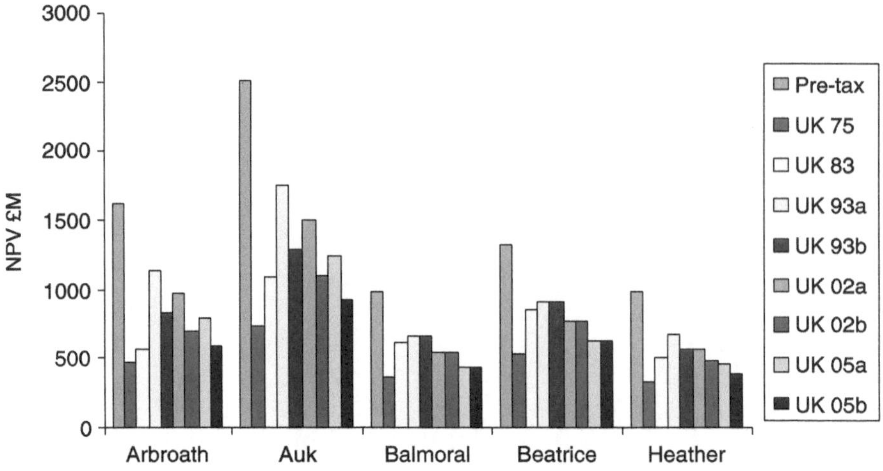

Figure D9 Small fields.

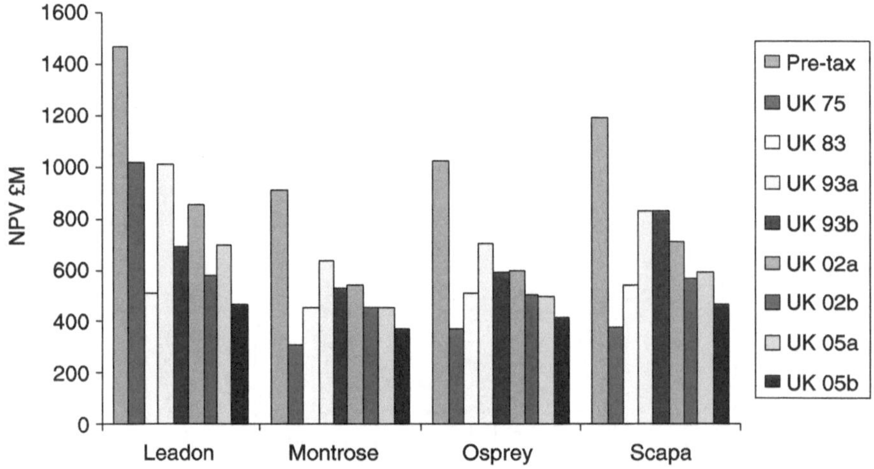

Figure D10 Small fields (continued).

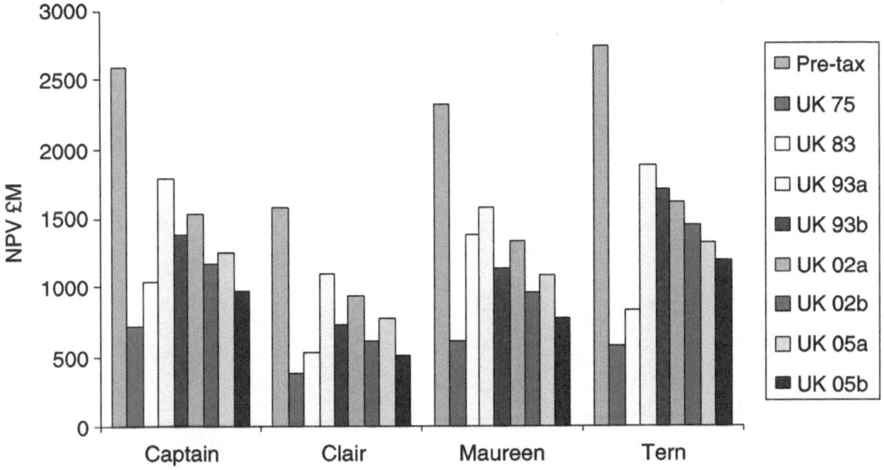

Figure D11 Medium fields.

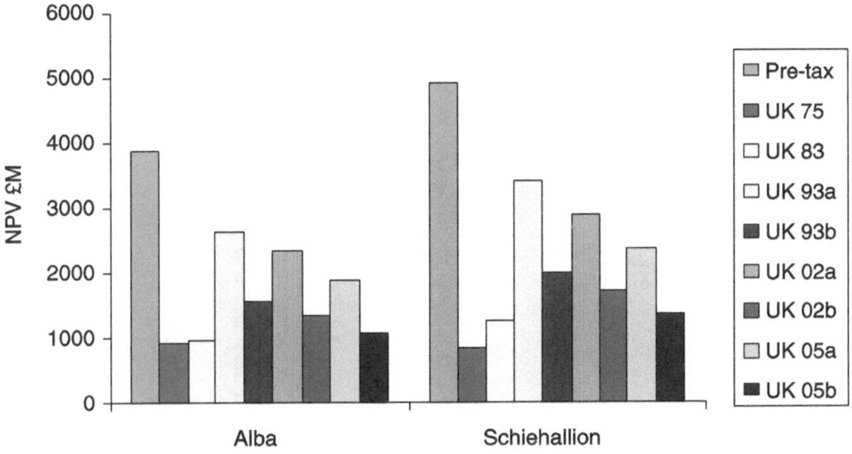

Figure D12 Large fields.

Government take percentage for all fields under different tax scenarios using low oil price.

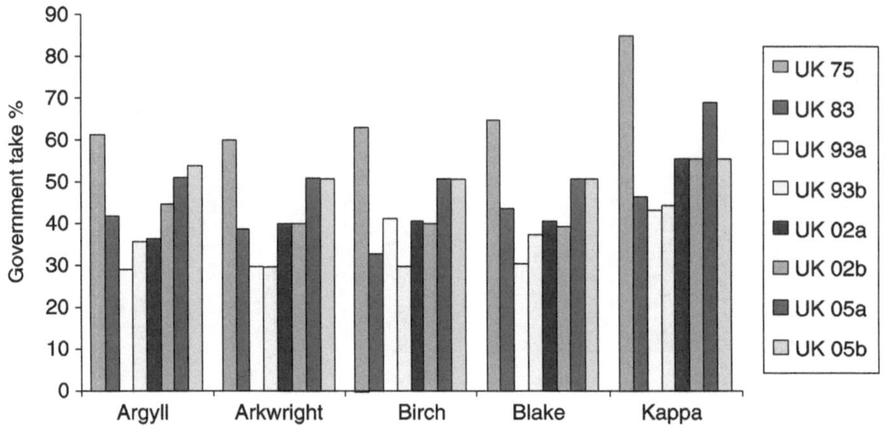

Figure D13 Very small fields.

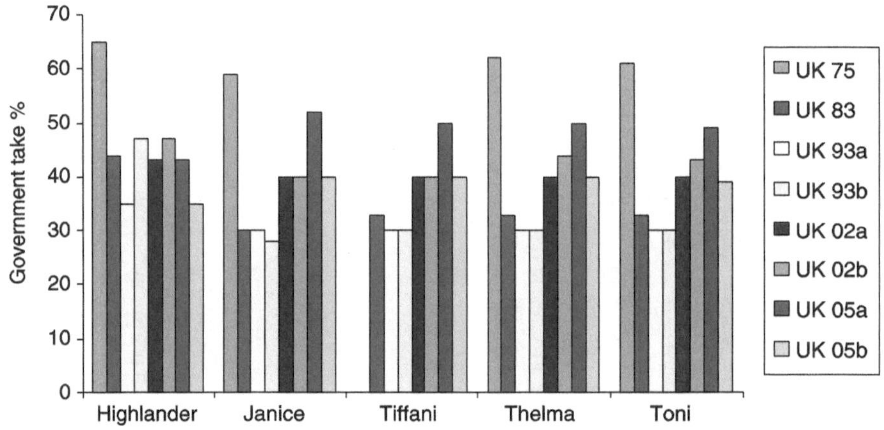

Figure D14 Very small fields (continued).

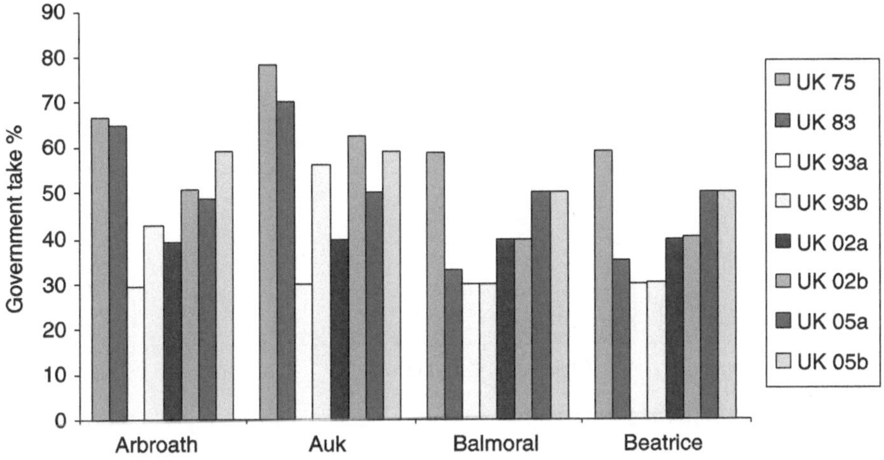

Figure D15 Small fields.

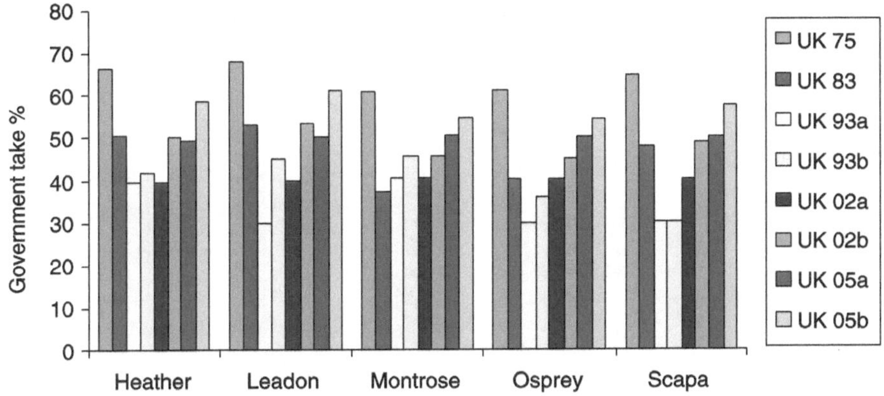

Figure D16 Small fields (continued).

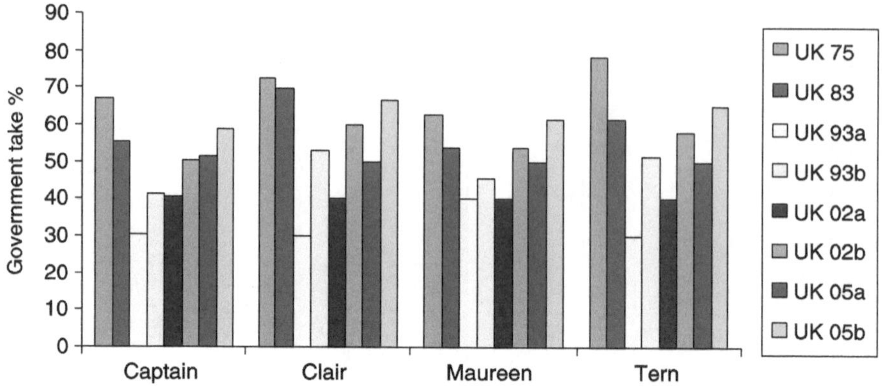

Figure D17 Medium fields.

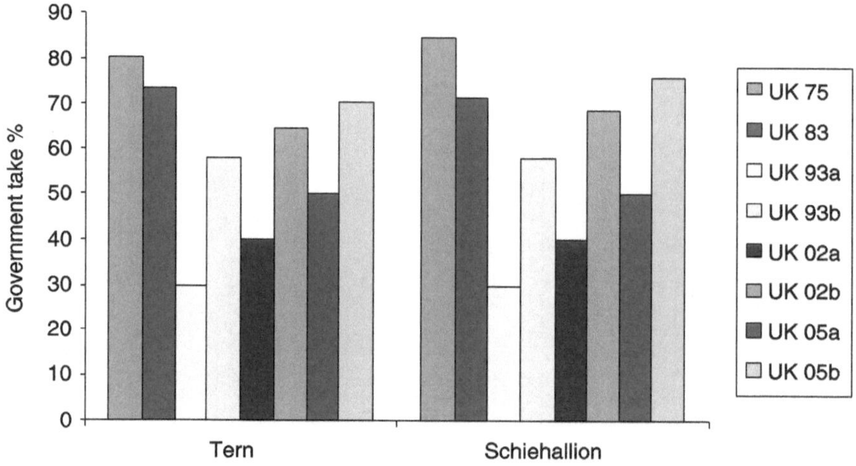

Figure D18 Large fields.

Government take percentage for all fields under different tax scenarios using high oil price.

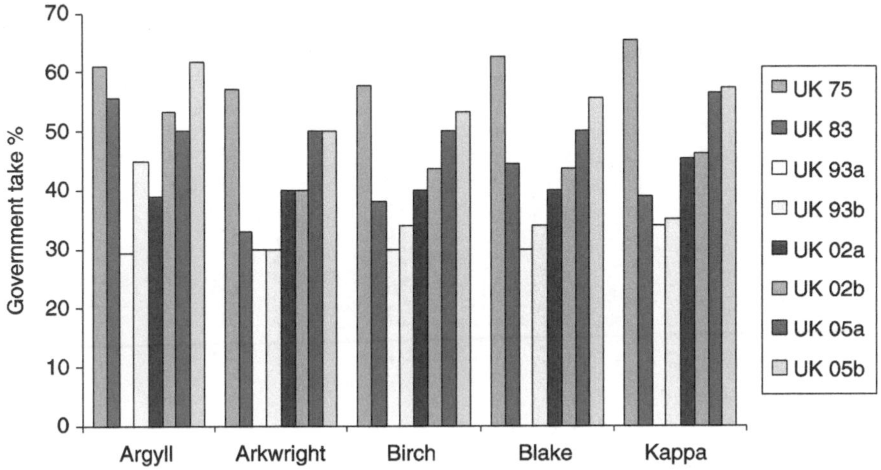

Figure D19 Very small fields.

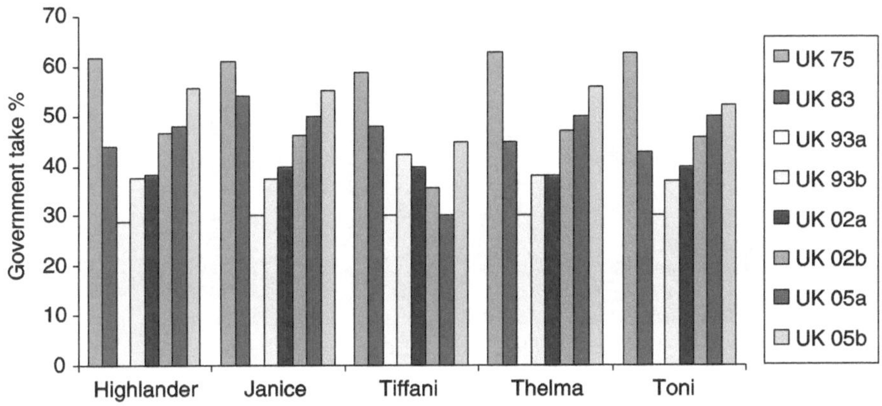

Figure D20 Very small fields (continued).

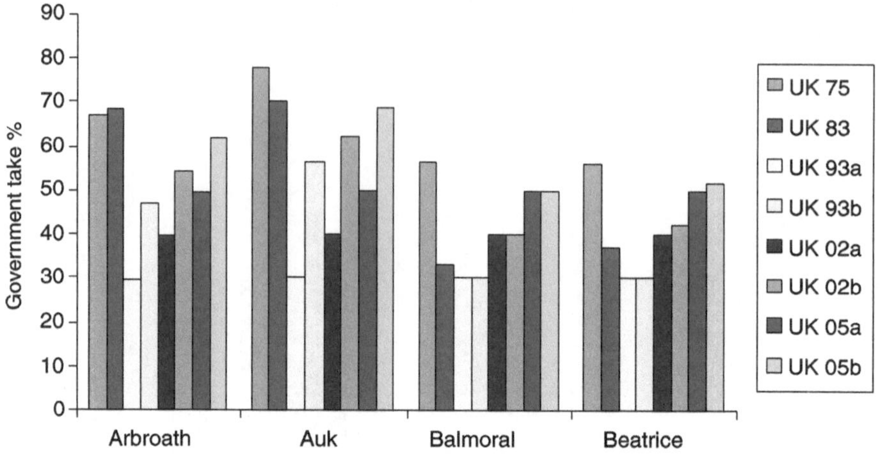

Figure D21 Small fields.

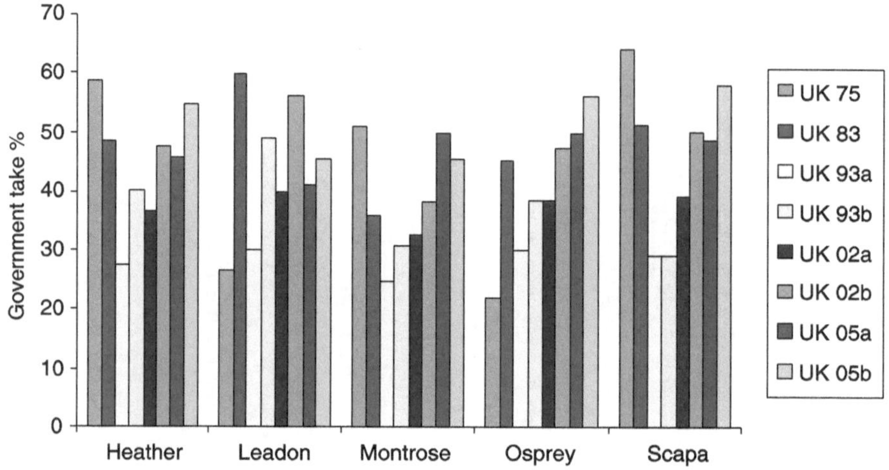

Figure D22 Small fields (continued).

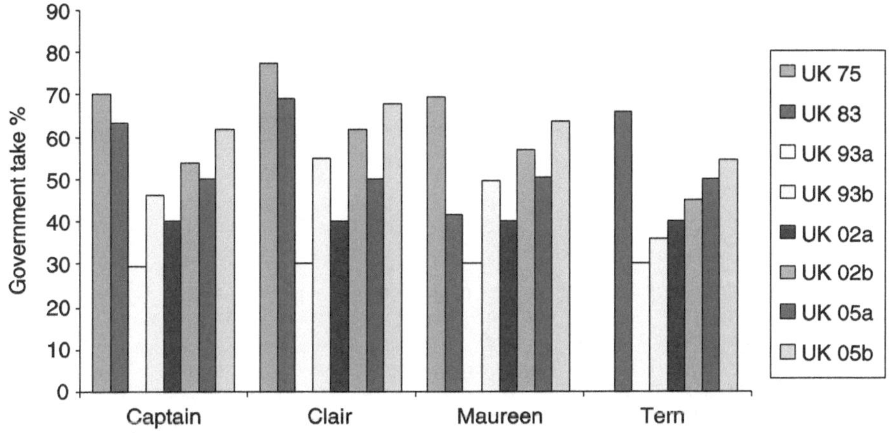

Figure D23 Medium fields.

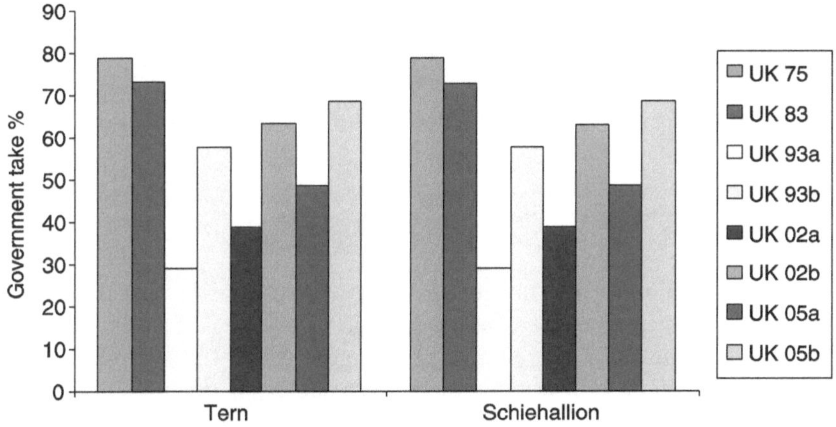

Figure D24 Large fields.

Appendix E
Oil price model

Geometric brownian motion[1]

The GBM considers price changes in terms of two components: a constant drift, α, and a random deviation from the tendency written as the product of a volatility parameter, σ, and an error term, u_{t+1}:

$$\frac{(P_{t+1} - P_t)}{P_t} = \alpha + \sigma u_{t+1} \qquad \text{(E.1)}$$

Over a short interval of time, *dt*, the discrete time process is illustrated as:

$$\frac{(P_{t+1} - P_t)}{P_t} = \alpha dt + \sigma \sqrt{dt u_{t+dt}} \qquad \text{(E.2)}$$

When *dt* approaches zero, hence $dP_t = \lim(P_{t+dt} - P_t)$, the left hand side becomes an instantaneous percentage change in price: $\frac{dP_t}{P_t}$. The first term on the right side of the equation remains unchanged. As for the second term, the uncertain component, the series of discrete variables, u_t, are substituted with a term, *dz*, called the standard Brownian Motion, where $dz = \lim u_{t+1}\sqrt{dt}$, as *dt* approaches zero.

The continuous time equation illustrating the GBM process is:

$$\frac{dP_t}{P_t} = \alpha dt + \sigma dz \qquad \text{(E.3)}$$

Because the percentage changes in P are normally distributed, and since these changes are in the natural logarithm of x, the absolute changes in P are lognormally distributed.

If P(t) is given by equation (F.3) then F(t) = log P is given by:

$$dF = (\alpha - \frac{1}{2}\sigma^2)dt + \sigma \mathrm{dz} \qquad \text{(E.4)}$$

Over a finite time interval t, the change in the logarithm of P is normally distributed with mean $(a - \frac{1}{2}\sigma^2)t$ and variance of $\sigma^2 t$. For P itself, if P(0) = P_0, the expected value of P(t) is:

$$\varepsilon[P(t)] = P_0 e^{at} \tag{E.5}$$

and the variance of P(t) is:

$$v[P(t)] = P_0^2 e^{2at}(e^{\sigma^2 t} - 1) \tag{E.6}$$

Mean reversion model

Brownian Motion tends to wander far from its starting point (Emhjellen, 1999). However, under MRM price might fluctuate as a consequence of various events, but in the long run it might be drawn back towards an initial value.

The continuous time equation illustrating the MRM process is:

$$dP = a(P' - P)dt + \sigma dz \tag{E.7}$$

where λ is the speed of reversion and P' is the normal level of P.
If the value of P is currently P_0 and P follows Equation (E.7), then the expected value of P(t) is:

$$\varepsilon[P_t] = P' + (P_0 - P')e^{-\lambda t} \tag{E.8}$$

and the variance of $(P_t - P')$ is:

$$v(P_t - P') = \frac{\sigma^2}{2\lambda}(1 - e^{-2\lambda t}) \tag{E.9}$$

As t becomes large, $\varepsilon(P_t)$ converges to P' and the variance converges to $\frac{\sigma^2}{2\lambda}$. Also, as λ tends to infinity, the variance tends to zero, and when λ tends to zero, P_t becomes a simple GBM.

In both GBM and MRM the distribution of futures prices is lognormal. However, under GBM, oil prices in the future have a lognormal distribution with variance growing proportionally to the time interval. Whereas under MRM, the variance of the distributions grows in the beginning until a certain time t and remains constant after this.

Appendix F

The Black-Scholes Model[1]

Original Black Scholes Formula

The original Black-Scholes formula for the price of a European call option on stock has five parameters, four of which are directly observable and which are the price of the stock, the exercise price, the risk free rate and the time to maturity of the option.

The formula is:

$$C = N(d_t)S - N(d_2)Ee^{-rT}$$

$$d_1 = \frac{\ln(S / E) + (r + \sigma^2 / 2)T}{\sigma\sqrt{T}} \tag{F.1}$$

$$d_2 = d_1 - \sigma\sqrt{T}$$

Where:

- *C*: the price of the call
- *S*: the price of the stock
- *E*: the exercise price
- *r*: the risk-free interest rate (the annualised continuously compounded rate on a safe asset with the same maturity as the option)
- *T*: the time to maturity of the option (in years)
- σ: the standard deviation of the annualised continuously compounded rate of return on the stock
- *ln*: the natural logarithm
- *e*: the base of natural log function (approximately 2.71828)
- *N(d)*: the probability that a random draw from a standard normal distribution will be less than *d*

Derivation of the partial differential equation[2]

The Paddock, Siegel and Smith model is the most popular model for petroleum real options applications. The model is based on the Black-Scholes formula and is used to derive the option value of a petroleum project. This model has practical advantages due to its simplicity and few parameters estimation.

The following are the variables used in the model, where:

- B_t: the number of barrels of oil in the developed reserve
- V_t: the value per barrel of the developed reserve
- R_t: the return over an instant of time to the owner of the developed reserve. This return consists of the flow of profits from production and the capital gain on the remaining oil.
- $t = T$: the time to expiration.
- a_v: the risk adjusted expected rate of return to the owner
- σ_v: the standard deviation of the rate of return to the owner.
- dz: Wiener increment (random increment)
- ω: the fraction of oil in the reserve produced each year.
- Π: the after tax profit from a barrel of oil
- δ: the dividend yield from a unit of developed reserve
- i: the risk-free interest rate (real and after tax)
- I: the investment cost per barrel

R_t is assumed to follow a GBM:

$$R_t dt / B_t V_t = a_v dt + \sigma_v dz \quad \text{(F.2)}$$

The production from a developed reserve is assumed to follow an exponential decline:

$$dB_t = -\omega B_t dt \quad \text{(F.3)}$$

Then, R_t can be written as:

$$R_t dt = \lambda B_t \Pi_t dt + d(B_t V_t) = \lambda B_t \Pi_t dt + B_t dV_t - \lambda V_t B_t dt \quad \text{(F.4)}$$

Combining (D.2) and (D.4) gives the equation for the value of a barrel of oil (V):

$$dV = (a_v - \delta_t) V dt + \sigma_v V dz \quad \text{(F.5)}$$

Where:

$$\delta_t = \lambda(\Pi_t - V_t) / V_t \quad \text{(F.6)}$$

Using equation (F.5) and letting the F(V,t) denote the value of an undeveloped barrel of oil, with the use of Ito's Lemma, F(V,t), must satisfy:

$$\tfrac{1}{2}\sigma_v^2 V_{et}^2 F''(V) + (i-\delta)V_{et}VF'(V) - iF = 0 \qquad \text{(F.7)}$$

Equation (D.7) must be solved subject to the following boundary conditions:

$F(0,t) = 0$

$F(V,t) = \max(V_t - I, 0)$

$F(V^*,t) = V^* - I$

$F'(V^*,t) = 1$

Where:

- I is the project development cost
- $F(0,t) = 0$ condition arises from the observation that if V goes to zero, it will stay at zero. Therefore the option to invest will be of no value when V=0
- V^* is the price at which it is optimal to invest
- $F(V^*,t) = V^* - I$ is the value matching condition whereupon investing the firm receives $V^* - I$
- $F'(V^*,t) = 1$ is the smooth pasting condition, where if F(V) were not continuous and smooth at the critical exercise point V^*, one could do better by exercising at a different point.

Appendix G

DCF versus MAP results

Table G1 Pre tax scenario

	Base Scenario			*DCF*			*MAP*			
Year	*Revenues Liquids £M (A)*	*Total OPEX £M (B)*	*Total CAPEX £M (C)*	*Pre-tax NCF £M (D)*	*Real NCF £M (E)*	*Discounted NCF £M (F)*	*Revenues Liquids £M (G)*	*Pre-tax NCF £M (H)*	*Real NCF £M (I)*	*Discounted NCF £M (J)*
2002	0.0	0.0	110.0	–110.0	–110.0	–110.0	0.0	–110.0	–110.0	–110.0
2003	0.0	0.0	235.0	–235.0	–229.2	–207.4	0.0	–235.0	–229.2	–224.7
2004	0.0	0.0	220.0	–220.0	–209.3	–171.3	0.0	–220.0	–209.3	–201.1
2005	224.8	54.0	50.0	120.8	112.1	83.0	189.3	85.3	79.1	74.5
2006	364.0	58.7	25.0	280.3	253.6	170.0	293.6	209.9	189.9	175.3
2007	375.8	58.8	58.0	259.0	228.6	138.6	291.9	175.2	154.6	139.9
2008	506.3	66.8	73.0	366.5	315.4	173.1	380.7	240.9	207.3	183.9
2009	456.9	68.4	121.0	267.4	224.5	111.5	333.9	144.5	121.3	105.4
2010	424.3	69.3	37.0	318.0	260.3	117.0	302.5	196.2	160.6	136.9
2011	460.1	65.7	11.0	383.4	306.2	124.5	321.1	244.4	195.2	163.0
2012	474.7	63.9	70.0	340.8	265.4	97.6	325.1	191.2	148.9	121.9
2013	460.7	64.1	50.9	345.7	262.6	87.4	310.4	195.4	148.4	119.1
2014	548.8	72.4	10.4	466.0	345.2	104.0	364.6	281.8	208.7	164.2
2015	484.0	68.8	5.4	409.8	296.1	80.7	317.6	243.4	175.9	135.6
2016	402.3	63.1	0.0	339.2	239.0	58.9	261.2	198.1	139.6	105.5
2017	329.9	57.4	0.0	272.5	187.3	41.8	212.2	154.8	106.4	78.8
2018	295.8	49.4	0.0	246.5	165.2	33.4	188.7	139.4	93.4	67.8

2019	245.5	48.5	0.0	197.0	128.8	23.5	155.5	107.0	70.0	49.8
2020	214.6	46.8	0.0	167.8	107.0	17.7	135.1	88.3	56.3	39.3
2021	189.6	47.3	0.0	142.4	88.5	13.2	118.8	71.5	44.4	30.4
2022	182.7	41.9	0.0	140.8	85.4	11.6	113.9	72.0	43.7	29.3
2023	175.3	34.9	0.0	140.5	83.1	10.2	108.8	74.0	43.8	28.7
2024	179.7	32.6	0.0	147.1	84.9	9.4	111.2	78.6	45.3	29.2
2025	167.5	30.4	0.0	137.0	77.1	7.7	103.3	72.9	41.0	25.9
2026	154.5	30.9	0.0	123.6	67.8	6.2	95.0	64.1	35.2	21.8
2027	140.8	31.7	0.0	109.1	58.4	4.8	86.4	54.7	29.3	17.8
2028	126.2	32.5	0.0	93.8	49.0	3.6	77.3	44.8	23.4	13.9
2029	110.9	33.3	0.0	77.6	39.5	2.7	67.8	34.5	17.6	10.2
2030	0.0	0.0	110.0	–110.0	–54.6	–3.3	0.0	–110.0	–54.6	–31.2
2031	0.0	0.0	0.0	0.0	0.0	0.0	0.0	0.0	0.0	0.0
Totals:	7695.7	1291.4	1186.7	5217.6	3728.0	1040.1	5265.9	2787.7	1976.2	1501.3

Table G1. Pre Tax Scenario Explained

(A) Oil Revenue = Oil Price × Output

NPV DCF Calculation

(B) Pre-tax Net Cash Flow = Revenues – OPEX – CAPEX
(D) = (A) – (B) – (C)

(C) Real pre-tax NCF = Pre-tax NCF (D) / Inflation Factor

(D) Discounted Real NCF is equal to Real NCF multiplied by the discount factor

$$(F) = (E) \times e^{-rt},$$

where r is the discount rate assumed to be 10% in real terms and, t is the period, with year 2002 considered as period 0.
The total of column (F) gives the NPV using DCF technique.

NPV MAP Calculation

(G) Revenues adjusted for oil price risk. They are equal to revenues multiplied by the Risk Discount Factor (RDF), as given in Table G2, Column L.
(G) = (A) × RDF

(H) Pre-tax NCF is Revenues adjusted for risk less OPEX and CAPEX
(H) = (G) – (B) – (C)

(I) Real pre-tax NCF = Pre-tax NCF (H) / Inflation Factor

(J) Discounted Real NCF is equal to Real NCF discounted for time only, i.e. it is equal to Real NCF multiplied by the Time Discount Factor TDF, as calculated in Table G2, Column K.
The total of column (J) gives the NPV using MAP technique.

Table G2 Discount factors comparison

Risk adjustment factor of oil prices	$\phi = 0.3503$
Volatility factor of oil prices	$\sigma = 0.2$
Rate of mean reversion	$\lambda = 0.139$
Real risk free rate	$i' = 0.02$

Year	*Period*	*TDF (Real) (K)*	*RDF (Mean Reversion) (L)*	*Total MAP Discounting (M)*	*DCF Discounting (N)*
2002	0	1	1	1	1
2003	1	0.9801987	0.9366845	0.9181369	0.9048374
2004	2	0.9607894	0.8848569	0.8501611	0.8187308
2005	3	0.9417645	0.8420943	0.7930546	0.7408182
2006	4	0.9231163	0.8065664	0.7445546	0.67032
2007	5	0.9048374	0.7768711	0.702942	0.6065307
2008	6	0.8869204	0.7519204	0.6668936	0.5488116
2009	7	0.8693582	0.7308607	0.6353798	0.4965853
2010	8	0.8521438	0.7130145	0.6075909	0.449329
2011	9	0.8352702	0.6978393	0.5828844	0.4065697
2012	10	0.8187308	0.6848964	0.5607458	0.3678794
2013	11	0.8025188	0.6738287	0.5407602	0.3328711
2014	12	0.7866279	0.6643429	0.5225906	0.3011942
2015	13	0.7710516	0.6561968	0.5059616	0.2725318
2016	14	0.7557837	0.6491892	0.4906466	0.246597
2017	15	0.7408182	0.6431519	0.4764586	0.2231302
2018	16	0.726149	0.6379437	0.4632422	0.2018965
2019	17	0.7117703	0.6334458	0.4508679	0.1826835
2020	18	0.6976763	0.6295574	0.4392273	0.1652989
2021	19	0.6838614	0.626193	0.4282293	0.1495686
2022	20	0.67032	0.6232799	0.417797	0.1353353
2023	21	0.6570468	0.6207558	0.4078656	0.1224564
2024	22	0.6440364	0.6185676	0.3983801	0.1108032
2025	23	0.6312836	0.6166697	0.3892935	0.1002588
2026	24	0.6187834	0.6150228	0.3805659	0.090718
2027	25	0.6065307	0.6135932	0.3721631	0.082085
2028	26	0.5945205	0.6123518	0.3640557	0.0742736
2029	27	0.5827483	0.6112736	0.3562186	0.0672055
2030	28	0.5712091	0.6103368	0.3486299	0.0608101
2031	29	0.5598984	0.6095228	0.3412708	0.0550232

(G) $TDF = e^{-i't}$
(H) $\text{RDF} = \exp(-\varphi\sigma(1 - \exp(-\lambda t))/\lambda)$
(I) Total MAP Discounting = TDF × RDF
(J) DCF Discounting = e^{-rt}

References

Aaron, H. and Boskin, M. (1980) 'The Economics of Taxation', Studies of Government Finance, The Brookings Institution, Washington DC.

Alexander's Gas and Oil Connections. (1998) 'Shell Expro Warns UK Government on Tax Issue', vol. 3, (June 15).

Altay, A. (2000) The Theory of Optimal Taxation and New Approaches: A Survey, Dokuz Eylül Üniversitesi. Online. Available: <http://www.sbe.deu.edu.tr/SBEWEB/dergi/dergi05/altay.htm> (accessed December 2002).

Ambler, S. (1999) 'Les Modeles a Agent Representatif et la Politique de Taxation Optimale', CREFE- Universite de Quebec a Montreal.

Amimer, D. (2001) 'Economic Evaluation and Optimization of Assets in Petroleum Industry', Unpublished Thesis, University of Dundee.

Amundsen, E., Andersen, C. and Sannarnes, J.G. (1993) 'Rent Taxes on Hydropower Generation', *The Energy Journal*, 13: 97–116.

Andersen, A. (2000) 'Guide to Upstream Oil and Gas Taxation in the UK', Tax Services.

Andersen, S. (1993) 'The Struggle Over North Sea Oil and Gas: Government Strategies in Denmark, Britain and Norway', USA: Oxford University Press.

Andrews-Speed, P. (1998) 'Fiscal Systems for Mining: the case of Brazil', *Journal of Mineral Policy, Business and Environment*, 13: 13–21.

Atkinson, A. and Stiglitz, J. (1980) 'Lectures in Public Economics', London: McGraw-Hill Book Company UK Ltd.

Auerbach, A. (1985) 'The Theory of Excess Burden and Optimal Taxation', in 'Handbook of Public Economics' 1: 61–127; (edited by Auberbach, and Feldstein) 1:61–127, Elsevier Science Publishers.

Baker, M., Mayfield, S., and Parsons, J. (1998) 'Alternative Models of Uncertain Commodity Prices for Use with Modern Asset Pricing Methods', *The Energy Journal*, 19: 115–148.

Banfi, S., Filippini, M. and Mueller, A. (2003) 'Rent of Hydropower Generation in Switzerland in a Liberalised Market', *Centre for Energy Policy and Economics*, Federal Institute of Technology, Zurich.

Bank of England, (2002) 'Interest and Exchange Rate Data'. Online. Available HTTP: <http://www.bankofengland.co.uk> (accessed October 2002).

Barrows, G. (2000) 'World Petroleum Arrangements', The Barrows Company Inc.

Beckman, J. (1998) 'Industry Confounded by UK Tax Hiatus', *Offshore Journal*, Offshore Europe Section, May.

Bhattacharyya, S. (1998) 'Energy Taxation and Environmental Externalities: a Critical Analysis', *The Journal of Energy and Development*, 22: 199–220.

Bierman, H. and Smidt, S. (1984) 'The Capital Budgeting Decision', Mcmillan Publishing Company, Seventh Edition.

Bijur, P. (1991) 'Comment: Here's how to Assure Adequate Investment Levels in North Sea', *Oil and Gas Journal*, 89: 29, July 22.

Bittker, B. (1980) 'Equity, Efficiency, and Income Tax Theory: Do Misallocations Drive out Inequities?' Yale University Law School.

Bjerkedal, N. (2000) 'The Report from the Norwegian Tax Expert Commission', Paper presented at 11th International Petroleum Tax Conference, Odlo, Norway, November 9–10.

Bjornland, H.C. (1998) 'The Economic Effects of North Sea Oil on the Manufacturing Sector', *Scottish Journal of Political Economy*, 45:5.

Black, F. and Scholes, M. (1973) 'The Pricing of Options and Corporate Liabilities', *Journal of Political Economy*, 81: 637–659.

Bland, D. (1988) 'UK Oil Taxation', Arthur Young, 2nd edition.

Blinn, K., Duval, C. and Leuch, H. (1986) 'International Petroleum Exploration and Exploitation Agreements – Legal, Economic and Policy Aspects', Barrows Company Inc.

Bodie, Z. and Merton, R. (2000) 'Finance', Prentice Hall, Inc.

Bond, S. and Devereux, M. (1995) 'On the Design of a Neutral Business Tax under Uncertainty', *Journal of Public Economics*, 58: 57–71.

Bond, S., Devereux, M. and Sunders, M. (1987) 'North Sea Taxation for the 1990's', The Institute for Fiscal Studies.

Boskin, M. and Robinson, M. (1985) 'Energy Taxes and Optimal Tax Theory', *The Energy Journal*, Special Tax Issue, 6: 1–15.

Bradley, P. (1998) 'On the Use of Modern Asset Pricing for Comparing Alternative Royalty Systems for Petroleum Development Projects', *The Energy Journal* 19: 47–81.

Brealey, R. and Myers, S. (1991) 'Principles of Corporate Finance', 4th ed. McGraw-Hill, New York.

Brennan, M. and Schwartz, E. (1985) 'A New Approach to Evaluating Natural Resource Investments', *Midland Journal of Applied Corporate Finance*, 3: 37–47.

Brennan, M. and Schwartz, E. (1985) 'Evaluating Natural Resource Investments', *Journal of Business*, 58: 135–157.

Brent, N. (1991) 'The State Offshore: Petroleum, Politics, and State Intervention on the British and Norwegian Continental Shelves', New York: Praeger Publishers.

Brown, E. (1948) 'Business Income Taxation and Investment Incentives', in *Employment and Public Policy*, Essays in Honor of A.H. Hansen, New York, as referred to in Watkins (2001).

Buchanan, J. M. and Dwight, L. R. (1982) 'Politics Time and the Laffer Curve', *The Journal of Political Economy*, 90:4: 816–819, August 1982.

Burns, J., Lewis, I. and Sick, G. (1992) 'Valuing Petroleum Investments Using Discrete Option Pricing Theory', Society of Petroleum Engineers, Paper 2: 44–75.

Cappuccio, N. and Morettor, M (2001) 'Comments on the Investment-Uncertainty Relationship in a Real Option Model', University Di Padova, Department of Economics, Italy.

Coelen, N. (2002) 'Black-Scholes Option Pricing Model', Paper Posted at Trinity

Education. Online. Available HTTP: <http://www.trinity.edu/departments/mathematics/studpapers/s11pdf> (accessed December 2003).

Common Consolidated Corporate Tax Base Working Group (CCCTB WG), 'General Tax Principles', European Commision Directorate-General Taxation and Customs Union. Brussels, 10 December 2004.

Committee on Energy Taxation (1980) 'Energy Taxation: an Analysis of Selected Taxes', National Academy of Science, Washington DC.

Condray, A. (2002) 'North Sea Investment and Strategy – a Global Context', Speech Presented at the 'Future for Investment in the North Sea Conference', London, May.

Copeland, T. and Antikarov, V. (2001) 'Real Options – A Practitioner's Guide, Texere LLC Publishing, pp.372.

Copeland, T. and Keenan, P. (1998) 'How Much is Flexibility Worth?' *The McKinsey Quarterly*, 2: 38–49.

Cox J., Ross, S. and Rubenstein, M. (1979) 'Option Pricing: A Simplified Approach', *Journal of Financial Economics*, 7: 229–263.

Crawford, R. (2006) 'Gordon's own goal?' Parliamentary Brief, 10:5: 21–23.

Creedy, J. (1999) 'Tax Models and Their Uses', The University of Melbourne.

Crowson, P. (2004) 'Astride Mining: Issues and Policies for the Minerals Industry', Mining Journal Books Ltd.

Crum, F. R. (1985) 'Capital Tax Distortions in the Petroleum Industry', *The Energy Journal*, Special Tax Issue, 6: 155–169.

Dasgputa, P. and Heal, G. (1979) 'Economic Theory and Exhaustible Resources', Oxford: Cambridge University Press.

Dasgputa, P. and Stiglitz, J. (1971) 'Differential Taxation, Public Production and Economic Efficiency', Review of Economic Studies, 38: 151–74.

Davis, G. (1998) 'Estimating Volatility and Dividend Yield when Valuing Real Options to Invest or Abandon', Quarterly Review of Economics and Finance, Special Issue, 38: 715–754.

Deacon, R. (1992) 'Taxation, Depletion and Welfare: A Simulation Study of the U.S. Petroleum Resource', *Journal of Environmental Economics and Management*, 24: 159–187.

Deloitte and Touche (2003) 'Perspectives on UK Oil and Gas Taxation', Deloitte and Touche LLP.

Dentskevich, P. (1991) 'The Applications of Option Valuation Techniques to the Valuation of Physical Investment Opportunities', PhD Thesis, Imperial College.

Department of Trade and Industry (2003) 'Oil and Gas Directorate', DTI. Online. Avaiable: <http://ww.og.dti.gov.uk/upstream/taxation/index.htm> (accessed December 2003).

Department of Trade and Industry (2002) 'Abolition of North Sea Royalty-Consultation on Appropriate Timing', DTI. Online. Available HTTP: <http://www.og.dti.gov.uk/consultations/roycon.pdf> (November 2002).

Department of Trade and Industry (2001) 'Industry Activity Survey, 2001', Notes kindly provided by Mr. Earp, DTI.

Department of Trade and Industry (DTI) (2005) 'Digest of United Kingdom Energy Statistics', DTI.

Department of Trade and Industry (2000) 'Development of the Oil and Gas Resources of the UK- Brown Book' DTI. Online. Available HTTP: <http://www.dbd-data.co.uk/bbonline/index.htm> (February 2001).

Devereux, M., Griffith, R. and Klemm, A. (2004) 'Why has the UK Corporation Tax Raised so Much Revenue?' The Institute For Fiscal Studies IFS Working Papers.

Devereux, M. and Morris, C. (1983) 'North Sea Oil Tax Revenue: a Disaggregated Model', *The Institute For Fiscal Studies IFS*, Working Paper no. 40.

Diamond, P. and Mirrlees, J. (1971a) 'Optimal Taxation and Public Production I: Production efficiency', *American Economic Review*, 61: 8–27.

Diamond, P. and Mirrlees, J. (1971b) 'Optimal Taxation and Public Production II: Tax Rules', *American Economic Review*, 41: 277–96.

Dias, M. (2001) 'Real Options in Upstream Petroleum: Overview of Models and Applications', Online. Available: <http://www.puc-rio.br/marco.ind/overview.html> (December 2003).

Dias, M. (1999) 'A Note on Bibliographical Evolution of Real Options', in Lenos Trigeorgis, Edition, 'Real Options and Business Strategy- Applications to Decision Making', pp.357–362.

Dias, M. (1997) 'The Timing of Investment in E&P: Uncertainty, Irreversibility, Learning and Strategic Consideration', Paper presented at 1997 SPE Hydrocarbon Economics and Evaluation Symposium, Dallas, Proceedings pp.135–148.

Dias, M. and Rocha, K. (1998) 'Petroleum Concessions with Extendible Options Using Mean Reversion with Jumps to Model Oil Prices', Paper presented at the 3rd Annual International Conference on Real Options, June, Netherlands.

Dickson, T. (1999) Taxing Our Resources for the Future, Online. Available HTTP. <http://www.eraweb.net> (accessed March 2000).

Dixit, A. and Pindyck, R. (1995) 'The Options Approach to Capital Investment', *Harvard Business Review*, May–June, 105–115.

Dixit, A. and Pindyck, R. (1994) 'Investment Under Uncertainty', Library of Congress Cataloguing in Publication Data.

Eckbo, P. L. (1987) 'Worldwide Petroleum Taxation: the Pressure for Revision', Massachusetts, MA: Institute of Technology Press.

Ekern, S. (1988) 'An Option Pricing Approach to Evaluating Petroleum Projects', *Energy Economics*, 10: 91–99.

Emhjellen, M. (1999) 'Valuation of Oil Projects Using the Discounted Cashflow Method', Unpublished PhD Thesis, University of New South Wales.

Emhjellen, M. and Alaouze, C. (2001) 'The Discounted Net Cashflow Method and a Modern Asset Pricing Method – Implications for Project Selection and Government Policy', The University of New South Wales.

Emhjellen, M. and Alaouze, C. (1999) 'A Comparison of Oil Project NPV's in the North Sea Obtained using the Weighted Average Cost of Capital Discounting Method and a Modern Asset Pricing Method', The University of New South Wales.

Energy Committee, (1987) 'The Effect of Oil and Gas Prices on Activity in the North Sea', House of Commons, Third report from the Energy Committee.

Fane, G. (1987) 'Neutral Taxation Under Uncertainty', *Journal of Public Economics*, 33: 95–105.

Faris, S. (2007) 'All Eyes North: why Norway is keeping watch on its reserves, resources and Russia', Monocle, 2: 25–39, April.

Favero, C. (1992) 'Taxation and the Optimisation of Oil Exploration and Production: the UK Continental Shelf', *Oxford Economic Papers*, 44: 187–208.

Financial Secretary (1994) 'Speech to Petroleum Economist Conference'. Energy Now and for the Future, (2006) *UKOOA Oil and Gas for Britain Economic Report*, July 2006.

Fraser, R. and Kingwell, R. (1997) 'Can Expected Tax Revenue be Increased by an Investment Preserving Switch from Ad Valorem Royalties to a Resource Rent Tax?' *Resource Policy*, 23: 103–108.

Fullerton, D. and Henderson, V. (1983) 'Differential taxation, Public Production and Economic Efficiency', Urban Institute, Washington DC.

Garnaut, R. and Clunies Ross, A. (1983) 'Taxation of Mineral Rents', New York: Oxford University Press.

Garnaut, R. and Clunies Ross, A. (1979) 'The Neutrality of the Resource Rent Tax', *The Economic Record*, 55: 193–201.

Garnaut, R. and Clunies Ross, A. (1975) 'Uncertainty, Risk Aversion and the Taxing of Natural Resource Projects', *Economic Journal*, 85: 272–87.

Ghouri, S. (1996) 'Pakistan's New Petroleum Policy', *Energy Policy*, 24: 477–488.

Gibson, R. (2003) 'Real Options Theory as an Investment Decision-Making Tool', Zurich University, Switzerland.

Gilbert, R. (1976) 'Optimal Depletion of an Uncertain Stock', Technical Report no. 207, Stanford University, May.

Giles, C. and Hoyos, C. 2006 'North Sea tax revenue cut by £1.5bn' Financial Times, 25 March.

Global Insight (2007) 'United Kingdom – Norway: The End of an Era? The Outlook for Oil Production in the North Sea and Surrounds', June.

Gray, L. C. (1914) 'Rent Under the Assumption of Exhaustibility', *Quarterly Journal of Economics*, vol. 28.

Harberger, A. (1980) 'Tax Neutrality in Investment Incentives', University of Chicago.

Harberger, A. (1961) 'The Tax Treatment of Oil Exploration', The Proceedings of the Second Energy Institute, Washington DC, The American University, pp.259–269.

HarrisonLovegrove Co. (2003) 'The UK Continental Shelf-Still an Attractive Place', Online. Available HTTP: <http://www.hargrove.co.uk> (accessed July 2003).

Harvie, C. (1994) 'Fool's Gold: The Story of North Sea Oil', London: Hamish Hamilton.

Hayllar, R. and Pleasance, R (1977) 'UK Taxation of Offshore Oil and Gas', Butterworth and Co. Ltd.

Heady, C. (1993) 'Optimal Taxation as a Guide to Tax Policy: a survey', *Fiscal Studies*, 14:15–41.

Heaps, T. and J, Helliwell. (1985) 'The Taxation of Natural Resources', *Handbook of Public Economics*, Elsevier Science Publishers, vol. 1.

Helliwell, J. (1982) 'Taxation of Oil and Gas Revenues of Four Countries: Canada', *The Energy Journal*, 3: 20–30.

Henderson, D. (2004) 'North Sea Industry Experiences Renewed Interest', Alexander's Gas and Oil Connections, vol. 9, April 7.

H M Treasury and Customs, 2006 'Regulatory impact assessment for changes to the North Sea tax regime'. Online. Available: <http://www.hmrc.gov.uk/ria/ria-north-sea-regimes>

Horngren, C., Sundem, G and Elliott, J. (1993) 'Introduction to Financial Accounting', 3rd ed. Prentice Hall.

Hotelling, H. (1931) 'The Economics of Exhaustible Resources', *Journal of Political Economy*, 39: 111–119.

Howell, D. and Nakhle, C. (2007) 'Out of the Energy Labyrinth', London: I.B.Tauris.

Inland Revenue, (2003a) 'International – The North Sea Fiscal Regime a Guide to UK and UK Continental Shelf', Online. Available HTTP: <http://www.inlandrevenue.gov.uk/international/ns-fiscal3.htm#b> (November 2003)

Inland Revenue (2003b) 'Oil Taxation Manual', Online. Available http://www.inlandrevenue.gov.uk/manuals/otmanual/contents.htm (November 2003)

Inland Revenue (2003c) 'Petroleum Revenue Tax: Exemption for New Tariffing Business', Budget 2003, 9 April.

Inland Revenue (2000) 'PRT: Misuse of Safeguard Relief', Inland Revenue Press, 21 March 2000.

Institute of Fiscal Studies Committee (1981) 'The Taxation of North Sea Oil', The Institute For Fiscal Studies IFS.

The Institute of Petroleum (2001) 'Industry Information: Leading Oil Companies in the UK', London.

International Energy Agency (IEA) (2007) 'World Energy Outlook'.

International Petroleum Enterprises (2001) 'Reopening of Upstream Oil and Natural Gas to Foreign Interests: Views and Actions of Iran, Iraq, Kuwait and Saudi Arabia', Report Published by IPE.

Jacoby, H. and Laughton, D (1992) 'Project Evaluation: A Practical Asset Pricing Model', *Energy Journal*, 13: 19–47.

Jacoby, H. and Laughton, D (1991) 'Project Evaluation: A Practical Asset Pricing Approach', Institute for Financial Research, University of Alberta, Working Paper no. 1–91.

Jankowski, E. (2000) 'Nature of the Iranian BuyBack Contracts', Paper Presented at the IBC's Production Sharing Agreements/Host Government Contracts Conference 11th April, London.

Johnson, C. (1979) 'The Improvement of the North Sea', *Journal of Institute of Fiscal Studies*, 1: 39–51.

Johnston, D. (2003) 'Petroleum Contract Analysis and Design. State-of-the-Art-State-of-the-Industry', Daniel Johnston and Co., Inc.

Johnston, D. (2002) 'International Petroleum Fiscal System Analysis', Daniel Johnston and Co., Inc.

Johnston, D. (2001) 'International Production Sharing Contract Cash Flow Model', Johnston and Co. Inc.

Johnston, D. (1998) 'International Petroleum Fiscal Systems and Production Sharing Contracts', PennWell Books.

Johnston, J. and Reynolds, A. (1985) 'A Natural Resource Theory of Unitary Taxation', *The Energy Journal*, Special Tax Issue, 6: 309–323.

Jorgenson, D. and Slesnick, D. (1985) 'Efficiency versus Equity in Petroleum Taxation', *The Energy Journal*, Special Tax Issue, 6: 171–187.

Kellas G. (1993) 'Tax Reforms Raise Questions for Oil Industry in the UK', *Oil and Gas Journal*, 91:35.

Kemp, A. and Stephens, L. (1997) 'The UK Petroleum Fiscal System in Retrospect', University of Aberdeen.

Kemp, A., Stephens, L. and Masson, K. (1997) 'A Reassessment of Petroleum Taxation in the UKCS', University of Aberdeen.

Kemp, A., Rose, D. and Dandie, R. (1992) 'Development and Production Prospects for UK Oil and Gas Post-Gulf Crisis – A Financial Simulation', *Energy Policy*, 20: 20–29.

Kemp, A. (1990) 'An Assessment of UK North Sea Oil and Gas Policies, *Energy Policy*, pp.599–623.

Kemp, A. and Rose, D. (1982) 'The Effects of Taxation on Petroleum Exploitation: a comparative study', University of Aberdeen.

Kemp, A. and Crichton, D. (1979) 'Effects of Changes in UK North Sea Oil Taxation', *Energy Economics*, pp.224–240.

Kemp, A. and Crichton, D. (1978) 'A Review of the Proposed Changes in North Sea Oil Taxation', North Sea study occasional papers – University of Aberdeen.

Kooten, C. and Bulte, E. (2001) 'The Economics of Nature – Managing Biological Assets', Blackwell Publishers.

Laffer, A. (2004) 'The Laffer Curve: Past, Present and Future'. Backgrounder no. June 1975.

Laine, J. (1993) 'Option Valuation of Field Development Projects', Society of Petroleum Engineers, Paper 37965.

Laughton, D. (2002) 'A Brief Primer on the Use of Modern Asset Pricing for Project Evaluation in the Upstream Petroleum Industry', Notes provided by Laughton to the author.

Laughton, D. (1998a) 'The Potential for Use of Modern Asset Pricing Methods for Upstream Petroleum Project Evaluation: Introductory Remarks', *The Energy Journal*, 19: 1–11.

Laughton, D. (1998b) 'The Management of Flexibility in the Upstream Petroleum Industry', *The Energy Journal*, 19: 83–114.

Laughton D. (1998c) The Potential for Use of Modern Asset Pricing Methods for Upstream Petroleum Project Evaluation: Concluding Remarks, *The Energy Journal*, 19: 149–153.

Laughton, D. (1997) Spreadsheet presented at the Norwegian Petroleum Directorate Workshop on Modern Asset Pricing and Project Evaluation, Stavanger, Norway, May.

Laughton, D., Sagi, J and Samis, M. (2000) 'Modern Asset Pricing and Project Evaluation in the Energy Industry' Western Centre for Economic Research, University of Alberta, Bulletin 56, September.

Lazzari, S. (2005) 'Energy Tax Policy: An Economic Analysis', Congress Research Service Report, June 28 2005.

Leith, D. (2002) 'Death and Taxes not Necessarily', Ernst and Young LLP, Aberdeen, Scotland.

Loury, G. (1976) 'The Optimum Exploitation of an Unknown Reserve', Unpublished paper, University of California, February.

Lund, D. (2002) 'Petroleum Tax Reform Proposals in Norway and Denmark', *Energy Journal*, 23: 37–56.

Lund, D. (2001) 'Rent Taxation when Cost Monitoring is Imperfect', *Resource and Energy Economics*, 24: 211–228.

Lund, D. (1992) 'Petroleum Taxation Under Uncertainty: Contingent Claims Analysis with an Application to Norway', *Energy Economics*, 14: 23–31.

Lund, D. (1987) 'Investment, Taxes and Uncertainty with Applications to the Norwegian Petroleum Sector', PhD Dissertation, Massachusetts Institute of Technology.

Lund, M. (2001) 'Real Options in Offshore Oil Field Development Projects', Paper presented at the 3rd Annual International Conference on Real Options, 6–8 June, Netherlands.

Lund, M. (2000) 'Valuing Flexibility in Offshore Petroleum Projects', Annals of Operation Research, p.325–350.

Macalister, T. (2002) 'Oil Tax Threat to 50,000 jobs', The Guardian (May 24).

Managi, S., Opaluch, J., Jin, D. and Grigalunas, T. (2005) 'Technological change and petroleum exploration in the Gulf of Mexico', *Energy Policy*, 33: 619–632.

Mannekes, B.V. (2007) 'Oil and Gas Productions', Netherlands Oil and Gas Exploration and Productions Association, Paper presented at Brussels, 28 March 2007.

Martin, S. (1997) 'Tax or Technology? The Revival of UK North Sea Production', Oxford Institute for Energy Studies.

McDonald, R. and Siegel, D. (1986) 'The Value of Waiting to Invest', *Quarterly Journal of Economics*, pp.707–727. November 1986.

McKellar, K. (2006) 'Going Dutch? A Parallel Development beside the SNS', Deloitte.

Mercier, D. (1999) 'Royalty that Slides with Oil Prices Can Add Value to Producing Fields', *Oil and Gas Journal*, 97: 92–95.

Merton, R. (1973) 'The Theory of Rational Option Pricing', *Bell Journal of Economic Management Science*, 4: 141–183.

Miller, M. (2000) 'Why We Must Make More of Black Gold', The Observer- Business section, October 8.

Miller, M., Ireland, N., Cripps, M. and Zhang, L. (1999) 'Collecting Economic Rents on North Sea Oil and Gas: A Proposal', Research Report Submitted to ESCR, University of Warwick.

Mirrlees, J. (1976) 'Optimal Tax Theory: a Synthesis', *Journal of Public Economics*, 6: 327–358.

Mitchell, J. (1982) 'Taxation of Oil and Gas Revenues of Four Countries: The United Kingdom', The Energy Journal, vol.3, pp.39–50.

Mohiuddin, A. and Ash-Kuri, S (1998) 'Measures to Promote Exploration and Production Investment in Pakistan', *Oil and Gas Law and Taxation Review*, 7: 263–269.

Mommer, B. (2001) 'Fiscal Regimes and Oil Revenues in the UK, Alaska and Venezuela', Oxford Institute for Energy Studies.

Mommer, B. (1996) 'Bernard Mommer Defends Petroleum Royalty as an Efficient Rent-Collecting Device', Energy Forum, Oxford, May 1996.

Moose, J. (1982) 'British and American Tax Treatment of UK North Sea Oil Fields', *Energy Journal*, Special Issue, 3: 55–63.

Morgan, O. (2000) 'Can Gordon Soak the Oil Man?' The Observer – Business section, October 8.

Muttitt, G. and Marriott, J (2000) 'Pump and Circumstances', The Guardian, October 4.

Musgrave, R. (1982) 'A Brief History of Fiscal Doctrine', in 'Handbook of Public Economics', vol. 1 (edited by Auberbach A. and M. Feldstein), Elsevier Science Publishers, pp. 1–59.

Myers, S. (1977) 'Determinants of Capital Borrowing', *Journal of Financial Economics*, 5: 147–175.

Nakhle, C. and Hawdon, D (2003) 'The Impact of Oil Taxation on Fields' Profitability in the UK North Sea – A Comparison with Five International Representative Regimes', Paper Presented at the 26th Annual IAEE Conference, June, Prague.

Nakhle, C. and Hawdon, D (2002) 'The Impact of Oil Taxation on Field's Development in the UK North Sea', Paper Presented at the 25th Annual IAEE Conference, Aberdeen.

National Audit Office (2000) 'Petroleum Revenue Tax', Report by the Comptroller and Auditor General HC 5, Session 2000–2001. December 14.

Nelsen, B. (1991) 'The State Offshore: Petroleum, Politics, and State Intervention on the British and Norwegian Continental Shelves', New York: Praeger Publishers.

Nelson, Y. and Nix, D. (1997) 'Results of the Delphi IX Survey of Oil Price Forecasts', California Energy Commission.

Newbery, D. and Stern, N. (1987) 'The Theory of Taxation for Developing Countries', A World Bank Research Publication, Oxford University Press.

Noreng, O. (1980) 'The Oil Industry and Government Strategy in the North Sea', British Library Cataloguing in Publication data.

North Sea Energy Data Statistic and Analysis: Oil, Gas, Electricity and Coal by Country Analysis Briefs January 2007. Online. <www.eia.dow.gov>

OGJ (1993a) 'UK Job Loss Seen in PRT Changes', *Oil and Gas Journal*, vol. 91. April 19.

OGJ (1993b) 'UK Operators React to PRT Changes', *Oil and Gas Journal*, vol. 91. March 29.

OGJ (1993c) 'UK Plans Big Changes in Taxes on Oil and Gas', *Oil and Gas Journal*, vol. 91. (March 22)

Oil and Gas UK (2007) UKOOA (2007) 'Activity Survey' UKOOA Oil and Gas for Britain February 2007. Energy Now and for the Future, (2006) *UKOOA Oil and Gas for Britain Economic Report*, July 2006.

Oil and Gas UK (2006) UKOOA (2006) 'Energy Now and for the Future', UK Offshore Operators Association Economic Report 2006

Oswald, A. (2000) 'Oil and the Real Economy: an Interview with Andrew Oswald', University of Warwick, March 17.

Paddock, J., Siegel, D. and Smith, J. (1988) 'Option Valuation of Claims on Real Assets: the Case of Offshore Petroleum Leases', *Quarterly Journal of Economics*, 103: 479–508.

Palmer, K. (1980) 'Mineral Taxation Policies in Developing Countries: An Application of Resource Rent Tax', International Monetary Fund: Staff Papers, 61: 65–73.

Pechman, J. (1980) 'What Should be Taxed: Income or Expenditure?' Studies of Government Finance, The Brookings Institute, Washington DC.

Perman, R., Ma, J. and McGilvray, J. (1998) 'Natural Resources and Environmental Economics', Singapore: Longman Publishers Ltd.

Petroleum Review (2004) 'Enhanced UK Tax Relief for New North Sea Entrants', February Issue, 58: 3.

Pickles, E. and Smith, J. (1993) 'Petroleum Property Evaluation: A Binomial Lattice Implementation of Option Pricing Theory', *Energy Journal*, 14: 1–26.

Pike, R. and Neale, B. (1996) 'Corporate Finance and Investment- Decisions and Strategies', 2nd edn, Prentice Hall Europe.

Pindyck, R. (2001) 'The Long-Run Evolution of Energy Prices', *Energy Journal*, 20: 27.

Pindyck, R. (1993) 'Investments of Uncertain Cost, *Journal of Financial Economics*, 34: 53–76.

Quinlan, M. (1998) 'North Sea Oil and Gas Province, *Petroleum Economist*,

August 98, Online. Available HTTP: <http://wuda.hypermart.net/characters/cjhuang.html> February 2001.

Raabe, B. (2007) 'Europe's Indigenous Oil and Gas Production', International Association of Oil and Gas Producers, Brussels, 28 March 2007

Raja, A. (1999) Should Neutrality be the Major Objective in the Decision-Making Process of the Government and the Firm, Online. Available: <http.//www.dundee.ac.uk/cepmlp/reflist.docmain/html/car_article2.htm> (accessed December 2000).

Ramsey, F. (1927) 'A Contribution to the Theory of Taxation', *Economic Journal*, 37: 47–61.

Ray, R. (1997) 'Issues in the Design and Reform of Commodity Taxes: Analytical Results and Empirical Evidence' *Journal of Economic Surveys*, 11:4.

Reuters (2004) 'Analysis – UK Faces Future without North Sea Oil, Reuters News Service (January 14).

Ricardo, D. (1951) 'The Principles of Economy and Taxation', vol. 1 of 'Works and Correspondence', edited by Sraffa and Dobb, Cambridge University Press (as referred to by Watkins, 2001).

Ritchie, D. (1992) 'Mineral Sector Investment Criteria – An Industry Perspective', United Nations Seminar, December.

Robinson, C. and Rowland, C. (1978) 'Marginal Effect of PRT Changes', *Petroleum Economist*, 18: 501–503.

Robinson, C. and Morgan, J. (1978) '*North Sea Oil in the Future*', Macmillan Press.

Robinson, C. and Morgan, J (1976) 'World Oil Prices and the Profitability of North Sea Oil', *Petroleum Review*, pp.197–206. April.

Robinson, C. and Rowland, C. (1976) 'A Comparison of Tax Systems', *Petroleum Economist*, pp.170–171. May.

Rodriguez-Padilla (1991) 'Fiscalite Petroliere et Risque', *The Energy Journal*, 13: 91–113.

Rowland, C. (1983) 'The Economics of North Sea Oil Taxation', Unpublished PhD Thesis, University of Surrey.

Rowland, C. (1980) 'Changing North Sea Profits Taxation and the Gains from Offshore Oil', Surrey Energy Economics, Centre, Discussion Paper no. 3, University of Surrey.

Rowland, C. and Hann, D (1987) '*The Economics of North Sea Oil Taxation*', Macmillan Press.

Rowland, C. and Hann, D. (1986) 'UK Oil Taxation: Failings and Reform', Surrey Energy Economics Centre, Discussion Paper no.32, University of Surrey.

Ruairidh, S. (2003) 'The UK North Sea: 2003 a Year of Transition?' Simmons and Company International, Energy Industry Research, February 7.

Rutledge, I. and Wright, P. (2001) 'Taxing Petroleum: Don't Forget about the Upstream', Financial Times Energy Economist (Energy Economist Briefing), 2–12, October.

Rutledge, I. and Wright, P. (1998a) 'Profitability and Taxation in the UKCS Oil and Gas Industry: Analyzing the Distribution of Rewards Between Company and Country', *Energy Policy*, 26: 795–812.

Rutledge, I. and Wright, P. (1998b) 'North Sea Oil Taxation: Principles, Methods and Evidence', Centre for Energy, Petroleum and Mineral Law and Policy, University of Dundee.

Rutledge, I. and Wright, P. (1997) 'Profitability and Taxation in the North Sea Oil and Gas Industry', University of Sheffield, Energy Studies Paper.

Salahor, G. (1998) 'Implications of Output Price Risk and Operating Leverage for the Evaluation of Petroleum Development Projects', *The Energy Journal*, 19: 13–46.

Samuelsen, J. (2002) 'The Norwegian Petroleum Tax System', PriceWaterhouse-Coopers.

Samuelson, P. (1986) 'Theory of Optimal Taxation', *Journal of Public Economics*, 30: 137–43.

Sapsford, R. (2001) 'Survey Research', SAGE Publications Ltd.

Sarkis, N. (2003) 'Iran-South Pars Production above target Rate with Only 15 of the 20 Planned Drills', *Arab Oil and Gas*, 32: 5–14.

Sarma, J. and Naresh, G. (2001) 'Mineral Taxation around the World: Trends an Issues', Asia-Pacific Tax Bulletin, pp.2–10.

Sassoon, J. (2003) 'UKCS Exploration Consultation, HM Treasury Exploration Steering Group.

Scottish Council for Development and Industry (2002) 'The Implications of Recent Changes to the North Sea Fiscal Regime', Policy Paper.

Scully, G. (1994) 'Tax Rates, Tax Revenues and Economic Growth', National Centre for Policy Analysis.

Select Committee on Energy, Press Statement: North Sea oil depletion policy, HMSO, London, 18

Sem, T. Ellerman, D. (1997) 'North Sea Reserve Appreciation, Production and Depletion', Massachusetts Institute of Technology.

Siegel D., Smith, J. and Paddock, J. (1986) 'Valuing Offshore Oil with Option Pricing Models', *Midland Corporate Finance Journal*, 5: 22–30.

Siew, W. (2001) 'Financial Evaluation Techniques Used to Evaluate Risk and Appraise Projects in the Oil Industry', Unpublished Thesis, University of Dundee.

Smith, B. (1999) 'The Impossibility of a Neutral Resource Rent Tax', Faculty of Economics and Commerce, Australian National University, Working Paper no. 380.

Smith, J. and McCardle, K. (1999) 'Options in the Real World: lessons learned in evaluating oil and gas investments', *Operations Research*, 47: 1–15.

Solana, J. (2006) 'Towards an EU External Energy Policy' Speech given at the EU Energy Conference, Brussels, 20 November 2006

Stauffer, T. and Gault, J. (1985) 'Exploration Risks and Mineral Taxation: how fiscal regimes affect exploration incentives', *The Energy Journal*, Special Tax Issue, 6: 125–35.

Stiegeler, S. (1985) 'Dictionary of Economics and Business', Gower Publishing Company Limited. Swan. (1984) 'Resource Rent Tax', Economic Papers, 3: 1–11.

Stiglitz, J. (1975) 'The Efficiency of Market Prices in the Long Run Allocations in the Oil Industry', In Brannon (1975)

Stiglitz, J. (1972) 'Taxation, Risk Taking and the Allocation of Investment in a Competitive Economy', Studies in the Theory of Capital Markets, pp. 295–361.

Sunley, E., Baunsgaard, T. and Simard, D. (2002) 'Revenue from the Oil and Gas Sector: Issues and Country Experience', IMF Conference Proceedings on Fiscal Policy Formulation and Implementation in Oil Producing Countries, June 5–6, 2002.

Swan, P.L. (1984) 'Resource Rent Tax', *Economic Papers*, 3: 1–11.

Tax Principles Workbook: A Tool for Critiquing Tax and Fiscal Proposals and Systems, February 2003.

The Norwegian Petroleum Directorate (2007) 'The Norwegian Petroleum Sector – Facts 2007', Online. Available <http://www.npd.no>

The Norwegian Ministry of Foreign Affairs (2007) 'The Norwegian Government's High North Strategy'.

The Open Society Institute. 2005 'Iraqi Oil Wealth: Issues of Governance and Development' Recommendations from Discussions Policy, Paper presented at The London Conference, School of Economics, Policy, 29 June–1 July 2005.

Tilton, J.E. (2004) 'Determining the optimal tax mining', *Natural Resources Forum*, 28: 144–149.

Tjersland, R. (2007) 'Norway's role in contribution to EU Security of supply', paper presented at STATOIL Conference in Brussels. March 28 2007.

Trigeorgis, L. (1996) 'Real Options: Managerial Flexibility and Strategy in Resource Allocation', Cambridge, MA: Massachusetts Institute of Technology Press, pp. 308.

Trigeorgis, L. (1990) 'A Real Options Application in Natural Resource Investments', Advances in Futures and Options Resources, 4: 153–164.

UK Debt Management Office (2003) 'Quarterly Review – January–March 2003'. Online. Available HTTP: <http://www.dmo.gov.uk> (accessed November 2003).

UKOOA (2003) 'Exploration on the West Coast of Britain – West Britain the Search for oil an explanation'. Online. Available HTTP: <,http://www.ukooa.co.uk/issues/exploration/v001321.htm> (accessed December 2003).

UKOOA (2002) 'Survey Reveals Extent of Tax Hit on North Sea Exploration', Online. Available HTTP: <http://www.ukooa.co.uk> (accessed October 2002).

UKOOA (2001) 'Harnessing Talent and Technology- Economic Report', UKOOA Publications.

Van, M. P. (1997) 'World Fiscal Systems for Oil', Van Meurs Associates, 2: 509.

Varzi, M. (2002) 'Mobilising Iran's Natural Gas Resources – The Role of Foreign Private Capital', Oil and Gas Research, Dresdner Kleinwort Benson- UK.

Verleger, P. (1980) 'An Assessment of the Effects of the Windfall Profits Tax on Crude Oil Supply', *The Energy Journal*, 1: 41–58.

North Sea Energy Data Statistic and Analysis: Oil, Gas, Electricity and Coal by Country Analysis Briefs January 2007. Online. <www.eia.dow.gov>

Walker, R. (1988) 'Applied Qualitative Research', Gower Publishing Limited.

Watkins, C. (2001) 'Atlantic Petroleum Royalties: fair deal or raw deal', The AIMS Oil and Gas Papers, Atlantic Institute for Market Studies, Halifax, Nova Scotia.

Watkins, C. (2000) 'Characteristics of North Sea Oil Reserve Appreciation', Massachusetts Institute of Technology, Cambridge, USA.

Watkins, T. (2002) 'Real Options Theory', San Jose State University, Economics Department. Online. Available HTTP: <http://www.sjsu.edu/faculty/watkins/realoptions.htm> (November 2002)

Webb, A. (2006) 'Venezuela buys Russian oil to avoid defaulting on deals', Caracas. April 28 2006.

Webb, M. (2007) 'Oil and Gas UK: The continued importance of indigenous oil and gas Production', Paper Presented at UKOOA dinner debate, March 28th.

Weinthal, E. and Luong, P. J. (2002) 'Energy wealth and tax reform in Russia and Kazakstan', Resources Policy, 27: 215–223.

Westwood, H. (2007) 'UKCS – Looking Ahead', Petroleum Review, 61:722: 46–47.

WoodMackenzie (2000) 'UK Upstream Service- Country Overview', November.

Wright, P. (2003) 'Liberalising Upstream Oil and Gas: The UK Experience and Its Implications', OPEC Bulletin, 4: 16–22.

Wurtzen, A. (2007) 'EU Security of Supply – A Danish Perspective', Paper Presented at Brussels Dinner Debate, 28 March 2007.

Zettl, M. (2002) 'Valuing Exploration and Production Projects by Means of Option Pricing Theory', *International Journal of Production Economics*, 78: 109–116.

Zhang, L. (1997) 'Neutrality and Efficiency of Petroleum Revenue Tax: A Theoretical Assessment', *The Economic Journal*, 107: 1106–1120.

Zhang, L. (1995) 'Taxing Economic Rents in Oil Production: Assessment of UK PRT', Department of Economics, University of Warwick.

Zittel, W. (2001) 'Analysis of the UK Oil Production, A Contribution to ASPO (Association for the Study of Peak Oil), Online. Available HTTP: <http://www.energykrise.de (accessed March 2003).

Index

